920.04 C514p FV
CHECKSFIELD
PORTRAITS OF RENAISSANCE LIFE
AND THOUGHT

5.00

*Portraits of Renaissance Life and Thought*

# Portraits of
# Renaissance Life and Thought

M. M. CHECKSFIELD, B.A.

NEW     YORK

BARNES & NOBLE, INC.
*Publishers · Booksellers · Since 1873*

Published in the United States in 1965
by Barnes & Noble, Inc.
105 Fifth Avenue, New York

© M. M. Checksfield 1964
First published 1964

Printed in Great Britain by
Northumberland Press Limited
Gateshead on Tyne

# Contents

# *Plates*

## Decorative devices on the title-pages

## Maps

# *Preface*

THIS BOOK IS not intended simply as a series of biographies of people all living in a particular age. Still less is it an attempt to adumbrate a period of European History. The characters I have chosen are not necessarily key to an understanding of Renaissance Europe, although some would obviously qualify to be included in such a selection. They are presented here because they illustrate, in their lives, work and personalities, certain aspects of the life and thought of the time; and some knowledge of their activities should therefore assist the reader, who it is assumed will have made or be making a preliminary study of the general history, in building up a picture of fifteenth and sixteenth century Europe. I have tried to show aspects of broad movements (e.g. the Reformation; exploration) through the eyes of individuals who were closely connected with them, to reveal manners and customs through the lives of some who helped to form them, and to examine phases of the thought of the age through some of its writers.

While a number of the people selected will be more or less familiar, I have taken the opportunity to introduce some that may be new to inexperienced students. Bodin has been included because his analysis of the concept of sovereignty provides a useful introduction to the study of elementary political theory; Montaigne, because it seems that one of the most inspiring of European writers is not introduced sufficiently early to English students. In the case of the better known figures, the less frequently emphasised elements of their personalities have been included, so that we may, for example, take into account that Cervantes was as much man of action as author, and that Columbus had a marked strain of mysticism.

I hope that the chapters will not be regarded as completely self-contained, and that the reader will accept that there is a significance—other than the merely chronological—in the order in which they are placed.

The total background obviously makes a broad canvas, and one cannot specialise in very much. In history, as in everything else, the 'general' approach is becoming rare; yet it is occasionally needed, for there are always those at the stage where they want some notion of the layout of the wood before they begin to examine the trees.

The writing of a 'life', however brief, involves the risk that sympathy for a character with whom one has to some extent identified oneself will cause him to be presented in too favourable a light. We live in the age of the anti-hero and hero-worship was never less fashionable. The old adulatory view of the great men of the past has given way to a scepticism about almost every quality they might have possessed. We can only try to strike a balance, with the reader warned that a close study may have led the writer to be a trifle partisan. After all, we want to consider the distinguished men of other times as human beings, and to take a reasonably favourable view of their motives when they were performing commendable actions, seems to be a factor in doing this.

All biography is to some extent conjectural. We cannot know the men of the past; neither for that matter can we really know our next-door neighbours or our friends. History as well as our personal lives would be very dull if we did not make our approaches as human as possible.

Facilities for coming closer to history are improving every day, and particularly through increasing travel students are able to feel the reality of what they have read in books, and to envisage figures of enduring fame in their authentic atmosphere. In consideration of this there will be found in what follows frequent mention of places, buildings and works of art of relevant historical interest that can fairly easily be seen.

In giving the names of foreign places I have been consistent only in using the form that is likely to be most familiar to English readers; hence, some are anglicised and some kept in their native forms. The names of the characters as set out at the beginning range from soubriquet to full title out of a similar consideration and also because the particular form adopted seems best to express the personality as here presented.

My thanks are due to a number of people who have been helpful in the preparation of this book. I should like to thank here, especially, Mr and Mrs Ronald Wells who kindly read the typescript and made some valuable suggestions; officials of the

Royal Netherlands Embassy, and Mrs Agate of Penshurst Place who answered questions and supplied illustrative material; and Monsieur Maurice Berjaud of Bordeaux who not only answered questions and gave me numerous pictures, but also lent material he values to a total stranger whose only credential was an admiration for Montaigne.

M.M.C.

## ACKNOWLEDGEMENTS

We are grateful to Penguin Books Ltd. for permission to include material from *Don Quixote* by Miguel de Cervantes translated by J. M. Cohen. In the chapter on Montaigne all the quotations from Montaigne, with four exceptions which are the author's own translation, are taken from Donald M. Frame's translation. They are reprinted with the permission of Walter J. Black, Inc., publishers of the Classics Club edition, and of Stanford University Press, from *The Complete Essays of Montaigne* translated by Donald M. Frame, © copyright 1948, 1957, 1958 by the Board of Trustees of the Leland Stanford Junior University.

# Introduction

IT IS CUSTOMARY to divide history into conventional 'periods' for study, and although this is misleading if it distracts our minds from the essential continuity of all history, it is obviously a necessary practical preliminary to any study at all. The three centuries contained approximately within the years 1320 and 1620 saw such immense changes in the life of Europe that this period, known as the Renaissance, has perhaps come to seem particularly self-contained: this is certainly an illusion, but good reasons remain both for considering it as an epoch and for characterising its distinctive atmosphere in this way.

The Italian term 'rinascita' was first used during the period itself to apply to the revival of the classical style of architecture in Florence and it soon came to include the rediscovery of classical culture in all its aspects. It was not until the mid-nineteenth century that the French historian Michelet applied the word 'Renaissance' to a whole historical period. Since then the term has signified both the 'rebirth' of the knowledge and art of the Ancient Greeks which had been all but lost in the Middle Ages, and also the line of demarcation between the medieval and the modern worlds.

The nature of the new developments—the exploration of vast new lands, upheavals in religion which destroyed the unity of Christendom, the various results following from the discovery of printing, revolutions in methods of warfare, and the eventual growth of strong national states—cannot fail to give the impression that modern history, at any rate as the term applied until our own scientific age, began at this time. Even though we now know that many Renaissance changes—cultural, economic and constitutional—extend well back into the Middle Ages, and that more medieval attitudes than were previously allowed for persisted into Renaissance times, we are still compelled to recognise a significant phase in the evolution of Europe, placed within tentative dates.

If we could somehow acquire a total view of the life of Europe in 1400, and again in 1600, we should certainly observe that more changes had taken place in the interim than in any other two centuries between the collapse of the Western Roman Empire and our own time. Also we must be impressed by the fact that the men of the Renaissance themselves believed that they were living in a time of revival and that they were inaugurating a new era. Their whole literature is saturated with this consciousness and with pride in their historic rôle; and if the high confidence of the early exponents is later modified by the forebodings of more pessimistic writers, this itself is characteristic of a rapidly changing society in which the swift pace of adaptation at length begins to exact its toll.

We are dealing with a European movement, but since it had its origin in Italy it is necessary to grasp something of the attitudes and values prevailing there in the fourteenth and fifteenth centuries in order to understand the revolution in thought that was, in its progress, to affect the north to an equal extent.

For a variety of reasons Italy was the most likely place for the impulse towards the new learning to be felt. Urban development, which was a feature of the late Middle Ages had proceeded furthest there, and town life, bringing men together, sharpened their wits and broadened their outlook. A new progressive element appeared and intellectual curiosity was stimulated. This was soon to lead to an enthusiasm for experimentation in all the arts, but its first effect was, somewhat paradoxically, to concentrate attention on the past. Latin classics, and Latin translations from the Greek had been esteemed throughout the Middle Ages. Now they were studied with a fresh interest which also promoted a search for what had been lost; during the fourteenth century and increasingly in the fifteenth, there was a steady stream of discoveries of ancient manuscripts. Admiration for what they revealed fostered an interest in antiquities of all kinds.

Obviously it was in the Italian peninsula that there were the strongest ties with the classical past. Apart from the immediacy of the linguistic inheritance, treasures of antiquity were buried in the soil, ancient monuments abounded; the grandeur that was Rome was still a living tradition. Here too, sufficient wealth enabled libraries to be founded and books to be made more generally accessible. Above all, Italy had the most immediate contact with the Greek world from which much of the inspiration for the new learning was drawn.

Since the collapse of the Roman Empire in the fifth century, the Christian Church had been divided into two, the eastern (Greek) section, which had escaped the worst onslaught of the Barbarians, continuing to be organised from Constantinople while the Roman Church pursued its own way in directing the rest of Christendom. During the early fifteenth century the westward advance of the Turks had caused leaders of both Churches to think in terms of united resistance to the infidel, and a number of missions had been sent from the eastern Church to various Italian cities to discuss union. They all failed; but because of them the Italians were able to make the acquaintance of a number of Greek scholars who were later reinforced by refugees from Constantinople when it fell to the Turks in 1453. Italian scholars realised that since Latin culture was founded on that of Greece, a knowledge of Greek was the key to further progress; indeed, by the time of the Greek missions a number of Italians had already made their journey to Byzantium[1] to study Greek manuscripts. During the later fifteenth century it became the major preoccupation of Italian scholarship.

What was eventually recovered from the Ancient Greeks was perhaps not so much a belief in learning as a belief in man. To the Greeks of the classical period, man, developed through all his faculties, was the most perfect thing they could conceive. They thought it possible that humanity could fulfil its own highest intentions provided that all its potentialities—intellectual, æsthetic and physical—were developed in harmony and unity. They believed in the 'whole man' and they saw their gods as created in man's image.

This confidence in human possibilities returned with the revived humanism of the fourteenth and fifteenth centuries. During the Middle Ages men's eyes had been trained on the world to come and their minds had been preoccupied with a conception of service to their superiors in a restricted and relatively static world; now they began to scan wider horizons and to look for fulfilment in a host of fresh activities. The new spirit animated art, literature, philosophy and education; it led to new inventions, geographical discoveries and to a re-examination of religion itself.

1 Constantinople was built on the site of the old Greek city of Byzantium early in the fourth century. The term 'Byzantine' persisted as a description of the civilisation and culture of which it was the centre.

In the course of time it produced revolutionary changes in political and economic life.[2]

The word 'humanism' as it applied to the thought of this period should not be made to carry any of the overtones of scientific scepticism that it has acquired in our own day. Probably to the early humanists themselves their name simply denoted scholars of the culture of antiquity: it came to imply a belief in its values and the duty to express them through the uniquely human capacity for words. They were, indeed, imbued with a sense of responsibility to language in the basic way implied by their alternative title—grammarians. Language was at the service of man. Greek and Roman literature, *litterae humaniores*, had made his quest their theme.

If, therefore, we take the term 'Renaissance' to designate a period of history and also a movement of renewal, we must see the revival of learning as an essential factor in both. Certainly there must have been at work other factors unconnected with classicism, which helped to produce the great outburst of mental activity; the ground was being prepared before the revival of learning. Neither did the reassertion of antique values imply perpetual servitude to classical modes of thought and expression. There were phases of pedantic and uncritical imitation, but in the long run the very spirit engendered by the study of the ancient writings promoted intellectual independence. Adulation of the Greek thinkers yielded to a more judicious appraisal of their work; students of the classical languages turned with a new pride to polishing the vernacular and making of it a worthy literature.

It was impossible that all the results following from such a revolutionary movement should be equally beneficial. The picture presented by the Italian cities of the Renaissance is not entirely one of cultural charm. Brutality, violence and licence were equally features of their society; the citizens suffered from a bewildered lack of an accepted code. In an overcharged atmosphere of great intellectual excitement the line that divides glorious self-confidence from overweening arrogance is very thin, and undoubtedly many of the humanists were on the wrong side of it.

2 It is equally true that, from another angle, political and economic changes may be said to have promoted humanistic thought. Cause and effect are inextricably interlocked in this way throughout the Renaissance period.

The new spirit made men question everything, but they all officially—and no doubt most of them genuinely—remained Christian; later phases of humanistic learning were markedly religious in character. Greek learning, however, had brought with it a pagan influence, and many of the new interests had a strong secular pull.

The Greeks, living before the Christian era, had a confidence in man unmixed with a sense of guilt: they achieved a poise that could not be recaptured. Christianity, bringing its great concepts of mercy, brotherhood and the equality of all men before God, also brought with it the sense of sin. Between the Greeks and the Italians stretched over a thousand years in which men had regarded themselves as miserable sinners: it was an attitude that could not easily be abandoned. The Italian humanists' new-born confidence was lacking in poise. It suffered from a nagging conscience, and this persistent conflict caused it all too frequently to assume the form of a swashbuckling arrogance. Exhibitionism, ' nerves', fits of temperament, petty egoism were all marked attributes of the Renaissance scholars.

Italy received the first stimulus of the new movement, and her people had to make the most difficult adjustments; by the time the Renaissance spirit touched northern Europe it was somewhat less feverish, having been tempered by the German religious reformation and the cooling minds of scholars like Erasmus. But to understand its various manifestations—whether good or evil—it is necessary to turn first to the country of its origin. Actually ' country' was what Italy was not. It was, at the time, composed of a number of small independent states, and it was in one of these, Florence, that the Renaissance came to its full cultural glory.

# Lorenzo de' Medici

*(1449-1492)*

*My desire is that by my life or my death, my misfortunes or my prosperity I may contribute to the welfare of our city.*

SAVOY/
PIEDMONT

DUCHY OF MILAN

Milan

REP.
OF
VENICE

Venice

REP.-OF
GENOA

M F

REP. OF FLORENCE

Florence

R

REP.
OF
SIENA

STATES
OF THE
CHURCH

(TO VENICE)

ADRIATIC SEA

CORSICA
(to Genoa)

Rome

KINGDOM
OF
NAPLES

Naples

SARDINIA
(to Aragon)

TYRRHENIAN
SEA

ITALY
in the late
Fifteenth Century

SICILY
(to Aragon)

Miles
0   40   80   120  160

F   Ferrara
M   Modena
R   Romagna

THE CITY OF FLORENCE is permanently associated with the name of one of the most eminent families that Europe has ever produced. The word 'Medici' still retains a unique power to evoke ideas of lavish and enlightened patronage for many who give no thought to the political history of fifteenth-century Italy, and are even unaware of the precise nature of the Medicean services to the arts. The family, from which came two popes and a queen of France, as well as successive rulers of Florence, was in fact equally remarkable in its prime for the number of its members who filled positions of political importance, and for the diversity of their interests. Among the Medici whose names have been celebrated, it is probable that the most representative of his age and of his house was Lorenzo—called the Magnificent.

To appreciate the position of the family into which Lorenzo was born in 1449, and his own activities in manhood, it is necessary to see the city over which the Medici ruled in relation to the peculiar political structure of Italy at that time. The feudalism of the Middle Ages had developed much less emphatically there than in other parts of Europe, for whereas in other countries, despite the growth of towns, the great territorial lord had become the most powerful factor in society, in the northern half of the Italian peninsula the City had come to hold the most powerful position, and the great lords had had to leave their mighty castles and come to dwell within the jurisdiction of the city in 'castellos' of a much less pretentious nature. It is true that they did not always settle down quite peaceably—we can see a reflection of their family bickerings in *Romeo and Juliet* where the squabbles of the great men's servants are miniatures of the bloodier battles between the barons' retainers in northern countries—but the fact remains that in the north of the peninsula, the City, or rather the City-state, was the effective political unit.

There were a large number of these City-states among which Venice, Milan and Florence were pre-eminent, while others such as Genoa, Ferrara, Siena, Mantua and Modena were also playing

an important part in the Renaissance movement. The term 'City-
state' is used for a city which controlled a large area of land
around it, including smaller towns brought under its sway; it was
independent of any superior authority, having all the powers
which we now associate with the larger unit of the nation. In the
organisation of the City-state it was the city itself that was all-
important: the rural inhabitants usually had no political rights,
but even within the city only a small proportion of those dwelling
there ranked as citizens. In the fifteenth century, Florence had a
population of some 90,000 of whom only a little over 3,000 were
qualified to vote.

South of these Cities, the States of the Church stretched from
Rome right across central Italy and northwards up the east coast,
including under their nominal dominion a number of towns
whose rulers were virtually independent. Further south, occupying the remaining half of the peninsula, was the Kingdom of
Naples, long the subject of contention between the Spanish House
of Aragon and the French House of Anjou. From 1442 it was ruled
by the House of Aragon.

In the fifteenth century, since Italy was the most advanced part
of Europe, these states regarded themselves as the most important
political entities and would have seen the Italian peninsula in
which they manoeuvred and intrigued against each other as the
central civilisation of the western world—a foreshadowing to some
extent of the way in which the larger nation-states were to come
to regard themselves and Europe.

During the twelfth and thirteenth centuries most of the Italian
City-states were free burghs where there had been intermittent
attempts at some rudimentary form of democracy. In Naples the
monarchy was always all-powerful, and the States of the Church
presented a varied and complex political structure within which
there was room for some democratic elements. During the fourteenth and fifteenth centuries things changed, and most of the
states passed under the control of 'despots', men who had seized
power or, like the Medici, had gradually bought it and then kept
it in their families while steadily reducing the rights of the citizens
to intervene. This did not happen to Venice; that city had always
been much more oligarchic than democratic, and within that
limitation it remained a free republic throughout. The other

cities succumbed to their new rulers—retired condottieri,[1] merchant princes, the offshoots of royalty and mere adventurers— but having succumbed, proceeded to blaze with a fresh glory as the despots proved themselves to be ardent patrons of the new learning.

It is difficult to be precise about the constitution of Florence which the Medici perverted because it consisted of a tangle of interrelated councils which acted as checks upon each other, and in any case it was from time to time subjected to various experiments. During the thirteenth and fourteenth centuries power had passed increasingly to the people, and the rise of families like the Medici was partly due to the fact that the old nobility were excluded from office. Supreme authority lay with a body known as the Signoria which was presided over by an officer called the Gonfalonier, and which was changed every two months. It was chosen by lot from among those eligible for office, and eligibility depended on membership of one of the 'Arts'. These were guilds into which the bulk of the citizens were divided according to their occupations. The seven 'Greater Arts' were corporations of those interested in great basic industries such as the textile trades, or in the legal and banking professions; the 'Lesser Arts' were guilds of tradesmen who depended for their living on supplying goods to the Greater Arts and to wealthy families; and a host of smaller guilds incorporated the ordinary artisans. All the citizens of Florence had at least a theoretical right to attend a Parlamento of the whole people in the open square, for the purpose of approving government measures. As Florence moved from a limited democracy to despotism, the number of councils multiplied, but this was substantially the constitution which the Medici steadily undermined. There was no dramatic seizure of power; the head of the family did not take a title; he did not usually hold high office, but gradually the Councils of State became dominated by Medici nominees and the people of Florence came to accept them as the power behind the government, and the head of their house as the figurehead of the state.

1 Leaders of mercenary troops who supplied rulers with trained forces in return for payment, and who were occasionally able to seize principalities for themselves. One of the most famous was an Englishman, Sir John Hawkwood (d. 1394).

The secret of their power lay in their wealth; they had considerable interests in the alum mines and the woollen industry, and on this basis they founded a banking business with branches in all the important cities of Europe and even in the Levant. Officially the Church still forbade its members to lend money for interest, but the practice was by this time widespread, with the popes themselves among the borrowers. Thus the Medici family were able to wield a power greater than that of many acknowledged potentates. By threatening to call in a loan or by refusing credit they could control the destinies of Florence and deflect the policies of rival despots.

The first Medici to gain eminence was Salvestro, who had taken the side of the people against the oligarchic cliques and emerged in 1380 as Gonfalonier of Justice—an officer whose main task it was to keep the nobles in order; but it was Cosimo, the grandfather of Lorenzo, who really made the Medici dynasty secure. In an unobtrusive way he gained control over the Signoria, and by his financial acumen and unscrupulous political manipulation he managed to triumph over considerable opposition and win from the grateful Florentines the title of 'Father of his Country'. They were doubtless impressed by the fact that it was during his period of power (1434-64) that Florence became the chief centre of the new Renaissance art and learning. Cosimo encouraged Greek scholars to come to Florence; he supported book collectors by allowing them credit at the Medici bank; he founded a library; he financed the building of churches and—perhaps most important of all—he established the Platonic Academy which, under the directorship of Marsilio Ficino, son of Cosimo's physician, was to become the principal centre of Greek learning. His home, which was always maintained as that of a private citizen, was the meeting place of scholars and artists, as it was also the repository of a noble collection of works of art.

When Cosimo died in 1464 he was succeeded as head of the Medici house by a son, Piero, who was a much less emphatic personality and who was an invalid suffering from chronic gout. He survived only a further five years, and in 1469, at the age of twenty, Lorenzo came into his inheritance.

The heads of all the most powerful families in Florence agreed that Lorenzo and his brother Giuliano should wield the authority of their father and grandfather. Lorenzo undoubtedly saw it as a single accession: 'The second day after my father's death, although I was very young, being only in my twenty-first year, the principal men of the city and of the state came to our house to condole with us on our loss, and encourage me to take charge of the city and of the state, as my father and grandfather had done. This I did, although on account of my youth and the great responsibilities and perils arising therefrom, with great reluctance, but for the sake of our friends and our possessions. For it fares ill in Florence for any who possess wealth without any control in the government.'

By this time the Medici were so popular with the majority of the Florentines that there was no question that, young as he was, Lorenzo would be looked to as head of the state. Everywhere the Medici arms[2] displayed on public buildings commanded the respect usually given to national flags. Still today in Florence medallions with the Medici *palle* can be seen in various parts of the city on buildings which were, in Renaissance days, associated with its most famous family.

Lorenzo's childhood had been one which had prepared him for his high destiny. His mother, the beautiful and intelligent Lucrezia Tornabuoni was a remarkable woman who gave him and his brother and three sisters their early training, based on practical piety, and he had the advantage of his grandfather's stimulating household. His tutors had been some of the most famous scholars of the age and under excellent tuition he had been quick to learn and eager to excel. Now, at the age of twenty, he was a very attractive young man. Not that he was handsome. There is a representation of him at the age of twelve, painted by Benozzo Gozzoli on the walls of the Medicean palace in Florence, in which he is riding in a procession on a magnificent gaily-caparisoned white horse, attended by a flock of pages, and this certainly gives the impression of a very beautiful youth, but the portrait was probably conceived in flattery and it is most likely that it is Lorenzo's charming dress, the carefully arranged curls and the

2 These comprised six balls (*palle* in Italian)—five red, and one blue with the lilies of France. The right to this last had been bestowed on Lorenzo's father by the French king Louis XI. The arms as a whole may indicate the origin of the Medici banking business in pawn-broking.

highly decorative setting which really catch the eye. The portraits of Lorenzo as a man do not show him as handsome, but it is an interesting face, with its firm square jaw, the long flattened nose, and the forehead which suggests thoughtfulness. Certain salient character traits are reflected in all Lorenzo's portraits: firmness, humour and shrewdness. Some of the representations seem to have caught a struggle taking place between his sense of humour and his inflexibility of purpose. For if Lorenzo was trained for high place, he was by nature a merry pleasure-loving lad. He threw himself wholeheartedly into the gay and rapid social life of Florence at its most expansive period. He joined in the carnivals and the tournaments, and the riotous games of the other city boys. The Medici never held themselves aloof and with the advent of Lorenzo and his even more charming and popular brother Giuliano to lead the social life, youth was at the helm.

In the temperament of the Florentines was an element of child-like spontaneity which made them able to abandon themselves to the passing moment with the greatest enthusiasm. Florence became famous for its festivities of all kinds. Two tournaments in particular found fame in contemporary poetry and painting— that held to celebrate Lorenzo's betrothal just before his coming to power, and another some years later in honour of his brother —and we have eye-witness accounts of the pageantry of this mimic warfare. The jousting took place in one of the great squares of the city. Knights of all the principal families attended, followed by heralds, trumpeters, men-at-arms, all gorgeously dressed. The crowds were all round the square, on the roofs, balconies and improvised galleries. On the first of these occasions we are told that Lorenzo wore a velvet surcoat, and a cape of white silk edged with red. His silk scarf was embroidered with roses and pearls, and his cap ornamented with rubies and diamonds. His helmet was adorned with three blue feathers and his horse draped with red and white velvet scattered with pearls. Significantly, his shield bore the device of a bay tree part dead, part green, and the motto: 'The spring returns'.

The return of the spring perhaps expressed itself most characteristically in the carnivals. These riotous frolics—sometimes elaborately planned and sometimes entered upon almost spontaneously —took the form of processions through the streets, beginning in the late evening and often going on till dawn. The carnival on appointed festival days would include decorated wagons illustrating scenes from legend and history with bands of sumptuously dressed attendants dancing round them and singing specially written songs. At intervals masques on set subjects would be performed. But often on warm summer evenings, without even the excuse of a festival day there would be heard the cry of 'The masquers are out' and a small impromptu procession would be joined by parties of masked men on horseback and flocks of torch-bearers on foot, and would swell into night-long revelry.

Lorenzo gloried in the variegated life of the city that he had come to think of as his. At a time when the great families vied with each other in commissioning works of art, he was a patron of scholars and artists alike. As all his family, he lived his private life with no show of grandeur. Although he went on official journeys with some state and a retinue of twenty or thirty, in Florence there was nothing in his appearance to pick him out. Certainly he dwelt in the Medici palace[3] which his grandfather had built in the Via Larga—a building whose austere exterior concealed an elegant home—but family life was simple and his clothes were the un-ostentatious garb of a plain citizen.

If he went about his ordinary business with the mien of an ordinary burgher, so with his pleasure he joined in on equal terms. He would go round with the wild absurdly-dressed singing parties. He even wrote some of their songs, for Lorenzo was no mean poet even if he was a poor singer. His voice we are told by some was like that of a bull-frog, but he loved music and did his best, and his companions' united voices could drown his. Not all of his activities were creditable to him, any more than were the more ribald of his songs. What is certain is that in his vigorous and varied life, in his virtues and in his vices, Lorenzo accurately reflected the spirit of Renaissance Florence: and nowhere more plainly than in Florence can we see what the Italian Renaissance outlook was.

Perhaps Lorenzo himself had early forebodings of the shadows that were to fall which impelled him to snatch eagerly at the pleasures of youth. As he said in one of his best known masque songs:

3 See Plate 1.

' Fair is youth and void of sorrow
But it hourly flies away—
Naught ye know about to-morrow . . .

Young and old together playing
Boys and girls be bright as air;
Every sorry thought forswear!
Keep perpetual holiday.
Youths and maids enjoy to-day;
Naught ye know about to-morrow.[4]

For mixed with all this joy and excitement was a good deal of violence and corruption. The state of the Church, which was soon to call forth Luther's protest, was such that serious men could no longer respect it; each successive pope seemed to be more worldly than the last. If the citizens of Florence, like those elsewhere, remained officially loyal members of the Church, they did not give much thought to the graver issues of life, and they had far too many distractions to allow much time for examining their own moral conduct. The violence too sometimes came very close home.

Popular as the Medici undoubtedly were, they did, after all, exercise power through control of a faction, and it was only to be expected that other factions in the city would occasionally challenge their supremacy. They had always to be on the alert for intrigue. During Lorenzo's boyhood the chief rival party had formed round the Pitti—a family who had pushed themselves into prominence during Cosimo's last years—and there had been one serious attack on Piero, when the promptitude and resource of Lorenzo probably saved his father's life. In 1478, when Lorenzo was twenty-nine, he and Giuliano were the victims of a more deeply-rooted conspiracy. Pope Sixtus IV, like most holders of the office in this period, participated in the political rivalries of Italy on the same terms as the secular rulers, and he was prepared to support the attempt of another family—this time the Pazzi— to exterminate the Medici. The Pazzi were rivals both because they too were bankers and also because they coveted a greater share in the administration of Florence, and when Lorenzo, for

4 Symonds's translation.

reasons of state policy, had refused advances from the Medici bank
to assist the Pope in setting up his nephew as a petty count in the
region to the north east of Florence, it was perhaps natural that
Sixtus should turn to the Pazzi house for the loan. It was certainly
an opportunity for the Pazzi to get the support of the Pope for
their designs against the Medici.

The plot against the brothers was timed for the morning of 26
April so that they should be attacked when they were attending
mass in the Cathedral. As the two brothers approached the altar,
armed men leapt forward and attacked them with daggers.
Giuliano was killed on the spot, but Lorenzo, wounded in the
neck, struggled free from his assailants and managed to reach the
sacristy where his friends gathered round him and barred the
door, although one lost his life in holding up the pursuers. Meanwhile panic reigned in the cathedral, and rioting began in the city
where troops had arrived in support of the Pazzi. An attempt to
gain possession of the Palace of the Signoria was foiled by the
Gonfalonier who managed to imprison the intruders The assas-
sins themselves were captured (some immediately and some a few
days later) and all were killed on the Gonfalonier's orders without
trial or confession. Most were beheaded in the courtyard, but some
half dozen were hung out of an upper window of the Palace and
died horribly in sight of the public—a punishment which illustrates the intermittent barbarity of the times. As the Cathedral
had emptied, Jacopo dei Pazzi, the head of the house, had ridden
round the city calling 'Liberty!' and trying to rouse the populace; but the crowds replied with 'Palle! Palle!'[5] and assembled
outside the Medici palace. Lorenzo, his neck swathed in bandages,
appeared at the window of his house, and calmed the crowd, dis-
suading them from further looting of the Pazzi palace. But
between seventy and eighty were killed as a result of mob violence
and many must have been innocent.

The tragic death of the charming young Giuliano and the
miraculous escape of Lorenzo seem to have rallied waverers to the
Medici cause. There were great public demonstrations, and a
special medal was struck to commemorate the occasion. Lorenzo
had never been more popular.

5 This is a reference to the arms of the Medici.

Later, his successes in the field of foreign affairs were to confirm him more soberly in the people's favour. All the important states of Italy were at that time engaged in the game of political manœuvring known as 'the balance of power', and Lorenzo was one of its chief, if gentler, exponents. He always desired peace. He was himself without military ability or military training, and in any case peace was necessary if he was to make Florence the city of his dreams. The basis of Lorenzo's policy was friendship between Florence, Milan and Naples. This secure, he felt able to deal with dangers that might come from Venice or the Papal States. At this time, however, Milan and Naples were becoming hostile to each other for dynastic reasons, and when the Pope, exasperated by the failure of the Pazzi plot and the subsequent hanging of an archbishop, declared war on Florence he was able to persuade Naples to join in on his side.

King Ferrante[6] and his son Alfonso were doubtless lured on by military ambition, but the actual campaigns were somewhat lacking in glory as also in decisiveness. Lorenzo, for his part, knew that Florence could not go on fighting long with her former ally against her. Her apparent wealth was very largely that of the Medici family, and extensive as that might be, it was, after all, only a private fortune. During a truce in 1479, Lorenzo took the important and quite private decision to go to Naples himself to negotiate a peace.

All his life he had had experience of foreign missions. We get the first glimpse of his public life when, at the age of twelve, in a splendid new suit, he received Duke John of Anjou and we are told he made his speech with great confidence. At sixteen he went to Rome to represent his family in some commercial business. After that had come foreign politics and now he proposed to take an unprecedented risk for the sake of Florence. It is possible that the actual hazards were not as great as the Florentines thought; Naples had strong reasons, which Lorenzo well knew, for wishing to be out of the war. All the same King Ferrante was not a person to trust and was actually known to have murdered an ambassador who had come with a safe-conduct, after fêting him for a month. However that may be, Lorenzo was successful in persuading Fer-

6 Sometimes written as Ferdinand.

rante that the dominance of the Papal States would be bad for Naples and that Florence was still his most useful ally. After a stay of three months he returned to Florence with reasonably satisfactory terms, and a little later a surprise attack by the Turks on the south east coast of Italy made the Pope also glad to be reconciled with the Medici city.

Lorenzo's popularity could go no higher. Henceforth his power was truly autocratic, and although he had yet another war to fight against the Pope (and Venice) in 1482-84, it may be said that for most of his time he did hold Italy in a balance of peace. But for every citizen who was able to appreciate fully his services in the diplomatic field, there must have been a hundred who loved Lorenzo as a leader of the social life of Florence and as one of the chief ornaments of its far-famed culture.

Since the tragedy of the Pazzi plot life had been more serious for Lorenzo. The loss of Giuliano must have hurt him deeply, for there was always much affection and no jealousy between the brothers, and as we have seen, fresh troubles pressed on Florence. Yet it was true that in no part of Italy was the tingling excitement of the Renaissance mood more in evidence. The Florentines had passed beyond the phase in which the chief interest was centred on learning as a concern of the few. The cultural revival now manifested itself in a wealth of activities and above all in art. Some of the greatest artists of the world were Florentines and their sense of vocation was never a restricted one; to be an artist was also to be a craftsman. Botticelli was a jeweller and goldsmith before he was a painter, and if the many-sided Leonardo da Vinci —the Renaissance man par excellence—was allowed to slip away to Milan and France, it was in a Florentine bottega that his career began. The streets of Florence were crowded with botteghe, half workshops half studios, where the craft of the jeweller and the art of the painter were practised side by side, usually by the same masters and apprentices. The fervour of creation had spread to the whole people, and Florentine boys dreamed of the day when they would enter a bottega as boys of a later age were to long to become engine drivers. Filippino Lippi, Ghirlandaio, Pollaiuolo and Verrochio were among other great names of Florentine art and the greatest artist of all, Michelangelo, as a boy of sixteen entered Lorenzo's garden school of sculpture. Her cultural fame and her newly won importance in the international field brought Florence enhanced prestige, and testimony to it came from all quarters.

Some of these expressions of respect seem to us a little quaint as, for example, the famous present of a giraffe from the Soldan of Egypt. This giraffe seems to have been a very amiable beast who attained great popularity, not only with the city urchins but also with the more exalted. It walked in processions and was taken round the monasteries for the inmates to see, but in spite of having fires kept up in its stables during the winter because it disliked the cold, it survived little more than a year. In this brief time it seems to have made its mark with some emphasis for it is to be encountered frequently in both pictures and writing of the time.

Lorenzo would not have been above being interested in the giraffe. A playful streak in his character persisted throughout and we see frequent glimpses in the records of his family life, entangled as that necessarily had to be with affairs of state. Lorenzo had married—at the age of twenty—Clarice Orsini, a member of a noble Roman family, and they had three sons and four daughters. In his dealings with his children he showed the typical Renaissance mixture of a genuine desire for them to have a good education for its own sake together with a worldly ambition that they should forward the fortunes of their house. He arranged for his daughter Maddalena to marry, at the age of fourteen, the son of Innocent VIII, a pope whom Lorenzo wished to placate after the hostility of Sixtus IV. Marriages of convenience were the custom of the age, but this particular one does draw attention to the fact that Innocent VIII (unlike his predecessors) openly acknowledged his illegitimate children; and also that political bargains in the game of the balance of power could be struck with the Papal State as much as with any other. Innocent needed alliance with Florence (and perhaps more specifically with the house of Medici) and in return Lorenzo's second son, Giovanni, was made a cardinal at the age of thirteen. Certainly the Pope felt constrained to say that he could not take up the office for three years, but it is a further reflection of the state of Rome that Lorenzo, the gay Florentine, should think it necessary when the sixteen-year-old boy left home in 1492, after advising regularity of life and perseverance in study, to add: 'As you are now to reside in Rome, that sink of all iniquities, the difficulty of conducting yourself by these admonitions will be increased:' Giovanni was to become Pope as Leo X and to have to face the Lutheran revolt.

Some of the pictures we have of Lorenzo as a father are more engaging. He took the greatest interest in his children's developing personalities. He said himself how different were his three sons—Piero the foolhardy, Giovanni the studious and Giuliano the good. Lorenzo joined them in their music, he wrote plays for them to act, and there is a story of an ambassador, come on an important errand, finding the Magnificent rolling on the floor with the children. His family, like all Florence, called him simply Lorenzo, and the childish letters that still exist reveal confidence and affection. Piero, at the age of seven, wrote: 'I have always written in Latin to give more tone to my letters, but I have not yet got that pony which you promised. . . . I am afraid that some misfortune may have happened . . . for if it were well I know that you would have sent it as you promised.' It (or another) must have come quickly. Soon after there was a letter of thanks which added: 'We are all well and studying. . . . Giovanni is able to spell. You can see for yourself how my writing is getting on. As for Greek, I work at it with Martino's help, but do not get very far.' Martino was a tutor, but the principal director of their studies was the famous scholar and humanist Angelo Politian.[7] Unfortunately their mother, who was responsible for part of their instruction, disagreed with his methods, and some of the very few hints of family discord concern this subject.

Can we judge how successful Lorenzo's educational methods were? Perhaps it is safest to say that his children turned out no worse and no better in character than most of the outstanding personages of that turbulent age. As patrons of art and learning they carried on the great Medici tradition.

It must be remembered, however, that there was another side to that tradition—the persistent strangling of the liberties of Florence. Under Lorenzo that process was carried a good deal further. The Parlamento was almost completely ignored. A new Council of Seventy was set up to override the old council. The members of it were all drawn from certain families (mainly mem-

7 Also written Politiano and Poliziano.

bers of the Greater Arts), they were all to be over forty years of age and they were replaced by simple co-option. Plainly, the democratic element was almost eliminated. Neither does Lorenzo come out with quite clean hands from his various financial transactions. It must be remembered that the Medici were never backed by a military force, they had to rule by personal popularity and by their wealth. Lorenzo did not possess the financial ability of his father, and the cost of Florence's position in the world was constantly increasing. In any case the accounts of the city and those of the Medici house must have been inextricably mixed, and there were some incidents which are suspicious. There was, for instance, the affair of the Dowry Bank. It was customary at that time for girls who married to be provided with a dowry by their parents; an unendowed girl was not very likely to find a husband. Most parents paid into this Monte delle Doti, and the money, which had gained a high rate of interest, was paid out on their daughter's marriage. During the war with Naples the fund had been so heavily drawn on by the government, that it had to suspend payment. Later it was arranged to pay one-fifth of the dowry at the time and to allow the rest to accumulate at a lower rate of interest than formerly, but this arrangement naturally found little favour with the citizens of Florence.

Corruption was not to go unchallenged either in the public or the personal sphere. By 1490, Savonarola, a Dominican monk fired with reforming zeal, was already preaching in St Mark's, Florence, thundering against pope and despot alike. Actually he seems to have exercised some fascination for Lorenzo: at any rate, the ruler of Florence was very tolerant of him, and although he did suggest that he should moderate his alarming prophecies of the wrath to come, he went to hear him preach, and remained unruffled when Savonarola refused to have any contact with Medicean circles. More important, he sent for Savonarola when he was dying. For some years Lorenzo had been suffering from the hereditary gout which caused him to age very early, and in 1492 at his country villa of Careggi, the end came. There are a number of stories of doubtful authenticity about what happened at the death bed. Savonarola was certainly present and it is most likely that he gave the blessing Lorenzo asked for after receiving the sacrament from his own confessor. The funeral was unostentatious and Lorenzo was buried next to his brother in the Old Sacristy of the church of San Lorenzo.[8]

Florence was plunged into mourning—and that for more reasons than the passing of Lorenzo. The whole peninsula of Italy was entering troublous times. The same year that Lorenzo died, Rodrigo Borgia, worst of all the popes, was elected as Alexander VI, and the prophecies of Savonarola were spreading a sense of doom; Lorenzo's heir, Piero,[9] was in every way a lesser man than his father; the stability of the Medici house itself seemed uncertain. Two years later the storm broke. Charles VIII, the young king of France, having by his marriage with Anne of Brittany, completed the process of unifying his country, was looking for a field for his martial ambitions. He revived old family claims to the kingdom of Naples, and as Naples was at this time quarrelling with Milan, Charles sought to ingratiate himself with Ludovico Sforza, the Milanese despot. He succeeded in persuading him to admit French troops to Milan, and from there he moved southwards. As he approached Florence, Piero de' Medici went out to the French camp in the hope of persuading him to pass through Florentine territory by the coast road without aggression against the city itself. Soon the bewildered Florentines learnt that their city had been handed over to the French. Their wrath was such that Piero had to flee and Florence revived its old republican constitution which, first under the austere Savonarola and later under a Gonfalonier, lasted till 1512, when Piero's son returned.

Lorenzo the Magnificent and the family from which he came have exerted a permanent fascination over men's minds; and in view of the variety of their activities it is not surprising that judgements should be divided. For some, the fact of their political tyranny remains the major consideration and they—like Savonarola—can never forgive the family who destroyed the republican liberties of Florence. For others the very word 'Medici' is almost a symbol for cultural aspiration, and for these Lorenzo's political perfidies simply do not exist. His appeal to his own time undoubtedly sprang mainly from his adaptability and confident vitality. He must have been one of the world's best mixers. A keen sportsman who could join in the ball games, the wild horse riding

8 The remains were later removed to the New Sacristy, where they now are.
9 Sometimes written Pietro.

and the hunting, he could also carry on philosophical disputations with the wisest of his generation. A landowner with a practical knowledge of farming and a deep love of the countryside, he could throw himself with zest into the feverish gaiety of the capital. He was more than a patron of artists, he was something of a connoisseur; he was an esteemed man of letters who wrote plays and poetry both sacred and profane. And all the time he had to be the active politician. This many-sidedness, the quick turns about, may give an impression of inconsistency. His very speed of adaptation can make him appear a hypocrite. Alternatively one might say that his vivid concentration on the affair of the moment was proof of the strong sincerity of his spontaneous responses.

The account of any historical figure—like that of anyone else—must ultimately be drawn with a credit and debit side. There are few saints and only a few to occupy the gallery of monsters. Perhaps for Lorenzo, some words of the Florentine historian, Guicciardini, written a few decades after his death, strike a balance: ' Florence did not become free under Lorenzo, but a better master no society could have had. Incalculable good resulted to it . . . while the evils that are inseparable from a tyranny in any form, were limited in their workings—rendered almost harmless in fact, when his will came into play. There were doubtless many who rejoiced at his death; but all who took any part in the administration, regretted it deeply, even those who thought that they had grounds of complaint against him for none can tell what a change of rulers might bring about.'

The change of rulers in 1494 certainly brought about a very different Florence. Although the Medici house was to be restored, its great days were past. The pope who was Lorenzo's son, and another who was his nephew were to continue the family tradition in raising the papacy to the height of its cultural glory; but in the city of their origin, the Medici—perhaps the greatest patrons of learning known to history—were never again to have the far-reaching influence they had held under Lorenzo the Magnificent.

## FURTHER READING

FERDINAND SCHEVILL. *The Medici.* Gollancz 1950.

———— ————. *A History of Florence.* Bell 1937.

C. M. ADY. *Lorenzo dei Medici and the Italian Renaissance.* English Universities Press 1955.

# Thomas More

## (1478-1535)

*I die the King's servant, but God's first.*

In 1534 HENRY VIII declared himself Supreme Head of the English Church, and in 1535 Thomas More was beheaded for refusing to take the required oath. The relationship between these two events illustrates the great change that was coming over sixteenth-century Europe and it also points to one of mankind's permanent dilemmas.

More's biography has to be composed of three strands: his family life which has become a model of Christian domesticity, his service to his King and country, and his writings, one of which is a classic of English literature. The three strands were very closely interwoven, for More's devotional spirit influenced his every activity; he was essentially of those who would wish their

'days to be
Bound each to each by natural piety.'

Thomas More was born in the City of London on 6 February 1478,[1] the son of a lawyer who later became a judge and a knight. He was sent to St Anthony's School in Threadneedle Street at a time when English education was first faintly stirred by the ideas of the New Learning, though it is probable that St Anthony's was hardly yet affected by the intellectual revolution, and More's education at this stage would have been on the medieval pattern. At about the age of twelve the boy was placed, according to the custom of the time, in the household of John (afterwards Cardinal) Morton, Archbishop of Canterbury and Lord Chancellor. He seems to have acquitted himself well in his service at Lambeth Palace, and also to have enjoyed the life. We have records of his participation in the amateur theatricals, and the evidence that he liked and respected his patron is to be found in his *Utopia* where he describes Cardinal Morton as 'a man not more honourable for his authority, than for his prudence and virtue'.

1 Or possibly 1477.

Cardinal Morton, on his side, was struck by the boy's unusual intelligence and in 1492 he sent him to Oxford to study at Canterbury College (on the site of what is now Christ Church), where he would have had to live in the very austere manner of the Oxford students of his time. The day's work was long, the food plain and scanty, and there were few comforts. But there was ample nourishment for the mind, for at Oxford there was great enthusiasm for the new classical learning. Grocyn, whose lectures More attended, was just back from Italy and throughout the University a great debate was raging between those who supported Grocyn in his encouragement of Greek studies and those who wished to preserve the medieval type of scholarship. How much Greek More actually learnt at Oxford is uncertain—seven years later he is talking of 'perfecting' his Greek—but certainly he was immensely interested in the ideas of the Ancient Greeks, as presented through the revival of classical studies in Italy. Unfortunately More's father had little sympathy with this line of thought, and as he was anxious for his son to pursue a legal career he removed him from Oxford in 1494 and placed him at New Inn (and later Lincoln's Inn) in London to study law. The Inns were like a university devoted entirely to legal studies, and More made good progress here as he had done elsewhere so that after qualifying in 1501 he remained as a lecturer. It was probably at this stage of his career that he first met Erasmus—not yet the world famous scholar—at the house of a common friend, and so began a friendship that was to last for life, with great benefit both to the participants and to European learning.

Between 1499 and 1503 More's mind was much occupied with another question. Should he take Holy Orders? At this time he was studying Greek, with Grocyn and Latimer, and his conception of humanism was that the new linguistic knowledge and the discoveries of original Christian writings should be used to 'restore Theology' and put the words of Christ more vividly and accurately before men.

Church or Law? It was for anyone as earnest and as scrupulous as More a very difficult choice. For almost three years he took the unusual position of sharing part-time the lives of the monks of the Charterhouse, lodging near them and accepting their discipline while he continued with his legal work. We find that in 1501 he gave lectures on St Augustine's *City of God* in the Church of St Lawrence, Old Jewry, where Grocyn had become Rector. But his father was pressing for the opposite decision, and More himself came to the conclusion that he was intended to live a family life rather than to withdraw from the world. In 1504, at the age of twenty-six, he was elected to Parliament, and the next year he married Jane Colt of Roydon, Essex. More's son-in-law, William Roper (who wrote a biography) quaintly tells us, whether accurately or not, that ' albeit his mind most served him to the second daughter, for that he thought her the fairest and best favoured, yet when he considered that it would be both great grief and some shame also to the eldest to see her younger sister preferred before her, he then of a certain pity, framed his fancy towards her, and soon after married her '.

Whatever More's reasons for marrying Jane, they seem to have settled down happily at Bucklersbury in the heart of the City, and during the next six years three daughters and a son were born to them. During this period of his life More began to go abroad on business, and on the first occasion he visited the famous universi-. ties of Paris and Louvain. His capacity as a lawyer was increasingly recognised, and in 1510, the year after Henry VIII came to the throne, he was made an Under-Sheriff of the City. This post was that of a permanent legal official who advised the Mayor and Sheriffs and also presided over a court as their representative. More was a popular magistrate and all the evidence is that he was conspicuous for his honesty and fairness at a time when practices which we should call corrupt were all too prevalent.

Indifference to both intimidation and flattery was an outstanding trait in More's character. He lived at a time when moral decision was particularly difficult because Europe had reached the dividing line between the medieval and the modern world, and it is impossible to understand More if we do not remember how much of him was medieval. All the values of the Middle Ages were part of his inheritance; those of the modern world were only slowly forming round him. More was a sincere Catholic who believed that heresy must be punished. He once ordered a boy in his household to be flogged for spreading heresies. He practised mortification of the flesh and constantly—though secretly—wore a hair shirt. Like Erasmus he believed in the necessity of preserving a united Christendom, and feared that if the Catholic Church were disrupted, endless conflicts of unprecedented violence would follow; unlike Erasmus he had a strong sense of patriotism at a time when that emotion was something of a novelty. The reformer in him wanted to attack many contemporary evils, but the scholar who always saw the temporal in the light of things eternal wished to keep much unchanged in a rapidly changing world. More had great personal charm; he had tenderness, humanity and self-control, and his sense of humour saved him from priggishness. It was a distinctive sense of humour with a strong vein of irony, and the fact that More could both joke very solemnly and preach pleasantly has led to considerable confusion in the interpretation of his views. He was not perfect; his speech to Parliament on the fall of Wolsey may be deemed ungenerous, he was not above small prevarications in a friend's interest, and he was bigoted in his refusal to believe that Lutherans might be moved by conscience; which is only to say that all men have their faults. But he had an ultimate integrity, and a sweetness of disposition that make him one of the most lovable and admirable characters in English history.

In 1511 More's star was rising in his profession, but he suffered a heavy domestic affliction when his wife died leaving him with four children under six years. Perhaps it was this last circumstance which caused him to remarry very quickly. His second wife, Alice Middleton was a widow seven years his senior with one daughter, and although she seems to have been completely incapable of appreciating the finer points of her husband's character and also somewhat sharp of tongue, she proved a devoted stepmother to his children and an excellent manager of the now considerable household.

The accession of Henry VIII to the English throne had been hailed with joy by More and his fellow humanists both in England and on the Continent because it was felt that he would be a generous patron of the new learning and its scholars. Certainly Henry called men of letters to his Court, but probably this was partly because he saw the advantages of having their brains in his diplomatic and administrative service. More's eminence in his profession led to his being sent on state missions and in 1515, at the request of some City merchants, he was included among those who went on the King's behalf to discuss commercial affairs in Bruges and Antwerp, an embassy which lasted some six months and is of interest on the personal side because it enabled him, through an introduction from Erasmus, to meet Peter Giles,[2] the Town Clerk of Antwerp, 'a man so learned, witty, modest and so true a friend that I would willingly purchase his company at the cost of a great part of my fortune'.

More's achievements as an ambassador and his successes in the courts made their impression on Henry VIII and in 1517, on his return from an embassy to Calais which resulted in a treaty with Francis I of France, he was called to the King's service. In October he was made a member of the King's Council, and in 1518 he became a judge in the Court of Requests,[3] resigning his office of Under-Sheriff in the City so that there could be no conflict of interests. He did not accept a political rôle without a stern debate with himself. He was well informed on the corruption of courtiers and he knew how difficult it is to touch pitch without being defiled; but he also knew that if better men did not go into politics, worse ones would.

It was the year of a general peace between the competing powers of Europe, but everyone knew that this was only a temporary pause in the rivalry of the three young monarchs, Henry VIII, Francis I and Charles of Spain and the Netherlands. In 1519 Charles was elected Emperor, and the following year saw the culmination of the first phase of Wolsey's policy at the Field of the Cloth of Gold. More was in the King's retinue on this occasion, but he seems to have been mainly employed away from the scenes of splendour, settling trade questions with foreign merchants. It is doubtful how much he ever knew about the intracacies of Wolsey's diplomacy. He was an intermediary between the minister and the King and it was his duty to read and explain Wolsey's dispatches to Henry, but he was not called upon to give advice, and acted rather as a confidential secretary.

England emerged from the Field of the Cloth of Gold with separate and incompatible alliances with both Charles and Francis, and More's mind probably dwelt more on the precarious state of the peace than on Wolsey's personal hollow triumph.

2 Or Pierre Gilles.
3 A court principally for poor petitioners.

He must have found great relief from his somewhat uncongenial labours in his happy home. We know this family life chiefly from the letters of Erasmus who was, from time to time, a guest, and it is a very attractive picture we receive of the household first at Bucklersbury and at a later date at their new house at Chelsea.

More ruled his domestic commonwealth on the principle that there are two authorities, the supernatural and the natural; and to this end he directed his children's religious exercises and laid down the lines of their secular education. He conducted household prayers every evening and church attendance was compulsory on Sundays and feast days. More himself always rose very early for a period of study and devotion, and later attended Mass. At the beginning of each meal passages of the scriptures were read by one of his daughters. On the secular side of education, More had very advanced ideas in that he believed the intellectual education of women to be just as important as that of men. 'They both have the same nature,' he wrote, 'which reason differentiates from that of beasts; both therefore are equally suited for those studies by which reason is perfectioned.' And so he insisted that his daughters should be well instructed in Latin and Greek. When More was away on state business, he expected that those of his children who were old enough should write him a letter in Latin every day, and he himself regularly replied. He was very proud of the scholarship of his eldest daughter, Margaret, especially of her powers as a Latinist. All the children had school in their own house and tutors were engaged to teach them Philosophy, Theology, Mathematics and Astronomy as well as languages. As might be expected, certain pastimes were rigorously forbidden, and these included all dice and card games. On the other hand, play-acting (of the kind More had enjoyed in Cardinal Morton's household) was a frequent activity, and gardening and music were encouraged as hobbies. Above all, More wished that his children should love what they did for its own sake, and not become prey to the exhibitionism which was already tainting the humanist learning of Renaissance Italy. Once when he was away from home he wrote to their tutor desiring that they 'should not get accustomed to praise or vainglory which makes us seek to please the greater number (always the worst)'.

When More moved to Chelsea—perhaps in 1524—he acquired a

considerable estate. There was a spacious house in a large garden
with fields and a farm adjoining and its situation afforded fine
views of the Thames and the wooded Surrey hills. He must have
needed his increased facilities, for besides his family, his house
also accommodated a flow of guests as well as a number of permanent extra dependants. His friends came from widely different
spheres, for More had a gift for friendship and he was quite indifferent to their social status, but among them would be some of
the greatest European scholars of the time. The artist Holbein
was there about the year 1526, having been introduced by Erasmus.
He painted the best known portrait of More as well as a family
group and portraits of individual children; and it is to the com-
missions which More's introductions obtained for him that we
owe many fine portraits of Tudor celebrities.

As his children grew up and married, More accommodated the
new young families as well, and they were also joined by his aged
father. Margaret had married a young lawyer, William Roper,
when they still lived at Bucklersbury and when she herself was
barely sixteen; and it is to her husband that we owe much of our
knowledge of More's character and the intimate details of his last
days. In the first four years of residence in Chelsea the two other
daughters, Elizabeth and Cecily and the son, John, all married,
and in the course of time there were eleven grandchildren in the
house. More also had an adopted daughter, Margaret Gigs,[4] and a
ward, John Harris, who acted as his secretary.

In spite of the framework of firm discipline, More's family life
was in no sense formal; he liked an atmosphere of freedom and
equality. He himself was rather careless of his appearance; he
dressed simply in an age of finery, and was not much interested in
food and drink. Erasmus has given a pen portrait of him which
describes a man of medium height, with auburn hair, blue-grey
eyes, a clear complexion and a thin beard. He emphasises his
cheerful expression, and there are many other witnesses to the
cheerfulness of More's disposition. It is perhaps characteristic of
his humour that, like his Utopians, he 'had singular delight and
pleasure in fools' and kept one—Henry Patenson, 'a man of
special wit unlike the common sort'—in his household. This fact
also serves to remind us how much More was a man of his time,

4 Or Giggs or Gyge.

34

before we go on to consider how much he belongs to all ages. He also delighted in birds and animals and kept numbers of these, including a very mischievous monkey, both for the pleasure they gave and because he made a study of them.

It must have been a happy little republic over which More presided in the decade after his first entering upon duties of state, and mercifully there could be no knowledge of the storms to come; for, from this group, apart from More's own tragedy, Cecily's husband was to be executed in 1540, Roper and John More were to suffer imprisonment, and both Margaret Gig's husband (John Clement) and John Harris were fated to die in exile.

Meanwhile, whatever misgivings might be locked in More's breast—and he was a very reticent person—the family life flowed on smoothly. At Chelsea, More had had the so-called ' new build- ing', containing a library, gallery and chapel, erected in the grounds, and here he spent every Friday in prayer and study. On Good Friday the whole household was assembled there to hear the Lord's Passion read. At all times it was where More retired for study and meditation, and to write, for by this time he was an author of some fame. Besides making translations he had written poems and plays, part of a history, and since coming to Chelsea, had completed a number of devotional works. Better known than any of these was the *Utopia*, published in 1516, the significance of which must be considered later.

Probably the period 1518-20 could count as the happiest and most prosperous of More's life. *Utopia* had made him famous throughout Europe; it was the time of his most cordial relations with Wolsey and Henry VIII when the King still delighted to talk with him on subjects such as astronomy and divinity; the stimulus provided by his new work was set off by the calm of his family life. In 1521 he became Under Treasurer of the Exchequer and was knighted, but the next few years of apparently rising fortune were also years of disillusionment. More was always an idealist rather than a careerist. About the time of his promotion, the ' judicial murder' of the Duke of Buckingham gave an unmistak- able sign of the royal tyranny that was emerging. Wolsey, whom More at first respected as a patron of learning, was now pursuing a foreign policy which was to plunge England again into the

European struggle, and war was declared on France in 1522. In 1523 More was Speaker in the only Parliament called during Wolsey's years of power, and in 1525 he was made Chancellor of the Duchy of Lancaster.[5]

By 1527 Wolsey had changed sides again, for the Emperor Charles V had neither shared with his ally the fruits of his victories, nor had he assisted the English cardinal towards the papacy. Furthermore there were already the first rumblings of the storm over the King's divorce. More's passion for peace and his dislike of the religious, political and personal implications of the 'King's affair' made him apprehensive. However he was still high in the King's favour, and Henry consulted him on the divorce question only to be met with the excuse that More considered himself ineligible to give such advice.

In 1529 the Peace of Cambrai between the Emperor and the King of France reduced Wolsey's policy to ruins; he was also failing to secure Henry's divorce and the King had no further use for him. After his fall More succeeded him as Lord Chancellor. The title implies that he was First Officer of State and Chief Adviser to the Crown, with functions administrative and judicial. He was also head of the legal system. When More accepted the Chancellorship he must have known that an attack on the Church was coming. In spite of his discreet silence, Henry must have been quite clear that he regarded the marriage to Catherine as permanently valid, but the King also knew that he would not attempt to influence others nor to bruit his opinions abroad. More generally respected the conscience of other people, and he was not much given to coat-trailing. In any case he was caught up in the King's service; only he could decide at what point his conscience would be irremediably affronted. Meanwhile he might possibly render some service to Queen Catherine.

Events began to move swiftly. In February 1531 the Convocation of Canterbury acknowledged the King their 'singular protector, only and supreme Lord, and, *as far as the law of Christ allows*, even Supreme Head' of the English Church. The same year More (speaking for the King) had the duty of announcing to Parliament the views of European Universities on the validity of the King's

5 This part of the King's inheritance was administered separately and the Chancellorship was an important office.

marriage. He began by reporting that the King declared himself troubled in his conscience for having married his brother's widow by papal dispensation, and that this was the principal motive in seeking a divorce. He declined to express his own opinion. He also declined to receive a communication from the Emperor Charles (Catherine's nephew) which presumably would have offered support for the Queen's cause. More was still the King's servant, but it was a very fine tightrope that he walked in loyalty to Henry.

In 1532 Convocation made the 'submission of the clergy' by which they swore to subordinate all ecclesiastical legislation to the royal assent. The next day More resigned the Chancellorship. He gave ill-health as an excuse and parted good friends with Henry. He was still anxious to avoid flaunting his views.

In May 1533, Cranmer (Archbishop of Canterbury since the preceding August) annulled Henry's marriage to Catherine. Five days later his marriage to Ann Boleyn, which had taken place secretly in January, was declared valid, and on 1 June she was crowned Queen.

More was not well off after his retirement, and he thought it too late to return to legal practice. He exhorted his family to plainer living and settled down to his religious writing. He was not left long in peace, however. The first trouble came early in 1534 in connection with the 'Holy Maid of Kent' prophecies. A poor girl, Elizabeth Barton, who had become a nun, claimed supernatural powers which enabled her to prophesy a terrible retribution for Henry. More was accused of encouraging her but the evidence against him was so flimsy that the King was persuaded to drop the charge. The incident is of interest because at a preliminary investigation it was suggested to More that he would be free from all interference if he would acknowledge the King's supremacy and the divorce. He refused, but wrote afterwards to both Henry and Catherine asserting his loyalty and defining his views. He must have seen in the suggestion a hint of what would happen if he remained intransigent.

In March 1534 Parliament passed an Act of Supremacy which included a clause stating that the King's marriage to Catherine was invalid and requiring confirmation by oath by the Lords Spiritual and Temporal and anyone else selected. More was among those selected. On 12 April he had notice served on him to appear before the Commissioners at Lambeth, and here he declared himself willing to swear to the Succession but not to the marriage clause. He was quite clear in his mind about his attitude. He was prepared to swear to the Succession because it rested with the secular authorities to regulate the choice of sovereign, but he was not prepared to say that Henry's marriage to Catherine was invalid. Neither could he acknowledge the Royal Supremacy because the supreme Head of his Church was the Pope, ordained, as he considered, by God. At the same time he was willing to remain silent and not propagate his views, for, as he told Margaret later 'I meddle not with the conscience of any man that hath sworn, nor take it upon me to be their judge'.

More was committed to the Tower as was also his friend Fisher, the Bishop of Rochester, for the same reason. He was fifteen months a prisoner and during that time he continued his writing, producing *The Dialogue of Comfort* and the unfinished *Treatise upon the Passion*. Sometimes his writing materials were removed and his work had to stop, but he always continued his letters to his family, using coal in the place of ink. Both Margaret and his wife had permission to visit him, and both, in their different fashions, tried to persuade him to take the oath. It was not difficult to convince his daughter of the power of his conscience and that 'Nothing can come but that that God will', but Dame Alice, although loyal to her husband, could never appreciate his attitude. Roper quotes her as saying to him: 'I marvel that you that have been always taken for so wise a man will now so play the fool to lie here in this close filthy prison, and be content to be shut up among mice and rats, when you might be abroad at your liberty, and with the favour and good will both of the King and his Council if you would but do as all the bishops and best learned of the Realm have done. And seeing you have at Chelsea a right fair house, your library, your books, your gallery, your garden, your orchards and all other necessaries so handsomely about you, where you might in the company of me your wife, your children and household be merry, I muse what a God's name you mean here still thus fondly to tarry.' Roper goes on, 'After he had a while quietly heard her, with a cheerful countenance he said, "I pray thee . . . is not this house as nigh heaven as my own?' To which she after her accustomed fashion, not liking such talk, answered "Tille valle, tille valle ".'

More's behaviour in prison was touchingly unselfish. He saw it his duty to comfort Margaret in her grief rather than to seek consolation for himself and he remained firm enough to give courage to a friend who broke down when they met. Like almost all who find the strength to resist to the end, he had moments of misgiving about his ability to face torture if that should come, and sometimes doubts about how he would face death. But fundamentally More was not afraid. To the Duke of Norfolk who had once warned him that the wrath of princes was death, he gave the immortal reply: 'Is that all? Then the difference between your grace and me is but this, that I shall die today and you tomorrow.'

A great part of his time in prison was given to meditation on his faith, and some part must have been given to reviewing his life and work and the development of his ideas. It is unlikely that in his last days More gave much thought to the ideas of the *Utopia*. Posterity has done that for him. Probably the author himself never took this book (or at any rate its more famous second part) as seriously as his readers have done, and the problem of reconciling some of the Utopian views with those More held in actual life is largely an artificial one. The book was conceived in 1515 when More was acting as ambassador to Flanders and had just made the acquaintance of Peter Giles in Antwerp, and it is Peter who is supposed to introduce More to a traveller, one Ralph Hythloday, who has news of the strange and admirable land called Utopia. His account constitutes the second book which was written first.

Before publication in 1516, More added Book I which contains some forthright criticism of the evils he saw in Tudor England. It is an indictment of the enclosure system by which arable land was being turned into pasture to increase the wealth of wool speculators and an exposure of the unemployment and profligacy which followed in its train. There is criticism of the harsh punishments inflicted on wrongdoers, such as hanging for theft, and of the lack of provision for the aged and sick; but it is noticeable that when More wishes to condemn the new nationalistic policies based on war, and the nonsense that had gathered round the idea of

D

chivalry, he has to use France as an example rather than reflect on the policy of Henry VIII and Wolsey. Ralph Hythloday suggests that most of these evils derive from the pursuit of private wealth, and that Utopia is a more nearly perfect state because there all goods are held in common. There follows the account of the island of Utopia.

It is a crescent-shaped easily-defended island containing fifty-four cities all within walking distance of each other. Outside of the cities there are farm households of not less than forty men and women, which are joined together in groups of thirty under one head ruler. Every year twenty persons from the farms are changed for twenty persons in the city where people have separate houses, but they are not privately owned, and every tenth year they are changed by lot. The whole island is ruled by a Prince who is elected for life, and who takes advice from a Council representing cities and farm groups. The lives of the inhabitants are carefully regulated. They all wear the same simple clothes, they all do a certain amount of agricultural work, to which each adds a craft of his choice. (The only exemption from this is for specially licensed scholars.) They work only six hours a day, but the amount of time for sleep and recreation is laid down, and all the permitted recreations are of an improving kind. They may enjoy music, attend lectures and play some few specified games. All production is commonly owned. Each city has four markets to which all produce is taken, and the head of each family unit fetches what is needed without payment. The size of this unit is prescribed, and if it does not contain fourteen children between the ages of ten and sixteen, some must be transferred from other, larger families. In the cities meals are taken communally with the men and women in separate halls and the older children serving. There are precise marriage laws and heavy penalties for a breach of them, but divorce is allowed for a variety of causes, which really add up to divorce by consent if the authority of the Council can be obtained. (This we are told was not lightly given.)

Neither war, slavery nor the death penalty are completely ruled out, but the Utopians never enter into leagues with other states, and fight only for defence or to help those who have been attacked. They prefer to overcome their enemies by 'craft and deceit' rather than by fighting, and the tactics described have a very 'fifth-column' flavour—an ironical reference to the Machia-vellian methods of sixteenth-century statecraft? Most important of all, the Utopians were not Christians, though many were drawn to the faith when Hythloday explained it to them. They had various kinds of worship: of the sun, the moon, and heroes as gods, but tolerance was enjoined upon all 'because it is no man's power to believe what he list'. So all could follow their own religion, provided only that they held the world to be ruled by a divine Providence, and accepted the immortality of the soul.

Remembering how much More was the jester with a straight face and that the book was fiction intended as a 'pleasant and witty work', it is difficult always to be sure when he was serious and how much to allow for irony. In any case *Utopia* abounds in the inconsistencies which are inevitable in works of its kind, and its author ran into the same stubborn difficulties that beset all social planners whether on paper or in the real world.

He has to ignore the demonstrable facts of human nature; and although he says Utopia has very few laws (and no lawyers!) it is quite clear that to preserve such a system, there would have to be a mass of regulations. He runs into one particular dilemma which illustrates this very well. The Utopians are not allowed to go abroad, and only to visit another city under licence. This is intolerably illiberal. Yet it was enacted to preserve the Utopian way of life, and it seems inescapably true that the standards of any society with a firm code are eroded by easy contact with people of different standards; possibly even liberalism itself could be diluted by its own liberty. The achievement of the Utopians remains what Hythloday claimed it to be; they did establish social equality, and government was in the interest of the whole community and not for the aggrandisement of rulers.

The more teasing problem is how far More was putting forward the ideas and customs of Utopia as desirable. If he agreed with their attitudes then there is a good deal that is inconsistent in his teaching and behaviour in life. But do we have to take the work as seriously as this? It was a work of fiction, written in Latin, per-haps to keep it from those who might draw the wrong conclusions. Since More's day the word 'Utopia' has become firmly planted in our minds as signifying a perfect state, but the word means 'nowhere' not 'ideal' and in the land of Nowhere anything, good or bad, may be allowed to happen. It is difficult to believe that More approved of the Utopian attitude to war; he can hardly have desired divorce by consent; and we know that both as a practical statesman and as a Catholic Christian he held that heretics could not be tolerated. It is not even certain that More would have approved of the socialist ideas of Utopia. It is easy to forget that the book is written in the form of a dialogue and that More in his own person tells Hythloday that there is much to be said on the other side. This does not alter the fact that More has made the book a repository of many of his cherished beliefs. Progressive as he was as a humanist and educationist, he was still a conservative reformer. He preferred the co-operative life of the medieval world, with its emphasis on community, to the competitive, individualist and nationalist society that he saw emerging. No man hated materialism more, and profit-making as the main motive power of the state was abhorrent to him. He held that the truth had been finally revealed in the Christian religion, and that because of this revelation there was no excuse for the heretic. It was essential to man's well-being both on earth and in the world to come that he should be held firmly within the community of the Church. The Utopians were without revelation, and as they had only reason to guide them, all its manifestations had to be tolerated until Truth should emerge, for, said More, ' Reason is servant to Faith '. *Utopia* was a lesson to Christians because it showed a society that, even with only natural reason to guide it, was in so many ways better than the allegedly Christian state. ' More did not mean that heathendom is better than Christianity. He meant that some Christians are worse than heathen.'[6]

From the point of view of an age that has accepted religious toleration (though it has unhappily transferred its intolerance to other spheres) More's religious policy when in office was grossly illiberal; but however much we may disagree with him we are compelled to respect him. As he looked over his past life he surely had less than most men to reproach himself with. Some men's lives, like some works of art, have the quality of timelessness. More's is among these. He demonstrated and resolved a recurrent human dilemma and he remains an example to mankind. When

6 R. W. Chambers. This view of the question of toleration in *Utopia* is stated and fully worked out in his book, *Thomas More*.

he was first invited to the King's service, he knew that since human institutions are imperfect, there is rough work to be done in public office, and that hands get soiled. He put the case to Hythloday in Book I of *Utopia*. 'If evil opinions and naughty persuasions cannot be utterly and quickly plucked out . . . yet you must not leave and forsake the Commonwealth; you must not forsake the ship in a tempest, because you cannot rule and keep down the winds. . . . You must endeavour to handle the matter wittily and handsomely, and that which you cannot turn to good, so to order that it be not very bad.' Hythloday objects that there is no room for philosophers in the courts of princes. 'Yes there is,' replies More, 'but not for a speculative philosophy that makes everything to be alike fitting at all times.' Hythloday can only warn him that a philosopher entering upon a court career might be taken for a spy or a traitor—and in this prognostication he proved only too correct.

More wanted to serve his country, and this meant to be practical; to be practical meant to compromise and this More was prepared occasionally to do. The difference between him and many who are willing to risk soiling their hands is that he knew exactly when his conscience was touched. Conscience was a trained and active part of his person. On first taking service under Henry VIII he received an assurance that 'in all his doings and affairs touching the King, he should first respect and regard God, and afterwards the King his master'. A large part of More's case against heretics was that they split the unity of Christendom; he had no desire to split the unity of the Kingdom.

Throughout the controversies concerning the divorce, the succession, the supremacy, he was willing to be silent about his own opinions in the cause of the peace of the realm, but he was never willing to utter false ones. This could be interpreted as mere time-serving, or even more uncharitably, but for one simple and over-whelming fact. Rather than swear to what he believed false, More laid down his life.

More was finally sentenced—probably on false evidence—on a charge of high treason. When the Act of Supremacy[7] was finally passed, after More's commitment to the Tower, it became high treason to assert that the King was *not* Supreme Head of the

7 Without the saving clause, 'as far as the law of Christ allows'.

Church. More was only refusing to assert that he *was*. Sometime in April or May 1435, Thomas Cromwell (now Henry's chief adviser) and other Councillors visited More and tried in vain to make him discuss the Supremacy question. In June the second group of Carthusian monks who had been sentenced for taking a similar stand went to their deaths, and a few days after More had seen them led by his window on their way to the scaffold, a further attempt was made to get a statement from him. His fellow prisoner, Bishop Fisher, was inveigled into denying the Royal Supremacy, and was beheaded on 22 June.

On 1 July More was put on trial at Westminster Hall, where he denied that his silence was ' *maliciously* depriving the King of his title '. ' You must understand that in things touching conscience, every true and good subject is more bound to have respect to his said conscience and to his soul than to any other thing in all the world beside.' The Solicitor-General (Rich) then asserted—falsely —that More had made the treasonable statement, to which More replied: ' If this oath of yours, Master Rich be true, then I pray that I never see God in the face, which I would not say were it otherwise to win the whole world.'

After the verdict of ' guilty' More insisted on his right to speak and gave plainly his views on the Supremacy. One could see society from a national or a supra-national viewpoint. Of the national society, the King was the Supreme Head, but the only ruler of the supra-national state was God. Ones membership of the nation was of less importance than one's membership of Christendom, and reckoning himself as a member of that greater society, he was not in a minority in his views.

For those views he was sentenced to the traitor's death (to be hanged, drawn and quartered) but it was commuted to beheading. A few more days were to be passed in the Tower before the end. When he arrived with his guard at Tower Wharf, his daughter Margaret pushed through the armed men and clung to her father in an agonised farewell. He tried to comfort her and asked her to pray for his soul; later he sent her his hair shirt together with the last letter he ever wrote.

His closing days show an extraordinary combination of austerity and humour. The messenger that brought him the notice of the time of his execution also brought a request from the King that he would not speak long on the scaffold. This More promised. He walked to his death wearing a rough robe and carrying a red cross, and as he went up the shaky steps of the scaffold he made his last joke. 'I pray you, Master Lieutenant, see me safe up, and as for coming down let me shift for myself.' He bound his own eyes and embraced the executioner. Then he begged the bystanders— who included some of his own household—to pray for the King, and, on the threshold of death, uttered the words that express so succinctly his whole philosophy: 'I die the King's loyal servant, but God's first.'


FURTHER READING

R. W. CHAMBERS. *Thomas More.* Cape 1935.
E. M. G. ROUTH. *Sir Thomas More and his Friends.* Oxford University Press 1934.

A recommended edition of More's *Utopia* (together with the *Dialogue of Comfort*) is that published by Dent (Everyman) 1955. Ralph Robinson's translation.

# *Erasmus*

*(1466-1536)*

*The worst side often wins in the field, and to kill one's fellow-creatures needs no great genius; but to calm a tempest by prudence and judgement is a worthy achievement indeed.*

It was part of England's good fortune that the Renaissance in this country was to be informed as much by the spirit of a Thomas More as by the enthusiasm of Italian humanists. The first English scholars to pursue their studies in Italy—Linacre, Grocyn, Colet, all men of More's circle—brought back with them a fine devotion to the revived classical studies, but they also retained a respect for the moral values that had previously sustained them.

Soon the Reformation would sweep away the old forms of their faith, and mingle itself inextricably with the Renaissance of northern Europe. For some of them it meant martyrdom, but by the end of the sixteenth century a great national culture had sprung from the original Italian impulse, tempered by cooler minds and spiritualised by a genuine feeling for reform.

The single mind that had done most to make the fusion possible was undoubtedly that of Erasmus. In spite of the fact that he would have wished to steer a different practical course, no-one did more to give the Renaissance its particular quality in northern Europe, and no-one better exemplifies the nature of its distinction. He was its central figure and its greatest scholar, a cosmopolitan to whom all the nations stood alike indebted.

The very circumstances of his life seem to fit him for his European rôle. Born illegitimate, he called himself Erasmus of Rotterdam after his birthplace, but he lived indifferently in France, Germany, Italy, England and the Netherlands. Although he must have spoken both French and German, his fluent and flexible Latin was his passport to educated circles in all countries. He wrote consistently in Latin at a time when many scholars and theologians were beginning to use the vernaculars. Attached to no family or country, he dedicated himself entirely to learning, believing that through enlightenment would come a higher quality of life and international peace.

Erasmus was always sensitive about the circumstances of his birth, the shame being the greater in that his father was a priest; and his falsifications together with an involuntary haziness about chronology have made it impossible for the dates concerning the first part of his life to have complete certainty.

The romantic story that he made up to soften the harsh facts of his birth is known to many English readers through the use Charles Reade made of it in his novel *The Cloister and the Hearth*. According to Erasmus, his father, having been discovered to be secretly betrothed to his mother, was driven away by her family and wandered as far as Rome. Here he received false news of her death, and in his despair he entered the priesthood. Thus when he returned home and learned of the birth of his son, he was bound by his vows and could only live apart, though he assumed responsibility for the boy's upbringing and education.

The story could not survive investigation—amongst other factors is the presence of a brother, Peter, three years older and an offspring of the same union—but it has helped to obscure the circumstances of Erasmus's early childhood.

He was born on 27 October, most probably in the year 1466, his father being a priest called Gerard and his mother the daughter of a physician. He was given the Christian name of Erasmus which, when he was adult, he converted into a sort of surname by putting Desiderius in front of it. Although he was born at Rotterdam, his father's family appear to have lived at Gouda[1] about twelve miles away, and it was there that he and his brother first went to school.

At the age of about nine he was placed by his father in a well-known school at Deventer and his mother moved into the province of Overyssel to look after him there. His teachers mostly belonged to the Brethren of the Common Life, an organisation outside the Church whose members lived according to monastic ideals though bound by no vows. They worked in the world, and part of their work was to teach.

Erasmus later wrote harshly about the Deventer school. The conditions, he said, were barbaric, and the teaching methods clumsy. Certainly it seems to have had little to offer intellectually to an eager, receptive intelligence, although towards the end of his time there a new headmaster began to shed a little light in the

1 Rotterdam and Gouda are in Holland, one of the provinces of the Low Countries at this time under the rule of the Duke of Burgundy, Charles the Bold. For further explanation of the Low Countries see Francis I p. 105 and William the Silent, p. 167 et seq.

dark places. In his own later thought, too, Erasmus showed that he had been influenced by the religious teaching which sought to substitute the actual gospel of Christ for the hair-splitting theology of medieval educationists.

His days at Deventer came to an abrupt end after some eight years when his mother died suddenly of plague and he was recalled to Gouda. His father died soon afterwards, and Erasmus and his brother found themselves in the care of guardians who obviously intended that their wards should become monks. They were placed in a school at Bois-le-Duc (or Hertogenbosch) which provided a preparation for the monastery rather than for the University towards which Erasmus was already being drawn.

At the end of their schooling, heavy pressure was put upon the brothers to accept the monastic life, and in 1485 Peter capitulated and disappears from our story. Erasmus himself resisted a little longer, and then, partly influenced by an older friend who had found the life congenial, he entered the monastery of the Augustinian order at Steyn, near Gouda.

He had no vocation for the life he was embracing; he had both a physical revulsion and a mental aversion from much that he knew he would find. He was fastidious in his tastes to the point of squeamishness, and he was always inclined to the kind of self-indulgence that sees discomforts and hardships as bearing more heavily on oneself than on others. Fast days were more than distasteful; fish made him ill. Wine was a necessity of his physical constitution. The ordinary monastic routine undermined his health because once he was roused from sleep he could never return to it. And so on. These were his retrospective complaints, made long afterwards; how much effort at adaptation he made at the time is not clear.

At this time many monasteries were decadent and great numbers of monks negligent and immoral. Thomas More said this degradation had been going on for at least a century. There is no evidence, however, that Erasmus was surrounded by depraved characters; he complained only of the idleness and illiteracy of many of his companions, and, somewhat more vaguely, of drunkenness. Obviously a more pressing cause of discontent was the lack of sufficient intellectual intercourse, the absence of respect for the 'good letters' which by now had become the lodestar of his life.

His account of his experiences at Steyn is contained in an extraordinary letter written in 1516—we shall see later how significant a date this was in his life—beseeching the Pope to release him from his vows. Looking back from the age of fifty with a good deal more experience of ecclesiastical corruption, he made the letter into a scathing generalised indictment of the monastic life. ' How few monasteries there are in which the inmates live sincerely according to their rule. . . . He who in his habit[2] indulges in daily intoxication, who caters to his palate and appetites, who associates secretly and openly with lewd women, who wastes the revenues of the Church in luxury, who has recourse to fortune-telling and other malignant arts, he is an upright monk and is promoted to an abbotship; but him who for any cause has laid aside his habit they execrate as an apostate, a name which in ancient times was deservedly a term of abomination given to those who fell away from Christ.'

He made this letter an occasion to detail the circumstances of his having entered the monastery, and his complaint against his guardians, on this score and others, is bitter. He accuses them of rapacity and carelessness—and hints at dishonesty—in their dealings with his inheritance. He stigmatises Peter as a stupid, drunken voluptuary who, by yielding easily to the pressure of his guardians, betrayed his younger brother into the hands of those who would ' leave no artifice untried against the mind of a simple boy of such importance did it seem to these worse than Pharisees to bury alive one breathing, living youth '.

Whether or not the middle-aged Erasmus exaggerated the boy's feelings, it is a fact that he became a monk by virtual compulsion, and that there was engendered an attitude, later reinforced by more objective judgement, that governed all his thought, and was not to be without influence on the affairs of Europe.

As far as Steyn was concerned, there are some things to be said on the other side. However much we may, from a modern point of view, condemn the guardians for propelling reluctant youths towards the cloister, we have to remember that in the fifteenth century it would have seemed a not unreasonable solution to

2 i.e. the dress of a monk.

their problem. They may have acted from respectable motives. Also we have to allow that Erasmus did get some benefits. He made a few friends of high intelligence, and he enjoyed a great blessing in the use of the extensive library. Here he found the best of the Latin classics together with translations from the Greek; here too, he was able to study the writings of the Fathers of the Church, especially those of St Jerome that were to come to mean so much to him. He developed rapidly as a humanist scholar; he also began to write poetry with the Greek and Roman poets as his models.

The fact that after his year's novitiate Erasmus took his vows may be some evidence that life in the monastery was not totally uncongenial. However, opportunities for uninterrupted study decreased after this, and the next six years were not happy ones. In 1493, some months after he had been ordained priest, release came. He was permitted to accept a post as Secretary to the Bishop of Cambrai, Henry of Bergen-op-Zoom and, armed with a dispensation of non-residence from the Pope, he began a new life which involved moving with the Bishop between Bergen, Brussels, Mechlin and Louvain.

At Bergen he became friendly with a schoolmaster named James Batt who afterwards became the town clerk. Batt had studied at the University of Paris and it was probably through his good offices that the Bishop was persuaded to provide Erasmus with a similar opportunity.

This was the realisation of a half-smothered dream. As a boy Erasmus had had some intimations of the new intellectual influences that were permeating Europe from their Italian sources; he had heard talk of the great Platonic Academy of Florence, of the University of Rome, of the splendid libraries in these and other cities. He had at first hoped that his service with the Bishop might take him to Rome, but that hope had been dashed. Now an alternative presented itself. True, Paris was by no means Rome, but his most pressing need was for the contacts and stimulus that any university would afford.

He must have already begun to read the classics while still at school, and as his knowledge deepened during his time at Steyn, a sense of destiny had begun to take possession of him. He came to feel that it was a duty laid on him to immerse himself in 'good letters ', to master their significance because what the ancient civilisations had to tell could be used to the advantage of Europe, not only culturally but morally. What Greece and Rome had to say was relevant even to the work of the Church. He must make himself a channel through which the fertilising streams of the revived culture could flow.

Erasmus's journey to Paris in 1495 marks the beginning of his independent migratory life. In those days it was necessary for a scholar to travel far in search of manuscripts, as well as to visit the widely separated libraries. In the infancy of printing, it was also often essential for him to be at the site of the press to supervise the production of his work. Erasmus's frequent travel was not all due to restlessness; it was often irksome to him, ill-suited as he was for the hardships involved. His various comings and goings are too complicated to be followed in detail, but the broad pattern of his residence in various countries is easily set out.

During his thirties he lived mainly in Paris with one brief visit to England in the middle of the period, and one rather longer one at the end. After that, he was for three years (1506-1509) in Italy, and then a further five in England. In 1514, when he was forty-eight, he went to live at Basle which was to be the city of his most permanent residence. He lived from 1517 to 1521 at Louvain, but returned again to Basle and only left in 1529 when religious fanaticism made it disagreeable to him. He then lived in Freiburg in the territory of the Austrian Habsburgs until 1535; in this year, the last of his life, he went back to Basle where he died, and is buried.

It will be convenient to follow his activities and achievements up to the years 1516-17 before examining the ideas which by then were clearly formulated and which constitute the main interest of his later life. These were decisive years both for him and for Europe because in 1516 were published the two works which he, at any rate, regarded as his most important, and in 1517 the breaking of the Lutheran storm involved him in the greatest crisis of European thought.

Erasmus arrived at the University of Paris still wearing the dress of an Augustinian canon, but he introduced himself as a poet. The specified object of his study was a doctorate in theology, but he certainly intended to advance his classical knowledge. Although the Sorbonne[3] was the stronghold of the old scholastic teaching, the University as a whole was stimulated by visiting Italian scholars, and at this particular time new visions had been opened up by those returning with King Charles VIII from his recent expedition against Naples.[4] They were full of stories of the wonderland beyond the Alps, and eagerness for the new learning increased. Greek had to struggle for its existence, here as in Oxford, but it had made some headway and it must have been possible for Erasmus to learn the elements of the language at this time.

He stayed first at the College of Montaigu and afterwards in private lodgings. In neither was he very comfortable, and he complained in the way becoming habitual to him of the uncleanliness and the poverty of the fare. All the same, he led a sociable life of less strictness than he had ever known before, and he made valuable friendships.

Some of his new friends were originally pupils he had taken to eke out his stipend, and among these was the young Lord Mountjoy who first persuaded him to come to England, and who was his host on a number of occasions in this country.

Erasmus's first visit here was in the early summer of 1499. It was a very important episode in his life. In London and at Oxford he moved in the circles of the English scholars, and among the friends he made were Thomas More and Dean Colet with whom he was to remain on affectionate terms until their deaths.

Association with these men helped towards the maturing of the purpose already stirring in Erasmus. A new dimension of seriousness was added to his thought as a result of his English visit. At Oxford, Colet was giving a memorable course of lectures on the Epistles of St Paul. Erasmus saw at once the significance of a new method of Bible interpretation; his scholarly interests, which had been weighted towards the classical, shifted to emphasise the theological. It was in the dissemination of the gospel of Christ that a new standard was required. After his first stay in England, Erasmus always had one over-riding purpose: to purify Christian teaching in such a way that it would still carry its message in the new world that he saw was dawning, to clarify its texts and eluci-

3 Strictly the Theological Faculty in the University of Paris.
4 See Francis I, p. 106.

date its doctrine so that there would be no conflict between religion and humanism. Scholarship itself would be the tool, and for this most Christian of tasks, scholarship would need Greek. He had sensed how much Colet had been handicapped in his New Testament teaching by ignorance of the original language.

Erasmus went back to Paris at the beginning of 1500. He was very pleased with everything in England—even the climate, ' as delightful as it is wholesome '; principally though, as he wrote to an English friend living in Italy, with ' the humane learning, not of the outworn commonplace sort, but the profound accurate Greek and Latin learning '. Even an unpleasant episode at Dover when all his money was confiscated in accordance with currency regulations did not long modify his enthusiasm. He complained vehemently of the ' robbery ' in his letters to his English friends, but had the good sense not to hold it against them.

Back in Paris, Erasmus entered the most difficult and least edifying period of his life. He was poorly off; his pension from the Bishop had become uncertain, and the loss at Dover was serious for him. His immediate aims were to master Greek and to edit the writings of Jerome ('spoiled, mutilated, entangled by the ignorance of divines' as they were) in such a way that their true meaning would be laid open. Meanwhile he had to live.

In his necessity Erasmus sought, as was the fashion, the patronage of the wealthy and great. Harassed by poverty, periodically terrified by outbreaks of plague, his self-respect reduced to its lowest ebb, he allowed himself to descend to a tone of whining and begging—if nothing worse—which makes this part of his correspondence disagreeable to read.

At this time his friend James Batt of Bergen had become a tutor in the household of the wealthy Lady of Veere who had already extended her patronage to Erasmus. She was now a widow living with her young son Adolf in her castle of Tournehem, near Calais. A letter that Erasmus wrote to Batt in the December of 1500, which certainly shows him at his least admirable, may be quoted, and then we can forget this regrettable glimpse of a wretched period in his life in considering the magnitude of his intellectual and moral achievement.

' Go yourself to the Lady ', Erasmus wrote, ' Take Adolf with you to present my petition that he may touch his mother's heart,

E

and do not let him ask too little. . . . Tell her that I am in
extreme distress . . . that I cannot degrade my profession as a
man of learning by reducing my scale of living below its present
level, and that Erasmus will do more credit to her liberality than
the theologians she has taken into her favour. They can only
preach sermons; I am writing books that will live for ever . . .
the like of me comes but once in centuries. . . . Do not be shy.
Do not mind telling a lie or two in a friend's interest . . . say that
I absolutely must have two hundred livres, with a year's salary
from the situation which she promised me. . . . You will not
mind a few good sound lies for Erasmus. See that Adolf presses
her too, and dictate to him what he shall say that may be most
moving. See also that whatever is promised shall be promised with
Adolf's knowledge so that if anything happens to the mother, I
may recover from the son.'

What can be said in extenuation? That it may not all be
meant quite seriously; that it was not quite so flagrant in the
context of its time; more cogently, that Erasmus was begging not
for money to squander but to make it possible for him to concentrate on his great task. There is no doubt of his single-minded-
ness. He had earlier declined church benefices both in England
and at Tournehem, and a year or two later he was to refuse a
professorship at Louvain University. Any of these posts would
have secured him a regular income; he preferred his self-dedicated
road.

He had travelled some way along this road by the time he left
Paris in 1505. He could now write all that he wanted to in Greek;
he had translated Lucian's *Dialogues* into Latin for practice, and
he had begun the most important of his literary and educational
work that was to occupy the next ten years. Two books that
attained popularity—*The Adages* and *The Manual of a Christian
Soldier*—were published during this second Paris period.

Erasmus left Paris in the autumn of 1505 to go to England again.
It was a fruitful eight months visit spent largely in London. His
circle was increased to include divines as well as humanists;
William Warham, Archbishop of Canterbury, Richard Foxe,
Bishop of Winchester and John Fisher, Bishop of Rochester all
became his friends. He translated several Greek plays into Latin
and prepared a larger edition of the *Adages*. Then came the

opportunity he had long wished for. The two sons of Henry VII's Italian Court physician were about to go to Italy to study in charge of a tutor. Erasmus was offered the post of supervisor of their studies without any duties of tuition. He had no hesitation about this, and in June 1506 the party set out.

They travelled by way of Paris where Erasmus had much to deliver to his printer, and, having arrived in Italy, they stayed first at Turin for Erasmus to receive the degree of Doctor of Theology. They then went on to spend a year in Bologna, with a six-week interval in Florence.

The situation in Bologna was disgusting to Erasmus. Pope Julius II, more warrior than priest, was personally leading his troops to recover territory claimed by the Papal States. Supported by French arms, he attacked Bologna which fell to him while Erasmus was in Florence. On his return he witnessed Julius's triumphal entry. He was more deeply impressed by the brutality and cruelty of the campaign than by all the glories of Italian Renaissance art; the stupidity of war was henceforth one of his constant themes.[5]

Erasmus did not get on well with the tutor he was supposed to be supervising, and at the end of his year's engagement he resigned his charge. He had, in any case, somewhere more interesting to go. He was already in correspondence with Aldus Manutius, the great Venetian printer who had so well served the revival of learning by his production of the Greek classics in cheap editions. The early printers were equally publishers; they were also men devoted to the cause of scholarship. Their work was obviously of immense importance to Erasmus's aims; by means of the press uniform copies of the works he revised and annotated would be spread all over Europe.

When Manutius agreed to print new editions of his translations of Greek dramas and also an expanded version of *Adages*, Erasmus removed to Venice where, lodged with Manutius's father-in-law, working in co-operation with the press, and stimulated by the

5 An amusing little sketch called *Julius Exclusus* describing Julius arriving at the gates of Paradise and being refused admission by St Peter was in manuscript circulation from 1513, and was printed in 1518. Erasmus several times denied having written it, but it is still generally held to be his work. It can be read in Froude's *Life and Letters of Erasmus.*

society of Italian intellectuals he passed a profitable year. Only one thing was amiss; it was here that he had the first attack of the painful kidney disease that was to harass him for the rest of his life.

In 1509 Erasmus at last visited Rome where he was well received by humanists and ecclesiastics alike, and found much to enthral him in the scholastic treasures of the libraries. A more confident personality was emerging. He was rapidly winning a European reputation as a scholar and those in high places sought to bestow their patronage. He could comfortably have remained in Rome. He rejected all offers, however; still he would not tie himself, or be deflected from his solitary purpose.

At this point—the summer of 1509—there was reason for going back to England, since Henry VIII, that hopeful young scholar, whom he had met as a boy ten years earlier, had come to the throne. Erasmus set out to meet old friends. As he rode over the Alps he conceived the book that was to be among his most popular and remains his best known. Thinking about his friend Thomas More, he began to let his mind play round the Greek form of his name (Moria=Folly) and to amuse himself on his journey he worked out *The Praise of Folly*. On reaching England he went to stay with More at Bucklersbury and there the book was rapidly written. It was published in 1511 in Paris.

This third stay in England lasted for five years and for two of them—the longest period he ever remained in regular paid work —Erasmus was lecturing in Greek and Divinity at Cambridge. The royal patronage was not forthcoming, for Henry was quickly entangled in war with France, but Erasmus was appointed Rector of Aldington in Kent, and allowed for the rest of his life to draw a pension for the office without the obligation of residence.

His next move was an important one that came about only by chance. His agent, entrusted with some of his manuscripts for publication, took them for some reason, not to the usual printing house in Paris, but to that of Johannes Froben of Basle. This proved to be the beginning of a most fruitful business association and an enduring friendship. Erasmus himself went out to Basle in the summer of 1514; he was cordially received by Froben and was soon again at work in the congenial atmosphere of a printing office.

During his years in England he had been working steadily at his two most important projects, the editing of the writings of St Jerome[6] and a fresh translation of the New Testament from the original Greek into Latin. At Basle he found a group of scholars who were also concerned with Jerome. From their combined efforts under Erasmus's editorship were produced nine volumes, of which the first four were his own version of the Letters. The complete work was published in 1516: so also was Erasmus's New Testament.

He was now a world-famous scholar, conducting a vast correspondence, proffering advice to princes and prelates and exerting influence in widely different spheres. He was nominated a Councillor to Charles, the young Duke of Burgundy who had just become King of Spain, and he took the opportunity to express his views on government in a treatise called *The Education of a Christian Prince* which was dedicated to Charles.

One other important event occurred during this year. On his way out to Basle he had received a letter which came as a shock for it was recalling him to the monastery at Steyn. Erasmus was now nearly fifty and it was twenty-two years since he had emerged from the cloister. For some ten years he had worn simple clerical dress instead of his monk's habit, but he was, in fact, still only on leave and his dispensation for it had long since expired. He had written at once to the Rector of Steyn refusing to return: in the late summer of 1516 he made a trip to England to consult his friend Ammonius who was papal agent there, and to compose the letter which has already been mentioned, beseeching the Pope for general absolution and final dispensation from his vows. The Pope, Leo X, replied favourably at the beginning of 1517, and Erasmus should now have entered a period of security and calm such as he had never known before. Unfortunately 1517 was the year of the first crisis in the Lutheran revolt, and although Erasmus always said he was merely a spectator of the drama, by the very nature of his position and influence, he had to be involved.

Before we discuss Erasmus's attitude to the Reformation it might be as well, at this point, when the most restless part of his

6 Among much other work St. Jerome was primarily responsible for the Latin translation of the Scriptures which became the Vulgate.

life is over and his most important works are already published, to ask ourselves what manner of man he was, and what view of life his books were publicising.

The best of Erasmus's character is so closely integrated with the views he expressed in his books that it is difficult to distinguish between his qualities and his opinions. His faults, as with many people, were mostly the obverse of his virtues. His persistent refusal to bind himself in any way is one expression of the individualism that was his most marked characteristic. All commitment was distasteful to him; he disliked the idea of service to a master or authority as much as he spurned attachment to any party. Always he had to be free, physically and spiritually, to move whither he would. The strength of this attitude was a genuine detachment which enabled him to judge questions with some impartiality; the weakness, the apparent unreliability of one who always keeps open his line of retreat. It was this factor that brought upon him the criticism, however unjust, of both sides in the Reformation controversy.

His individualism did tend to make him self-centred. He acquired a secluded donnish type of egoism which expressed itself in fussiness and self-coddling. He was always a little sorry for himself, never feeling quite happy or quite comfortable. He needed peace and harmony, yet trailed petty worries about his relations with others, springing from his self-consciousness about the impression he made.

Yet, if Erasmus was aloof, he was at the same time more in touch with ordinary people than were most scholars; if he did complain a great deal, he was more than averagely sensitive. He feared the harsh realities of life and sought to protect himself from them, but the age was a brutal one, and his fastidiousness emerged often as a good influence. His protest against dirt and disease was a cogent one.

The quality which has survived his weaknesses is his undeviating loyalty to intellectual truth, while his contemporaries were impressed by the modesty and humility with which, in his maturity, he had come to carry his great learning.

Charm of personality is not fully recaptured by posterity; he was apparently a fascinating conversationalist, and his sense of humour twinkles through all but his most austere or caustic writings. We see it, too, in the well-known portraits by Metsys, Holbein and Durer, where always the grave, delicate face of the scholar is enlivened by the play of humour and gentle irony.

It is not easy to get a firm grasp of what is comprised in Erasmus's total writing. Its enormous bulk and unusual forms, ranging from simple tracts to monumental volumes, the forbidding titles, the discrepancies between the dates of manuscript circulation and those of printing, the fact that he was constantly issuing new versions with additions that might later be published as separate works all increase the confusion. Here it is sufficient to say that warrant for the views attributed to Erasmus can be found scattered through his books, and to discuss some that have most interest for (and can fairly easily be obtained by) modern readers.

It is possible to distinguish five main groups of his work: (1) those that were intended to promote education in literacy, as *Letter Writing* and the original *Colloquies*; (2) the books of proverbs which had a partly similar intention, and are best exemplified by the famous *Adages*: (3) works which may perhaps be called moral manuals, dealing with questions such as war (*Complaint of Peace, War is Sweet to the Inexperienced*), religion (*The Manual of a Christian Soldier*) and marriage (*On Christian Marriage*, written for Catherine of Aragon);[7] (4) the great Christian works, the editions of the Church Fathers and the New Testament; and (5) the writings against Luther. The aforementioned *The Praise of Folly* stands somewhat apart from all these, and we have to remember that he was publishing translations from the Greek classics and selections from his own correspondence throughout a large part of his life.

The *Adages* which became so popular a book—there were sixty-two editions during his life time—was conceived originally as an introduction to classical thought and a means of improving the style of budding authors. It was, on its first appearance, a collection of eight hundred Latin proverbs chosen with these ends in view. With each subsequent edition the collection was increased so that the volume of 1508 is called *Thousands of Adages* and Greek proverbs are added to the Latin ones. Erasmus's method was

7 The subject matter of these groups overlaps, of course. An item in *Colloquies* or *Adages* often discusses a social question which also commands a whole book.

to print the proverb as a heading, then explain it, adding his own comments and frequently pointing his remarks to his own time. There is the occasional embellishment of fable or anecdote. Obviously the successive editions could increasingly be used to castigate the abuses he deplored. Adages like ' It is better to remedy beginnings than ends ', ' The discord of brothers is the most bitter ', ' There are as many opinions as there are men ', had only too obvious an application to what was happening around him. For today's reader it is amusing to find many of our own homely proverbs—' There is many a slip 'twixt cup and lip '; ' Where there's smoke there's fire '—in their classical dress. Others that Erasmus selected expressed the essential Greek wisdom that he was anxious to revive: ' Know thyself.' ' Nothing in Excess.'

The *Colloquies* did not appear in authentic printed form until after 1516, but their inception was in 1500 when Erasmus had prepared a few examples of conversation to instruct his Paris pupils in the correct use of Latin as a spoken language. For the rest of his life he was adding to these dialogues which reveal his humour at its best at the same time as they provide a picture of the life of Renaissance Europe. It was doubtless the genial tone of this book that made it one of the most read works of the age; it is easy to see how for Erasmus it became more and more a vehicle for his views on all questions.

*The Praise of Folly*, published in 1511, was so far his most direct attack on Church corruption: it had, indeed, given offence to the clergy and alarmed his friends. Its form, however, provided him with the excuse, if he wanted one, that it was all a joke. It is still most amusing to read, although a sudden shift in the angle from which the satire is directed makes it rather bewildering in terms of strict logic.

In the beginning Folly, arrayed in cap and bells, is in the pulpit addressing a congregation of her devotees. She explains how many acceptable things in life are due to folly. Without it men would neither marry nor perform heroic deeds. In fact, since life is short anyway, wisdom might suggest that suicide would save us all much trouble; but folly makes the world go round.

Nothing that Folly says in the first half need be taken very seriously, though it cannot be consistently inverted. Seen in terms of Erasmus's serious work, Folly is indeed talking in character when she derides matrimony, but she would be talking the highest sense when she says that it is a foolish sort of courage that leads men to war. In fact, she sometimes establishes that it is wise to be foolish; sometimes we have to remind ourselves that the point of view is only that of Folly.

In the second half Folly is only talking in dumb show. The voice is clearly that of Erasmus. He makes an onslaught on divines and monks, monarchs and popes. His old resentment against the monastic system, his growing dislike of empty ritualism, his disgust at the war-like propensities of Julius II, the Emperor and the kings all have full rein. Folly, if she be deemed to be occasionally speaking, does not claim them for her own. All that she can say is that by her means the mighty are diverted from the pressure of their responsibilities. ' By my assistance they leave all these cares to the gods, and mind only their ease and pleasure, and therefore will admit none to their attendance but who will divert them with sport and mirth.' She has ceased to praise herself: she is clearly condemning such foolishness. Or Erasmus is.

He re-establishes his fiction firmly at the end, however: ' If I have said anything too confidently or impertinently be pleased to consider that it was spoke by Folly.'

It must have been a perplexing little book to those who looked further than the jest, and did not know what was to come after.

These were Erasmus's popular works but they clearly indicated his uneasiness about the Church. His New Testament was the outcome of his dissatisfaction with such Latin copies of the scriptures as were available. It was a work of restoration that carried the seeds of a revolution.

We have to remind ourselves that the Bible was little read at this time. Parts of it were intoned during the church service; for the rest, the rare copies were only studied in libraries by theologians and scholars for the most part quite uncritically. Colet was doing something new when his lectures inquired what St Paul had really meant.

Erasmus's translation sought to bring out the true significance of the original words, to reveal the personality of Christ, and to make it possible for readers to compare pure Christianity with the teaching of the contemporary Church. There was a general introduction explaining his attitude and each Gospel and Epistle had its own preface and notes. As new editions were called for, Erasmus expanded these notes so that passages of Christ's teaching were paralleled by summaries of current practices. The effect was devastating, and it is not surprising that as the thousands of copies poured from the printing press across Europe there was a wail of protest from conservative theologians; 'as if', rejoined Erasmus fairly enough, 'I was rebuking Matthew or Luke instead of those whose ignorance or negligence had corrupted what they wrote correctly'.

What is astonishing is that Leo X permitted the work to be dedicated to him. The fact that he did so may have encouraged Erasmus's hope that there would be a peaceful reformation. Eighteen months after the publication of the New Testament, however, Luther posted his Theses on the door of the church at Wittenberg.

It is a commonplace of school history books that 'Erasmus laid the egg that Luther hatched'. It remains to elucidate this statement. There are two main points to be considered in any attempt to understand the circumstances that produced the Reformation: the first is the state of corruption into which the Roman Church had fallen, and this was plain for all to see; the second is that in view of the universal acceptance of the Christian faith and the great power of the Church, it was necessary to decide how much of its practice and doctrine corresponded with the wishes of its founder, and how much was the accretion of time and the addition of popes—Bishops of Rome whose authority, after all, might not be divine. This necessity impelled the efforts of both Luther and Erasmus.

When Luther visited Rome in 1510, he had encountered profound disillusionment. He performed all the rituals, visited the shrines and venerated the relics, but he could not fail to be struck by the frivolity and corruption of the priests. The worst scandals of the Renaissance papacy were all around him: Rome was still that 'sink of all iniquities' against which Lorenzo had warned his son.[8] Luther returned home with his eyes opened to see that such was also the state of the Church in other places. The most flagrant sinners, both lay and clerical, went regularly through the ritualistic observances with no noticeable improvement in their

8 Who was to become Pope three years later as Leo X.

moral lives. Earlier than this Luther's deep reading and earnest self-searching had led him to the opinion that there was little essential Christianity in such practices themselves. After his return from Rome, and particularly from the time of his appointment as Professor of Theology at Wittenberg in 1512, he was studying the scriptures even more intensively with the one object of finding out what Christ had really said. By 1515 he was preaching his findings. After 1516, he was greatly assisted by Erasmus's New Testament.

Luther was confirmed in his opinion that it was not the outward trappings of religion that promoted holiness, but the receptivity of the human heart. Observation of holy days, penances, fasts, pilgrimages, even confession, had not been enjoined by Christ, and were not necessarily conducive to a state of grace. When the communicant approached the altar, the one thing necessary was his faith in God. Nothing he had performed could justify him: there was only Justification by Faith.

Luther had thus reached complete conviction on the questions of repentance and salvation when the Dominican monk, Tetzel, arrived on the borders of Saxony selling the indulgences that had been issued by Leo X to provide funds to complete the building of St Peter's. To many people the basic principle of indulgences will not seem offensive; certainly it was not unreasonable. Equally certainly it had very little to do with the teaching of Christ. The Church habitually ordered penances to be performed in expiation of sins; it also, on occasion, issued indulgences to relieve people of these penances. It was not necessarily objectionable that some charitable donation, based on a genuine sacrifice, should take the place of the original penalty. But the line between this and a crude selling of indulgences was obviously very fine.

A combination of papal avarice and popular superstition had, long before Luther's time, reduced the whole system of indulgences to a traffic in redemption. People had come to believe that indulgences not only relieved them of earthly penalties but insured the forgiveness of their sins in the world to come; they were encouraged to believe that a sufficient number of paid-up indulgences could assist their dead friends in purgatory. A succession of popes tacitly—and in some cases by open declaration—condoned this view. The plenary indulgences which Tetzel was selling would remit all sins in this world and the next, even those that were not yet committed.

Luther's protest against this appalling state of affairs eventually took the form of his ninety-five theses posted on the church door; among other things he denied the Pope's power to forgive sins and condemned indulgences as a hindrance to salvation and a diversion of true charity. Then there began the stream of papal letters and bulls against Luther. Had the Pope, at this point, been prepared to discuss the abuses, as Erasmus was openly advocating, the violent cleavage might have been avoided. But Leo was not so minded; Luther was swept on to the Diet of Worms (1521) where he finally denied papal infallibility. Popes, as much as other human beings, were capable of error.

Where did Erasmus stand? Obviously, by what he had published up to 1517 he was in agreement with Luther about the abuses he attacked. He had his own quarrel with the monks, and he disliked the superstitious conventions that were a mask of so much evil-living. He too wanted religion to be based on true reading of the Bible, the Ten Commandments and a morality that was practised. He first saw the opponents of Luther as philistines obstructing the new learning. . . . 'They thought that they had found a handle wherewith to crush good learning', he wrote in a letter to him in 1519.[9] This was naturally a very important aspect for Erasmus.

In 1517 he expressed the hope that Luther would succeed in getting indulgences abolished, and he was writing favourably about him in letters to his friends. He also wrote to the Elector of Saxony recommending him to protect Luther. There were, however, always differences in their outlooks, representing as they did, very different types of men. The cool, rational, perhaps not very imaginative mind of Erasmus, could not understand the tempestuous, anxiety-ridden nature of a Luther. Erasmus endured considerable mental conflict, but he did not go through 'dark nights of the soul'. There was nothing of the mystic in him: much of Luther's religious experience was of this kind. So even when Erasmus agreed with Luther, he held his views more temperately.

Erasmus did not regard ecclesiastical law as permanently

9 Luther wrote to Erasmus first (in April 1519)—evidently attempting to feel his way towards an alliance.

established. He thought that pilgrimages, veneration of the saints[10] and many monastic practices[11] (all of which the common people had come to accept without question) were mere superstition; as for fasting, confession and holy day observances, it was perhaps better that they should not be neglected so long as they were not believed to be of primary importance. He continued to accept the doctrine of the Real Presence—as indeed did Luther—because he could not think God would have allowed His Church to have remained in error on this matter for so long.

The most important distinction between the two men was that Erasmus was often only indifferent to things which provoked Luther's downright hostility. For Erasmus it was preferable not to define too much. He would have stated as directly and briefly as possible the simple teaching of Christ, leaving a wide area in which men could think what they like—especially about the things that no-one could pretend to prove. Luther was busy defining a new dogma.

This was the position during the years (1517-21) that Erasmus lived at Louvain. He became an Imperial Councillor in 1519 since Charles of Burgundy and Spain was elected Emperor in that year.[12] Erasmus might have the favour of Charles V, but the theologians of Louvain University were intensely hostile to him, seeing him as an associate of Luther, and his works as a cause of all the trouble. In vain he strove to make his position clear. He would always be a faithful subject of the Roman See; among other things it was a bulwark against national strife. But it did need reform. He himself could not enter the struggle; he did not wish to be of any party, not even one of Erasmians. All the same, he reiterated that it was only just that Luther should be heard and his views objectively examined. 'Luther ought to be answered and not crushed.'

Throughout 1520 Luther's expression of his views became more passionate and the views themselves more extreme. He was denounced by the Pope as a heretic. His published writings were now demanding sweeping changes in the church services with the

10 ' Who canonised St Paul or the Virgin Mary? '
11 ' The New Testament knows nothing of monastic vows.'
12 For the Emperor's office and the importance of this election see Francis I, pp. 104 et seq.

abolition of most of the sacraments, and Erasmus, moved perhaps less by the sacraments than by the fear of a permanent division of Christendom, began to protest against the reformers. There had been frequent demands from both sides that Erasmus should publicly state his own opinions, but he had refused either to read Luther's work or to write about him. In the summer of 1521, however, after the Edict of Worms and Luther's temporary disappearance from the scene,[13] he wrote in a letter to Archbishop Warham: 'I suppose I must write something about him. I will read his books and see what can be done.' But he never retracted his own criticism of the contemporary Church. Neither did the monks of Louvain cease their vilification of him. In October 1521 he moved back to Basle where he still tried to preserve a liberal middle way through the surrounding intolerance.

Erasmus, whilst always jealous for the dignity of the Church, would have had compromise on religious practices. Let the clergy marry (in any case 'the celibates are many and the chaste few'), let the service be said in the vernacular tongue, let the laity receive the wine at communion. The essentials could still be retained and unity preserved. But the time for compromise was past. Vast numbers were now flocking to the Lutheran standard; in Wittenberg a completely reformed service was in use; in various towns of Europe image-breaking riots had broken out and altars were being overturned. Throughout Germany the turmoil was constantly increasing, and the violence which Luther himself deplored was taking charge. To Erasmus this was the worst of all worlds. He moved out of neutrality and penned his first writing against Luther. It was called *On Free Will*.

This may seem somewhat apart from the main issues, but it was really the heart of the permanent division between Erasmus and Luther. The core of Luther's doctrine was the rejection of overt works in favour of Justification by Faith, but faith was something that could not be commanded. It might be vouchsafed by the goodness of God, but no one could claim to have it as a personal decision. Hence the individual could not choose or even earn salvation. Those that lived righteously did not do so that they might be rewarded by grace; their behaviour was a manifestation of grace already bestowed. Human will did not enter into it; all was

13 He was back in Wittenberg within a year.

preordained, and the gloomy doctrine of predestination was the inevitable development. To Erasmus, this destruction of human responsibility was abhorrent. As a Roman Catholic he believed in original sin, but as a man of the Renaissance he believed in the uplifting of men through right education. His essay set out to show that there was no incompatibility.

Undoubtedly many people in Germany had sided with Luther because they resented the draining away of money to Italy for the support of a profligate papacy; many others approved of his attacks on superstitious observances. These points, where he and Erasmus were in agreement were easy for all to appreciate. Fewer gave thought to the deeper implications of his theology which was where Erasmus parted company with him: hence the charges against Erasmus of making a coward's retreat. In fact he retreated very little. His fundamental position remained the same throughout.

*On Free Will* was not acceptable to the extremists of either side. Erasmus strove still to maintain a middle position. On the one hand he was alarmed by Charles V's preparation to suppress the Reformation movement by force; on the other hand, it was the supporters of Luther who now seemed to him to be the opponents of ' good Letters '—they had ' brought learning into ill-repute '.[1]

As new sects inevitably began to splinter off from Lutheranism, Erasmus became more conservative in his attitude. In 1529, when Basle accepted the reformed faith, he moved to Freiburg to immerse himself again in his work on the Church Fathers and the classics.

The substantial charges made against Erasmus by his opponents are that having been the instigator of a religious revolution, he had not the courage to give it his active support, and that his attitude lacked consistency.

No one can read Erasmus's works up to 1516 without recognising a sure source of the ideas that the Reformation later developed. His New Testament was designed to promote the kind of Bible study which was to challenge the teachings of the Church. There was no reason, though, for him to give support to the activity of the reformers; he endorsed the criticisms they made and dis-

14 In *Ciceronian*, published in 1528, however, he himself suggested that too exclusive an attention to humanism, could be a danger to true religion.

sociated himself from violence and extremism. It is not always less courageous to pursue a middle course, though it is usually more lonely. If anyone is persuaded that Erasmus tried to keep in the good graces of all, it is only fair to remember that he felt he had incurred the hostility of all; and he continued to attack abuses in his later *Colloquies* long after the break with Luther.

He himself said he was not made of the stuff of martyrs. Perhaps not. But it is not always those who feel this who fail if brought to the test. We can hardly blame Erasmus for not seeking martyrdom. He resisted the attacks of Louvain and the blandishments of Basle; he showed courage in his frank addresses to both rulers and popes. He never allowed himself to be captured by a party.

The charge of inconsistency cannot stand if we bear in mind his complete views. He was, after all, occupied with much else. Of the purposes he set himself, for him the greatest was that of reconciling classical culture with Christianity. Next, probably came the cause of peace; he disliked conflict whether of class, nation or religion. His has been one of the clearest and strongest voices raised against national war, and he was anxious for a compromise that would preserve the states of Europe in one religion because he saw such unity as the greatest safeguard of peace. He was sufficiently in advance of his age to propose some sort of overall authority to compose the quarrels of princes.

Erasmus was never closely in touch with practical politics, and his economic and political views are rather superficial. Like most men of his time he favoured monarchy, though modified by some aristocratic and democratic elements. His writing is vague and somewhat contradictory about this. It is ' the consent of his subjects that makes a Prince ', yet there is to be no popular discussion of governmental questions. At the same time he insists that the purpose of laws should be to instruct rather than to punish. He obviously feared the absolutism he saw growing and would have preferred elective monarchies to hereditary ones. Since that was not to be, he put his trust, with true Renaissance optimism, in the right education of princes.

With social questions Erasmus was on firmer ground. He had experience of many places and contact with a great many people, and this was a basis for some advanced thinking. He advocated universal education for girls as well as boys, and he was concerned for the welfare of women. He wrote much about marriage, even going into details about the management of home and children. The forcing of young girls into reluctant marriages or into convents was a subject that always aroused his indignation. His fastidiousness about the condition of inns and lodgings had a strong social side. Anxious to check the spread of disease, whether caused by dirt or immoral living, he had practical remedies to suggest.

He always preached a morality that he believed to be within the grasp of all, free from superstition and informed with the Greek conception of the good life. Virtue and happiness were so much the same thing that it was only sensible to be good. His governing principle was always reasonableness, yet he was really no more a rationalist than he was a mystic. He reserved too large an area where the human mind could not operate. It was for him only reasonable to see that many questions are beyond reason.

Erasmus moved back to Basle in the summer of 1535, and for the remaining year of his life he was bedridden at the house of Froben's son. In Basle the religious turmoil had ceased, and the atmosphere was peaceful, but there was little consolation for Erasmus's last days. He was now very ill, and just before leaving Freiburg he had been saddened by the news of the deaths of Fisher and More. In Germany the Reformation pursued its way in the lull of an armed true. Since the Confession of Augsburg in 1530 he had been bringing himself to recognise that Christendom was irreconcilably divided: his counsels had not prevailed.

In estimating the influence Erasmus may have had, it is necessary to remember the great number of prominent persons with whom he was constantly in touch. Always he was swaying more minds than is suggested even by the extent of his writing.

Of the three chief results of his life's work, one is intangible, one was unintentional, and the third represents the goal of much of his endeavour. He must have contributed to the cumulative influence of liberal tolerant minds that persists in the European tradition. The Reformation—however we may regard it—sprang largely from Erasmus's thought, and no one can say now whether there could have been a better way. In the main field of his activity his intention triumphed: he made a massive contribution to the intellectual development of northern Europe.

# FURTHER READING

J. HUIZINGA. *Erasmus of Rotterdam* (1924), trans. F. Hopman.
Phaidon Press 1952.

MARGARET MANN PHILLIPS. *Erasmus and the Northern Renaissance.*
Hodder & Stoughton for English Universities Press 1949.

J. A. FROUDE. *The Life and Letters of Erasmus.* Longmans 1854.

ROLAND BAINTON. *Here I Stand* [Luther]. New American Library of
World Literature 1950.

*The Praise of Folly* may be read in an edition published by the
Oxford University Press, 1913. Edited by H. M. Allen; translated
by J. Wilson.

# Christopher Columbus

*(1451-1506)*

*All Christendom should rejoice and celebrate with solemn
thanks to the Holy Trinity both for the great exaltation
that may accrue to them in converting so many nations to
our Holy Faith, and also for the temporal benefits which
will bring great refreshment and profit, not only to Spain,
but to all Christians. . . .*

*I have done all that I could do. I leave the rest to God,
whom I have ever found propitious to me in my necessities.*

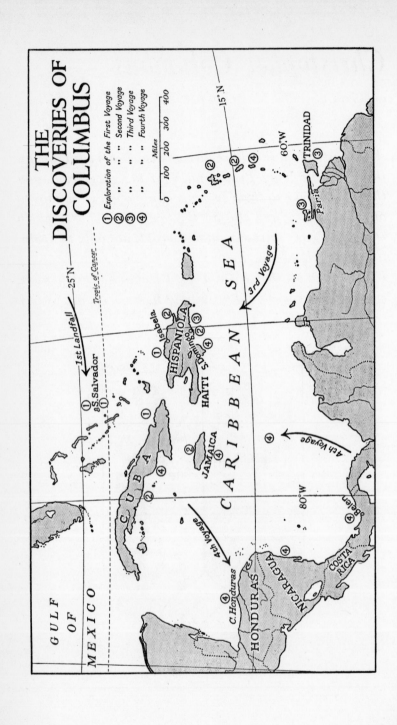

THE
DISCOVERIES OF
COLUMBUS

① Exploration of the First Voyage
② ,, ,, ,, Second Voyage
③ ,, ,, ,, Third Voyage
④ ,, ,, ,, Fourth Voyage

Miles
0    100   200   300   400

15° N

TRINIDAD ③
Paria
③
60°W

3rd Voyage

CARIBBEAN    SEA

25° N
1st Landfall
Tropic of Cancer

①S.Salvador
① ①

GULF
OF
MEXICO

CUBA
④
②

① Isabela ②
HISPANIOLA
S.Domingo ③
HAITI ② ④

JAMAICA
②

4th Voyage
④

80°W

4th Voyage

C.Honduras ④
HONDURAS

NICARAGUA
④

Belen
④

COSTA
RICA

IT IS POSSIBLE that of all the stirring events which occurred in the period of the Renaissance the discovery of the New World was of most importance to mankind's subsequent history. It is certain that its discoverer was among the bravest men who have lived at that or any other time. The character and personality of Christopher Columbus may well be differently judged by different people, but no student of his life and work can fail to remark that courage was its keynote.

The facts of Columbus's early life are somewhat confused, but it seems certain that the Colombo[1] family had lived near the Italian city of Genoa for some generations and that his father, Domenico Colombo, was a weaver who was also for a time a warden of one of the city watch-towers, and later kept a wine shop. Christopher, the eldest of five children, was born probably in 1451, and he may have received some elementary education from the Benedictine monks. If he did, it was very little; he never wrote in Italian, and the Spanish and Latin which he did use must have been acquired later in life. At about twelve years of age, he was assisting in the wine business, and when he was between fourteen and fifteen he first went to sea. The sea seems to have had the strong attraction for him that it had for many Genoese boys, and after some years' experience on trading vessels in various parts of the Mediterranean he joined—as a common seaman—a Genoese convoy that was going to trade in England and Flanders. This convoy was attacked off the south coast of Portugal by a Franco-Portuguese[2] war fleet; Columbus's ship was sunk and he managed to reach the shore not far from Lisbon whither he made his way. This adventure occurred in the year 1476 and proved to be a decisive turning-point in his life.

There were many Genoese at Lisbon, amongst whom was—or

1 The Italian form of Columbus's name was Christofero Colombo, but he is known to Spaniards as Christobal Colon.

2 France was at war with Burgundy and at least one of the Genoese ships was flying the Burgundian flag.

was soon to be—Christopher's brother Bartholomew, who had become a professional map-maker. The Republic of Genoa had, of course, strong sea-faring interests, and many of her sons were attracted to Portugal where King Alfonso V was still vigorously encouraging the exploration inaugurated by his uncle Prince Henry the Navigator. Lisbon was an international meeting place for sailors and cosmographers who had, indeed, a good deal to be excited about, for their world was seething with new ideas and conjectures about the nature of the universe and the possibility of undiscovered lands.

From early boyhood Columbus must have heard discussions on these topics; it is therefore worth while at this point to summarise the geographical conceptions that prevailed. Fifteenth-century Europeans were aware of the existence of Asia and Africa as continental masses. Trade was regularly carried on with the Indies, the Spice Islands (East Indies) and the coast of Cathay (a province of China) both by sea-route from Arabia, and overland across southern Asia. This had stimulated great interest in oriental commodities and also in the mysterious land of Zipangu[3] (Japan) which was thought to be a land of gold. As for Africa, apart from the north and the Nile Valley, which were, of course, known to antiquity, the West African coast as far as the equator had been explored by the Portuguese, who had also taken possession of Madeira, the Azores, and the Cape Verde Islands; and before Columbus's great expedition set sail they were to round the south of Africa and name the Cape of Good Hope. In the course of pioneering this type of exploration they had already acquired great experience of colonisation and its trading possibilities.

Since the sixth century B.C. there had been an intermittent belief in a lost land of Atlantis which was thought to have been submerged in the 'Ocean Sea' beyond Spain (i.e. the Atlantic), and there were tales that still, far in the west, there were a series of 'enchanted isles', the largest known as Antilia, which were stepping stones to a great continent beyond. Ancient Greek scholars had also held that the earth was round, but much ancient knowledge was lost during the Middle Ages and the medieval conception was of a flat world. Some held that the seas surrounding the

3 Also Cipangu, Cipango, Cypango, Ciganzu.

earth stretched flat to the borders of the Earthly Paradise which only the souls of the dead could reach. Others believed that the sea eventually curved down to a precipice and that no one who started to descend it could return. By Columbus's time probably most people thought of the earth as a disc floating on a vast ocean with the sky covering it as a great dome; but also by this time the idea of a spherical universe was generally accepted by scholars and enlightened men.

Columbus, who mingled so much with seamen and carto-graphers, certainly believed that the world was round, but in common with others he immensely underestimated its circum-ference and did not reckon on the existence of the American con-tinent. He was fired with the idea that if he could find the islands of the western ocean they would—since the world was round—be stepping stones to the mainland of Cathay and the Empire of the Grand Khan. We do not know exactly when Columbus became possessed by this ambition, but we do know that to its realisa-tion he dedicated the rest of his life. It must be remembered that there were no books of practical information; news of exploration was given by word of mouth and became a wild mixture of truth, legend and fantasy. Students, and some privileged persons, were able to get access to records of ancient Greek and Arab astronomy, and to the very inaccurate maps and charts of early explorers. Pro-fessional map-makers appeared who based their cartography partly on this data and partly on the reports of voyagers and interviews with seamen. 'Charting the universe' became a popular pastime for intellectuals.

Columbus must have taught himself a good deal about practical seamanship and the art of navigation between his first departure from Genoa and his arrival in Lisbon. During the eight years he lived in Portugal he learnt all he could about geography, astro-nomy and kindred subjects. He also, soon after his arrival, joined an expedition to England, Scotland and Iceland. All the time he was gathering information about the western seas, and when in 1479 he married Felipa Moniz Perestrello he became related to a churchman who had been corresponding with the famous Floren-tine cosmographer Toscanelli on behalf of the Portuguese King. Columbus was able to get from Toscanelli a copy of the informa-tion he had sent to the King, as well as a chart, and in the year

1482 he approached John II (who had succeeded Alfonso V) with a request for ships. Although the King himself was sympathetic, his advisers rejected the proposal for reasons unknown to us, but perhaps because Columbus's terms—if we are to judge from the ones he later asked from Spain—seemed extravagant.

In the years immediately following this rebuff Columbus's affairs do not seem to have prospered. Debts accumulated, his brother failed in his attempts to win the support of either the King of England or the King of France, and at this point, his wife disappears from the story. It is probable that she died, for some time in 1484 Columbus secretly left Portugal for Spain, taking with him his four-year-old son Diego. He found refuge in the Franciscan monastery of Our Lady of Rábida,[4] near the little port of Palos where the Prior consented to care for the boy and where he made a true friend in Father Marchena who had studied cosmography and was much interested in the religious implications of discovery. He was able to give him some useful introductions in Seville and there he gained the support of the Duke of Medina Celi who gave him a letter to Cardinal Mendoza, Archbishop of Toledo, and in January 1486 Columbus entered Córdoba where the Court was intermittently in residence. After a number of interviews with the Queen's confessor and the Castilian Comptroller of Finances, Columbus was granted an interview with the Queen herself.

Spain at this time was ruled by Ferdinand (of Aragon) and Isabella (of Castile) whose marriage in 1469 had eventually brought unity to Spain while leaving Isabella with a position more powerful than that of a mere consort. Her chief aim in life was to spread the Catholic faith and she was at once interested in the missionary possibilities that would be opened up if Columbus discovered a new route to the east. She therefore caused a Commission to be set up to examine the proposals, and meanwhile made Columbus a royal grant. The Commission seems to have been unconvinced by his calculations and perhaps swayed by old-fashioned theological objections; at any rate it reported unfavourably. Between 1489 and 1491 Columbus was back at La Rábida and was making overtures to the Court of France. Perhaps it was fear of France that caused Isabella to summon the Prior of La Rábida to Santa Fé where she and Ferdinand were encamped

4 See Plate 2a.

while conducting the siege of Granada, the last stronghold of the Moors. As a result of the interview another Commission was set up and Columbus was recalled to the Court. On 2 January 1492 Granada fell and Ferdinand and Isabella had achieved one of the major tasks of their joint reign—the destruction of the Moorish kingdom in Spain. Yet once more Columbus's proposal was rejected and he determined to carry it to France, but when he was already four miles out from Santa Fé, ambling along on his mule, a royal messenger overtook him and bade him return. The Keeper of the Privy Purse to King Ferdinand had persuaded the Queen of the advantages that might be gained from what would be, after all, a very small risk.

On 17 April 1492 a contract was drawn up which guaranteed support for the expedition, and also granted the far-reaching demands which Columbus always felt justified in making. The sum invested in the expedition would amount to about £4,000 in the money of today; and Columbus himself contributed one-eighth of the cost (which he had to borrow). Also it was conceded that Columbus would be Admiral of all Islands, and Continents he might discover, with honours similar to those of the Lord High Admiral of Castile, and that these privileges would descend to his heirs. He was also to be Viceroy and Governor over all lands discovered, with the right of nominating three candidates for the office of administrator of each island. One-tenth part of the profit from all precious stones, metals, spices and merchandise was to come to his family, and for ever they would have the right to contribute one-eighth of the cost of fitting out expeditions and to receive one-eighth of the profits. Finally, Columbus or his nominee was to be supreme judge in all disputes arising with other countries with regard to the traffic between Spain and her new lands.

In considering these terms it is important to remember that the rulers of Spain did not think of the discoveries as being likely to be more than a few islands on the way round the world to Zipangu and Cathay. The contract does not mention these eastern lands, but Columbus was provided with a letter of introduction to the Grand Khan, and his own Journal states that he had a commission to proceed to the East by a western route. What is stressed both by his royal patrons and by Columbus himself is that he has 'certain duties and enterprises affecting the service of God and the increase of the Christian faith, as well as our own advantage and profit'.

Having settled the terms, Columbus hastened to Palos where there lived the Pinzons, a family of shipbuilders and sea captains, to whom he had already been introduced. Martin Pinzon, the head of the family, already possessed some information about western lands, and he had been to Rome and inspected various maps and charts. He did not take altogether kindly to the suggestion that he should play second fiddle to the upstart Columbus of the mysterious origins, but he seems to have been placated by an offer of a share in the profits, and he and his two brothers joined the expedition. It was not easy to get ships. The Government insisted that two caravels due from Palos to the Crown should be handed over, but *Santa Maria*—the flagship—probably had to be chartered by Columbus himself. It was even more difficult to get crews. Some volunteers were forthcoming, but in the end it seems to have been necessary to waive the sentences of criminals if they would undertake the voyage, and the crews were thus in part composed of men released from jail for the service.

In spite of everything, within ten weeks the expedition was ready, and by the end of July 1492 the three little ships that comprised it were riding in Palos harbour: the *Santa Maria*, and the two smaller boats, *Pinta* and *Nina*. We have to imagine the flagship itself as a vessel no larger than could occupy a tennis court; they were all square rigged (at any rate from the time they left the Canaries), all had three masts and single decks. They each flew the royal pennon—a green cross with F and Y the (Spanish) initials of the sovereigns embroidered on it—and their sails also bore a cross. The *Santa Maria* also flew its own standard, showing a Christ crucified on a black background. They were armed with lombards—small short-barrelled cannon which threw balls of stone hooped with iron. They were, of course, equipped each with a mariner's compass, and Columbus also had an astrolabe, adapted from the old astronomer's astrolabe, for the purpose of calculating his position from the sun, but he had no knowledge of the currents in the uncharted ocean and his only means of telling the time was a half-hour sand glass. Martin Pinzon commanded the *Pinta*, his younger brother being in charge of the *Nina*. Also with the expedition were an interpreter who could speak Hebrew and some Arabic (as Arabic was supposed at this time to be the mother of all languages, this would do for the Grand Khan), an expert on metals, a doctor and a notary. The total complement was towards a hundred persons of whom about forty would have been on the flagship.

On 2 August all the ships' companies went to Mass and heard a sermon by the Prior of La Rábida. Just before sunrise on 3 August 1492 the expedition set sail. One of Columbus's most outstanding characteristics, his unwavering persistence, had borne fruit. Coupled with determination was pride. Although he must have suffered at times from a sense of inferiority, since it caused him to pretend to noble origins that were false, he had a genuinely high opinion of his own abilities, a self-confidence which is amazing when one considers all the circumstances; and he had never lowered his price.

The voyage was to test determination, self-confidence and courage all to the full. For seventy-one days the ships sailed doggedly westward through days of hope and through days of near-despair for all but the undaunted leader. Only the force of Columbus's personality persuaded a semi-mutinous crew to endure to the end.

In order to be within the zone of the north-east trade winds, they sailed first in a southerly direction to the Canary Islands[5] and were a month there because the *Pinta* needed repairs. On 6 September they left the islands and now sailed due west. Already by 9 September Columbus had decided that he must keep two logs, one true one for himself and one which gave only four-fifths[6] of the real distance so that the crews should not be alarmed if the journey were longer than he had estimated. This fact alone is a grim commentary on the morale of his seamen. After 13 September they were far enough west to observe the unexpected variation of the compass needle from the true north. No-one had previously encountered this phenomenon in the western seas, and the sailors were much alarmed, as they were also by meteors and the long absence of a 'returning wind'.

Occasionally there were signs that lifted their hearts, shoals of

5 Spanish possessions.
6 He was not consistent in this but the second log always showed less than the true distance.

fish, or birds flying westward which suggested that land was near, and during the third week of September they saw what they took to be bunches of grass—surely torn from some island? Actually they were entering the Sargasso Sea, and as the gulf weed increased until they seemed to be in the middle of a yellowish green meadow, their fears returned again. Perhaps they would never be able to get through to open water. A few days' experience, however, convinced them that sargassum is in fact no hindrance to navigation.

The distance logged by this time should, according to Columbus's calculations, have brought them to the archipelagoes which his maps told him flanked the coast of Asia, so he concluded that he must be driving between them and that they lay out of sight to the north and south; but this faith was not shared by his men. They all knew now that they had passed the estimated distance; they were afraid of food supplies running out, and perhaps old legends reasserted themselves. The mood was one of incipient mutiny when, on 25 September, Pinzon declared that he could see land. They believed in this landfall till the afternoon of the next day, and the crews had been assembled to give thanks, when they realised it was only a bank of cloud.

Some ten days later there was another false hailing of land, and further rumblings of mutiny, for 'the men could now bear no more', as Columbus wrote in his journal, but 'the Admiral heartened them as best he could, holding out to them bright hopes of the gains which they could make, and he added that it was in vain for them to complain, since he was going to the Indies and must pursue his course until, with the help of our Lord, he found them'. So he held his crew together until the memorable night of 11 October came.

That afternoon there were signs—a green branch floating, a stick worked with tools, and petrels flying. At ten o'clock Columbus thought he saw a light ahead but was not sure it was land. Queen Isabella had offered a prize of a yearly pension of 10,000 marvedis (about £25) to the first man who should see land. To this Columbus now added the offer of a silk jacket. At about two a.m. Rodrigo de Triana, a sailor who was look out on the *Pinta* which was leading, saw land about six miles ahead and shouted. Pinzon fired lombards—the agreed signal—and waited for the flagship. Sails were lowered and the boats lay to till morning; and then early on

Friday 12 October 1492 they dropped anchor on the western side of the island, now sometimes called Guanahani[7] and which Christopher Columbus christened San Salvador.

The natives of the island were a sturdy well-built race of people with broad chests and flat foreheads. Their skin was copper-coloured and their hair straight and coarse. They wore no clothes but were painted black, white and red, some over the whole body, and some only on their faces.[8] Rings and discs of gold hung from their ears and nostrils. They had no weapons and seemed to be a gentle people, regarding the newcomers with a mixture of fear and goodwill. Within a single generation of the white man's coming these people were exterminated. But at the time of Columbus's arrival, they crowded on the beaches to watch the approach of the armed boat that had been lowered from the flagship and to prostrate themselves before the miraculous beings who landed from it. Columbus was the first to set foot on land, dressed as a military commander in a dark velvet suit with a short cloak and violet silk stockings. He kissed the earth, had the royal standard planted on the beach, offered up prayers, and took possession of the island in the name of the Spanish sovereigns. The King's notary made an official record.

During the succeeding days Columbus cruised from island to island imagining them to be those between Zipangu and Cathay, and hoping to find the gold suggested by the ornaments of the natives. The islands were named in what was to Columbus the correct hierarchical order. The first had been The Saviour (San Salvador). In turn after that came Santa Maria, Fernandina, Isabela, and Juana (after the Crown Prince). Each island was ruled over by its own king—a person of few pretensions except that he wore some clothes and numerous ornaments. Among the marvels the sailors encountered was a breed of dog that were unable to bark, and men who seemed to be in thrall to a strange habit: '. . . the men always with a glowing piece of wood in their hands and certain herbs for smoking, these are dry herbs and placed in a leaf also dry after the manner of the paper tube muskets which the

7 Name from iguana—a reptile now extinct there.
8 Columbus afterward learned that this was done to protect them from the sun.

boys in Spain use at Easter. Having lighted one end, they draw in the smoke by sucking at the other—they absorb or receive it—and this gives a soothing feeling and almost intoxication, and according to their account relieves them from the feeling of weariness. These tubes, or muskets as we would say, they call by the name of tobacos.'

This encounter was on Cuba which Columbus took to be a continental province, but he could find no signs of the grandeur he associated with the lands of the Grand Khan, and so he sailed on southwards and landed on the island now called Haiti. Conditions there were idyllic; the people, though timid, were friendly, and the natives who had been brought from San Salvador to act as interpreters were able to prevail upon the local king—or cacique—to be entertained on board. He dined on the *Nina* splendidly arrayed in a shirt and a pair of gloves.

There was evidence of a little gold in the river sands, and Columbus decided to make a settlement on the island which he named Hispaniola.[9] On the north coast a small fortress was built in the centre of a clearing and the area surrounded with a wooden fence. This was to be the garrison of La Navidad (The Nativity), and thirty-nine men were chosen to remain there with provisions sufficient for one year. Columbus himself, taking the Indians with him, set out for home. He had to sail in the *Nina*, for the *Santa Maria* had struck a reef just outside the harbour and was lost. The return voyage—as indeed, were all subsequent crossings—was more difficult than the outward one because of contrary winds and high seas, but the spirits of the crew were high enough to face even the last tremendous tempest off the Azores with resolution. Were they not returning from the world's greatest adventure?

There was, however, one discordant note: the recurrent jealous resentment of Pinzon. During the exploration of the islands, he had sailed ahead without orders and separated his vessel for some six weeks from the flagship. Now, during a lull in the tempest, he took advantage of the *Pinta's* superior speed to make off for Spain in the hope of receiving the first acclamations. The *Nina*, with the last barrel of ship's biscuits already opened, was forced to put in at Santa Maria in the Azores where there were difficulties with the Portuguese governor. This hostility, which we may assume sprang

9 Actually in Spanish—Española.

from jealousy, was again manifested in Portugal itself a week later when the ship was forced to anchor off Restello[10] the outer port of Lisbon. Here one Bartholomew Diaz, who may or may not have been the Diaz who discovered the Cape of Good Hope, came aboard the *Nina* and ordered Columbus to return with him to give an account of himself. Columbus, striking a lordly note, said neither the Admiral of the Ocean Sea nor his subordinates could do this. Diaz inspected the *Nina*'s papers and returned to his superior, the Captain of the Portuguese man-of-war, who then paid a courtesy visit to the *Nina*. After four days the King commanded Columbus's presence at Court, thirty miles from Lisbon. There he was graciously received though the insincerity of King John was obvious. If he were plotting against Columbus's life the idea was abandoned, or at any rate postponed, for after a week Columbus was dismissed. Nevertheless he thought it prudent to decline the offer of an overland guide to Castile; he went by boat down the Tagus and sailed for home the next morning.

On 15 March 1493 Columbus anchored at Palos thirty-two weeks after his setting out. After all he was first: the *Pinta* arrived the following day, having first put in on the west coast north of the Portuguese border, and the same tide took the two vessels across the bar.[11] One of Columbus's first acts was to go shoeless and in sackcloth to give thanks at La Rábida. Then he went on to Seville where there was a letter from Ferdinand and Isabella to ' Our Admiral of the Ocean Sea, Viceroy and Governor of the Islands discovered in the Indies ', commanding him to the Court at Barcelona. There followed a triumphal progress through south and east Spain, from Seville by way of Córdoba where he met his two sons, on to Barcelona.

At this time Columbus was forty-two, a man of middle height, strongly built and well proportioned. His face was long with high cheekbones, strong features and bold eyebrows. He was of ruddy complexion, but his hair that was once red had turned white, giving him an appearance of dignity as well as of strength. He walked in the procession through the towns dressed in the simple garb of the Franciscan brothers, though his guards wore breastplates and carried pikes. Behind them came seamen bearing aloft

10 Now Belem.
11 Pinzon died shortly afterwards.

trophies of the adventure—bamboo reeds, parrots in cages, a
stuffed crocodile, Indian implements, branches of strange woods
and masks—and, following on that, the six[12] mysterious Indians
with their native accoutrements. At every chapel and altar devo-
tions were paid, and the Indians dutifully crossed themselves. The
procession was finally played into Barcelona by a band of drums
and fifes. Everywhere the people flocked to gaze in wonderment,
and we shall perhaps best enter into their feelings if we imagine
how we of the twentieth century might greet travellers returning
from the moon. The courage that had been required can have
been no less than space travel demands, for the unknown must
ever be awesome, and both enterprises are of the kind that challenge man to pit himself against infinity; the readjustment to
man's conception of his universe was perhaps the greatest he will
ever have to make until we acquire knowledge of another planet.

Columbus was received at Court with the highest honours and
accorded a seat next to the throne; but his heart and mind were
occupied with plans for a second expedition. First, however, there
were domestic affairs claiming his attention. During the earlier
time of his waiting in Spain a second son had been born to him,
about whose mother, Beatriz Enriquez very little is known. This
boy, Fernando, was now four years old and Columbus had to
make arrangements for him later to follow his brother Diego who
was already a page at Court. He also set great store on the spiritual
welfare of the Indians and arranged for them to be baptized in
the cathedral with the King as godfather. After he received the
letters of his nobility in March 1493, he was also preoccupied with
devising a suitable quartering for his escutcheon to which he
attached much importance. He was anxious to share his success
not only with his heirs but with his family in general, and it is at
this point that he summoned his brother Diego from his wool-
carding in Genoa and made him his aide for the new expedition.

The new fleet was fitted out in Cadiz and this time there was no
difficulty in getting volunteers to sail; there were, in fact, two
thousand candidates for a thousand places. In Seville, an administration for the new colonies was set up, and it was emphasised
that in all the new lands the Catholic faith must prevail. Actually
the Pope had already replied to King Ferdinand's request for a

12 One had died at sea and three were left at Palos.

monopoly of navigation and settlement in the newly discovered areas with a bull that was to prove of far-reaching importance. In order to obviate future conflict between the explorers of Portugal and those of Spain he had made a line of demarcation running north-south about a hundred leagues[13] west of the Azores and declared that all land discovered west of it should fall to Spain. Subsequent negotiations between Spain and Portugal resulted in the Treaty of Tordesillas in 1494 which fixed the line 270 leagues further west. As this line cuts through the easterly projection of South America which is now Brazil, it had the result of deflecting the main Spanish colonisation to the western coast.

The second expedition of seventeen vessels sailed from Cadiz on 25 September 1493. The whole Court had accompanied Columbus from Barcelona to see him off, and this time he was accompanied by a number of clerics in charge of Fray Buil, a Benedictine monk who was to act as Apostolic Vicar of the New World. The missionary note was never absent but there can be little doubt that the personnel of the second voyage was mainly bent on gold. They looked hopefully forward to arriving at a well-established settlement, and they took with them a selection of animals to introduce to the New World; pigs, sheep, goats, dogs, asses, horses, mules and chicken were all included since the Indies were almost devoid of mammals and domestic fowls.

Their hopes were woefully disappointed. They arrived to find a burnt-out fort and no Spaniards surviving. They found some of their corpses tied to wooden crosses, with evidence that they had been choked with grass and rope. Others had been burnt. The cacique's hut too was burnt out, and the natives, now timid and unfriendly, asserted that the whole settlement had been attacked by the warriors of another cacique, their hostility having been provoked by the behaviour of the gold seekers. It became plain that the lust for gold had led the Spaniards to treat the natives so cruelly as to produce reprisals, and that divisions among the adventurers themselves had rendered them incapable of warding off attack, even though the local cacique, Guacanagari, had remained loyal.

There was nothing for it but to start a new settlement, and this time, a little further east, Columbus plotted out a city—the first

13 One league = 3.8 nautical miles.

city of the New World—to be called Isabela. By the end of the year its church was ready for consecration. Unfortunately Columbus, who had proved himself without peer in command of a ship, was a poor administrator in the less rigid circumstances of a land community, and from this date his fortunes began to decline. His sailors, voyaging among the numerous islands, had found that at least some of the horrific stories of their Indian friends were true: other tribes were far from friendly, and some were certainly cannibals. Columbus, having found very little gold to send home, composed his first cargoes chiefly of aromatic woods and spices, but he put forward the suggestion that in future some of these more intractable savages should be sent to Spain as slaves because although they were 'ferocious of character' they were 'strong, able, soundly-built and of considerable intelligence', and he sent twenty-six men and women as specimens.

It must be remembered that Columbus was living when slavery was still widely accepted as an inevitable institution, and it is important not to judge him by a standard of ethics much in advance of his time. It is only the man of very great moral stature that can discern evil in what is generally approved by his age; and this is not Columbus's particular claim to fame. Neither is it correct to regard this suggestion as an indication of his moral decline. He was becoming more eager in the search for gold, but it seems to have been more from a desire to fulfil the expectations he had raised among his backers than for personal gain, and it is accompanied by no slackening of his missionary zeal. In fact his conception of himself as the instrument of divine providence for the proselytising of the heathen increased throughout the years. Columbus proved to be essentially a man of his time, and the opening up of the New World was soon to give scope for the vilest of slave trafficking, but some of his contemporaries were already beginning to feel qualms of conscience. King Ferdinand ignored this suggestion of Columbus's so we do not know what he thought; but Queen Isabella set herself against the notion of importing slaves from the beginning.

In Hispaniola there were plenty of other things to think about. Among the population of the new city there were far too many of the 'adventurer' type. They had joined the expedition in the hope of making their fortunes, and they strongly resented the necessity for manual labour. As the actual ships' crews were the only people entitled to draw a regular wage, the gentlemen-adventurers became extremely dissatisfied with their lot. Columbus, more than once, had to punish incitement to mutiny, and when he went on an expedition inland to build a fortress nearer to the area he imagined to contain gold, he had to have all guns and munitions stored on his flagship.

On this particular expedition the Spaniards met with little resistance. The interior Indians were overawed by the sight of men on horseback, imagining animal and rider to be one incorporated beast. When calmed they were friendly enough and indicated their belief that there was gold on the islands to the west. Columbus sailed thither, and touched at various points on the coast of Cuba which he still took to be part of Cathay. This belief became quite obsessional with him and he was so determined to establish his discovery of the continent he sought that he insisted on the notary taking testimony from all his men that they had found the mainland. The punishments proclaimed for any who withheld their testimony or ' ever said to the contrary ' were so fearful that no one ventured to disagree.

On his return to Isabela Columbus found all in confusion again. His other brother Bartholomew had arrived with three small boats, and although he was made Lieutenant-Governor, no more than Diego before him, had he been able to maintain authority and the whole island was in revolt. With difficulty the rebellion was suppressed, some Spaniards were sentenced to be sent home in irons, and the capture of an important native chief gave the opportunity to exploit the possibilities of ransom. Every Indian male over fourteen was required to bring a fixed quantity of gold dust every three months on pain of having his ears cut off if he failed. But the fact was that although a small mine had been discovered, it was not very productive, and in the parts of the island where gold did not exist, the Spaniards had to accept spun cotton as a substitute payment.

It was at this time that the Queen sent out various gifts for fitting out the vice-regal mansion. She expressed her satisfaction with the colonists' efforts, but Columbus was also receiving disturbing hints from Spain about gold. The returning ship took all that could be scraped together: it also carried 500 natives to be slaves, of whom 200 died on the voyage and most of the rest on landing.

There were strong reasons for Columbus himself to go back. He knew that those on the returning vessels would make disquieting reports, and also rumour had reached him that a government decree had now thrown exploration of the Indies open to all who cared to try to their luck. Only he could look after his interests in Spain. So on 11 June 1496 he arrived at Cadiz; but he came practically empty-handed to find enemies at Court working hard against him. It was a month before he received a summons to appear. He still had the Queen's confidence, however, and she fitted out a new expedition for him; but the condition and appearance of those adventurers who had returned from the New World discouraged recruiting and again there had to be recourse to commuting the sentences of criminals and confiscating boats. However the fleet of six vessels was eventually equipped and on 30 May 1498 Columbus set out to cross the Atlantic again.

The full complement of the third expedition was 350 and it is probable that it included thirty women. Columbus took a more southerly course in order that he might pass through fresh island groups, and also to test the theory of the King of Portugal that a continent lay across the equator between Africa and the New World, but three ships were sent on the direct route. By the end of July Columbus reached the island which he christened Trinidad—that is, 'The Trinity'. (Everything on the third voyage was done in the name of the Holy Trinity.) From there he sailed across the bay of Paria, and anchored on the tip of the Paria Peninsula on the coast of what is now Venezuela. He had landed on the continent at last! Not that he realised this at first. The exploration party that landed believed that they were on an island, and it was only as he left the coast that Columbus began to entertain the idea that it was a continent. Even then he still thought it was the mainland of Asia, and he surmised that there must somewhere be a strait through which Marco Polo had sailed to the Spice Islands.

Columbus sailed north-west across the Caribbean Sea and arrived at Hispaniola to find again conditions of confusion and rebellion. To complicate matters further, a private fleet now arrived under the command of one Alonso de Hojeda, and includ-

ing among its personnel a Florentine ex-pilot called Amerigo Vespucci. These explorers had already made a good haul of pearls
further south and were prepared to challenge the monopolies of
Hispaniola. The result was that the quarrel already existing
between sailors and gentlemen adventurers became a three-
cornered affair with the natives as victims of all parties.

The records of the third expedition are confused, but three
aspects of it are clearly memorable. It may be said to have made
the real discovery of America. Secondly, to those interested in the
man Columbus was, it is remarkable for evidences of growing
mysticism. From the outset of the third voyage he had stressed
more emphatically than ever its missionary nature. On the coast
of South America he had believed himself to be near the Earthly
Paradise, and thought that the four mouths of the Rio Grande
indicated the source of the river of which the Bible says that it
' went out of Eden to water the garden: and from thence it was
parted and became into four heads '.[14] Columbus had always seen
himself as the instrument of a divine purpose, and he began to
collect passages from the Bible and the classics that foretold his
mission from which he later compiled a ' Prophetical Book '. This
growth of religious fantasy was perhaps partly due to advancing
age, but it is also understandable when one considers the unreliability of his earthly supports. For our main impression of the
third expedition must be its tragic ending.

The rumours reaching the home country had been sufficiently
damaging to Columbus's reputation to make Queen Isabella decide
to send out a Commission of Inquiry. Perhaps the arrival of the
dying slaves had made her more willing to give credence to the
stories of maladministration. At any rate, a nobleman named
Bobadilla was sent to Hispaniola at the head of a Commission
with very wide powers. When he arrived at San Domingo, the city
on the south coast which had succeeded Isabela as the centre of
government, the first sight that met his eyes was a gallows from
which seven corpses of Spaniards were suspended. A fresh rebellion
had just been put down. Both Christopher and Bartholomew were
away on a tour of inspection, and Bobadilla promptly took over
the government from Diego. When the other two brothers returned

14 Genesis 2: 10.

all three were at once chained and imprisoned, and their property was confiscated. The ensuing inquiry into Columbus's administration was something of a farce. It was directed entirely towards the activities of Columbus's party and made no attempt to examine the rebels. The colony as a whole seem to have turned against their former viceroy and only the sailors of his ship stood by him. They refused to rivet the chains when the Commission decreed he was to be sent home in fetters, and one of the settlement workers had to perform this office. Throughout these ordeals and on the journey home, Columbus maintained an attitude of proud dignity, and increasingly withdrew for consolation into meditation on his faith. Once at sea, the Captain of the ship offered to strike off the chains of his illustrious prisoner, but Columbus refused this relief because he said it was in the name of the King and Queen he had been put in chains, and ' I shall wear them till they themselves order me to take them off, and I shall treasure them as relics, memorials of the recompense I have received for my services '.

Columbus was landed at Cadiz at the end of October 1500 and immediately contrived to get a letter to the governess of the Crown Prince who happened to be the sister of one of his most constant captains, by which means his complaints against Bobadilla reached the Queen's ears. After some six weeks she commanded his release, sent some money on account and even received him graciously. After consideration she agreed to restore his property in Hispaniola but not his position as viceroy.

These must have been weeks of bitter frustration to Columbus for at this time numerous explorers were following up his discoveries in Central America, and new expeditions were setting out from home, while the world's greatest navigator was kept hanging around at court, his advice unsought and his experience disregarded.

Eventually the King appointed a new Governor of the Indies, but he seems to have retained his faith in Columbus as a skilled mariner. In spite of gout, advancing age and disappointment, the Admiral was still looking forward to what he had come to regard as the final goal of his endeavours—the discovery of the strait through the mainland which he still took to be that of China to enable him to sail home to Spain by the circumnavigation of the world. At length he secured four small ships and was allowed to set out on further exploration on condition that he did not touch at Hispaniola except on the return journey if it should be absolutely necessary, and that he did not bring back slaves.

The fourth voyage of Columbus, which he described as 'of all my voyages the most honourable and advantageous', is of interest mainly to those who appreciate the art of navigation. It was a nautical feat which proved him to have developed into a seaman of consummate skill and his capacity, both as a deep-water mariner and as a coastal pilot, was fully tested throughout. On this voyage he was accompanied by his thirteen-year-old younger son.

Although he had been forbidden to touch at Hispaniola, storms forced him to seek refuge there. The new Viceroy, Ovando, refused to allow him to enter the harbour and so his fleet had to ride out the storm under the lee of the island. Well might Columbus lament in a letter home, 'What man was ever born, not even excepting Job, who would not have been ready to die of despair at finding himself as I then was, in anxious fear for my own safety, and that of my son, my brother and my friends, and yet refused permission either to land or put into harbour on the shores which by God's mercy I had gained for Spain with so much toil and danger?' He had seen Ovando's fleet ready to sail back to Spain with Bobadilla on board, and managed to send a warning to them not to set out, but his advice was ignored, storms overwhelmed the fleet, and the flagship was lost with all on board.

When conditions allowed, Columbus set out in a westerly direction, keeping south of Cuba, and then, changing to a southward course, touched the coastline of Central America at Cape Honduras. He then sailed east and south in sight of the land, putting in at several places on the coasts of what are now Honduras, Nicaragua and Costa Rica, finally attempting to establish a settlement at Belen on the coast of Veragua. They had erected a dozen houses or so when an Indian plot to exterminate them was discovered, and it was thought prudent to abandon the settlement. They set sail northwards on what proved to be the most hazardous part of the expedition. The ships were leaking, they encountered a cyclone, and on 25 June 1503 they ran ashore on the coast of Jamaica, where 116 members of the crew were marooned. The only ship's boat had been lost, so that any messengers sent to Hispaniola would have to use canoes. Columbus managed to get volunteers, and after one false start due to an attack by Indians of the interior, two canoes, each containing six Spaniards and ten Indians set out for the old settlement. They reached Hispaniola in five days and at very long last managed to persuade the authorities to send a ship with supplies. It was March 1504 when it arrived at Jamaica, and in the meanwhile Columbus had had to put down mutiny and force the natives by trickery to continue providing food for his men. Even now the ship was only to deliver supplies and to give a message that further help would come. It was the end of June before a rescue ship arrived, after they had been on the island just over a year. At Hispaniola, Ovando consented to receive them, but somewhat coldly, and Columbus made all possible haste to leave for Spain. He set sail on 12 September and after a very stormy crossing, landed on 7 November 1504 at Sanlucar, just north of Cadiz. It was the saddest of all his homecomings, and the eighteen months that remained to him form a tragic coda to a life of high endeavour.

He spent the first two weeks at Seville where news reached him that Queen Isabella, his most faithful supporter, was dying. With her passing, Columbus seems to have lost heart; the vitality which had hitherto been indomitable was waning; he felt old, exhausted, poor and lonely. How came the greatest hero of his age to have sunk so low? He was, as a fact, only in his early fifties, but he lived at a time when men aged early and his had been a life of no ordinary strenuousness. His finances—although he need not have been poor—were in utter confusion. He had never watched them very carefully, and he was not mercenary: the high demands he had made appear to have been part of his pride, and now he was unable to get the lavish promises fulfilled. For the rest, one of the less attractive manifestations of the Renaissance—perhaps of any age of sharp stimulus and speedy change—was the callousness which was engendered towards those in decline. Public attention could speedily be caught by the latest excitement; more opportunities were opening out for those who deliberately sought publicity. Amerigo Vespucci took care that his share in the voyages of discovery was brought to the notice of the right people, and so it was his name that was given to the new continent. Columbus was not to live long enough to learn this, but he did become aware that in some quarters there was acute jealousy, and that the general public had simply forgotten his name in the excitement of following the deeds of new heroes. Colonial fleets were now commanded by a new generation, Columbus's privileges were disregarded, even his pension came late or not at all.

In May 1505 Columbus decided to go from Seville to the Court at Segovia, but he found that the King had already ordered the sale of the Admiral's effects in Hispaniola to pay the debts that he had contracted, and although Ferdinand promised arbitration in the matter of the original contract, nothing was done—at any rate in time. It was only after his death that Columbus's family succeeded in retrieving a part of the titles and privileges that had been promised. The fact was that now substantial wealth was beginning to flow homeward from the New World Ferdinand realised for the first time what a colossal reward one-tenth of the discoveries would be. Had he honoured the bargain, Columbus would have become by far the wealthiest and most powerful noble in the land.

Living on loans, the frustrated hero made his last pathetic attempts to get justice. Travelling on a mule, he followed the Court to Salamanca and then on again to Vallodolid. By the time he arrived there his strength was almost exhausted. He hired a poor room in a small inn and on the wall he hung the chains in which he had returned from his third voyage. He cut a hole in the floor through which he could watch his mule that was stabled below. And there, alone, dressed in a Franciscan robe, he went over his papers, wrote letters, practised his religion, and surveyed the extraordinary activities of his life.

He must have looked back on his achievements with mingled pride and bitterness. How far could he be said to have had success? He knew that the Indians' lot had not been improved by the new régime, that they were indeed suffering from brutal mismanagement in conditions of total slavery; but this would not mitigate the sting of his own failure as an administrator. He had not found the strait which would lead to the Indian Ocean and prove that he had reached the East; and at home, his just rewards had been snatched from him. On the other hand, he must have been comforted in these last dark days by pride in his achievement. The vision that had been his as a boy had not deceived him. His faith, his obstinate persistence and his courage had enabled him to overcome seemingly insuperable difficulties, and to demonstrate the feasibility of sailing westwards to the lands beyond the ' Ocean Sea '. He may well have thought he had made the most important discovery in the history of mankind, and so he had, but since he died thinking the lands were Asia and the East Indies, it was of a different nature from his imagining. It was not till sixteen years after his death that Magellan's expedition was to prove the practicability of circumnavigating the globe.

As in all true tragedy, both the glory and the sadness spring from the character of the hero. Columbus was not one to be made by events; he made them. He was a man of marked individuality and strong personality, with vigour and imagination enough to express them in action without the support of circumstances. A man of little formal education, he had a natural delicacy of perception; of no social position, he had a superb confidence in his own powers; and in spite of his human weaknesses, he had an over-all integrity of purpose which makes most of his faults seem unimportant. Usually long-suffering, he could be violent (there were examples of it during the troubles at the settlement), he was often intolerant, and at least on one occasion he was mean. The sailor who first saw land at 2.0 a.m. at the end of the first voyage never got his reward because Columbus insisted on regarding his doubtful glimpse of a light at 10 o'clock on the previous evening as a prior claim.

Columbus's qualities, and some of his weaknesses too, sprang from the fervour of his powerful imagination. His stupendous vision of what could be done inspired the whole adventure. He was a visionary and man of action in almost equal proportions, and if this other-worldly element in his make-up was responsible for some of his most quixotic actions, it also enabled him to take refuge in mystical contemplation during the last dark days.

King Ferdinand did act at last. He offered Columbus a handsome estate in Castile if he would give up his claim to all the privileges promised in the original contract. Columbus refused. He was, in any case, almost past concern for the comforts and splendours of this world. He ratified his will, making his son Diego heir to all his possessions and privileges and the next day, 20 May 1506, in the presence of his son and a few friends from among his old shipmates, he received the last sacrament and died peacefully. His passing was so little noticed that for some years, acquaintances in Vallodolid believed him to be still living at the Spanish Court.

## FURTHER READING

CHARLES DUFF. *The Truth about Columbus,* rev. edn. Jarrolds 1957.

EDGAR PRESTAGE. *The Portuguese Pioneers.* A. & C. Black 1933.

*The Journal of Christopher Columbus* is published by the Hakluyt Society, 1960. Translated by C. Jane and revised by L. A. Vigneras.

# Francis I

*(1494-1547)*

*It has pleased God that a good, strong and loyal truce should be concluded between my good brother, the Emperor, and myself. Consequently, so that I may make use of a part of this time in honourable and virtuous relaxation, and also for the gain, profit and instruction which can come from it both to myself and to my subjects, I have taken steps to assemble and procure a goodly and great abundance of books. These will be in Greek as well as Latin, and by the best and most remarkable authors that can be found. They shall be placed and housed in a fine and sumptuous library which I am now having made in my kingdom. It shall be the same with some outstanding curios, if any can be found, and to this end I have charged my secretary to go forthwith into Italy to search for these books and curios.*

ON THE LAST day of May in the year 1520 Henry VIII of England set out to attend a meeting which was to become one of the most famous in European history, although its practical importance is perhaps fairly indicated by its popular title—the Field of the Cloth of Gold. For this celebrated interview between Henry and Francis I, King of France, was primarily a show, a calculated piece of stagecraft, entered upon in a competitive spirit by two monarchs who, throughout their reigns, were never able to remain firm either in friendship or in enmity. Not that the Cloth of Gold was without significance; the spectacular nature of its setting was itself symbolic, and it serves to focus attention on three young monarchs who in their persons represented the different order of things that was coming into being.

Francis needed an ally, for a year earlier Charles of Habsburg, the ruler of the Netherlands and Spain, although only nineteen, had been elected Holy Roman Emperor[1] in preference to himself, and the struggle between the French royal house of Valois and that of Habsburg, which was to continue throughout Francis's reign and beyond, had begun. A tentative treaty with England had been made eighteen months earlier, and Francis suggested the meeting in the region of Calais to confirm it. This territory of Calais was by then the last remaining English possession on the French side of the Channel, so that Francis was making a concession in proposing to meet on what was, in effect, conquered territory.

The ceremonies lasted for three weeks, and were fitted into a time-table specially designed to keep everything as equal as possible between the two parties, their every movement arranged with exact symmetry. On 31 May Henry crossed to Calais and went on a little further to Guines where he was to stay. On the same day, Francis and his entourage arrived at the little town of Ardres, about ten miles away, and here, along the river, sprang up a res-

1 See More, p. 32 and below p. 106.

plendent encampment shining with silver and gold. There were between three and four hundred tents of cloth of gold, surmounted by glittering golden apples. Francis's own lodging consisted of four golden tents joined together, surmounted by a six-foot statue of St Michael, clad in blue and gold, a spear in one hand, a shield enamelled with the arms of France in the other and the dragon at his feet. The tents and their embellishments had been designed by great artists of France. A temporary brick house had been built for receptions, and a model of a Roman theatre constructed for theatrical entertainments.

Henry's encampment was no less magnificent; indeed some French visitors felt compelled to record that he had surpassed his rival. The English created astonishment by erecting a wooden palace, constructed sectionally in England, then assembled at Guines, and finally painted to look like stone. Inside, it was hung with cloth of gold and silver, interlaced with green and white, the personal colours of Henry VIII. At each of its two main entrances fountains had been built—one as a model of Cupid, the other of Bacchus—both continually spurting wine. This splendid edifice was surrounded by lesser halls and houses, and altogether about 5,000 people, with nearly 3,000 horses, were accommodated there. This number was equalled more or less exactly by the entourage of Francis, and the nobles, advisers and eminent ladies in the train of each monarch were also fairly balanced. Henry was accompanied by Queen Catherine and his sister Mary Tudor: Francis brought with him his Queen, Claude, his mother, Louise of Savoy, and his sister, Marguerite Duchess of Alençon.

Between the two encampments was a superb pavilion of cloth of gold to serve as the actual meeting place of the Kings, and on a separate site the jousting lists were constructed, complete with spectators' galleries and vast, splendidly decorated withdrawing rooms for the use of the queens.

The first six days were passed by the ambassadors in business meetings partly concerned to guarantee exact equality between the two parties in the ceremonies ahead, and by the Kings in entertaining each other's royal ladies. Only on the afternoon of Thursday 7 June did the two sovereigns meet. On that day two vast processions approached, from opposite sides, the barriers which surrounded the official meeting place. Preceded by heralds, surrounded by grandees, and followed by dignitaries of the Church, the Kings, sumptuously attired, rode on magnificent horses to the music of drum and fife. Francis at this time was twenty-five, three years younger than Henry, and with a presence that was royal as well as youthful. He was six feet in height—very tall as European stature then went—proportionately broad, robust but slender. He had the reputation of a skilled athlete, an intrepid hunter and fighter, and he was by this time the hero of one great military victory. He was of fresh complexion with dark hair, and on this occasion wearing a beard specially grown to enhance his regality. Possessed of great personal charm and an agreeable voice, he had already made an impression on Henry's followers. Now, clad in cloth of gold sewn with diamonds, rubies, emeralds and pearls, his black velvet hat plumed and sparkling with precious stones, he rode to meet his 'friend and brother', the King of England. To the sound of trumpets the barriers went down as the two monarchs entered from either side and advanced to the centre of the enclosure. There they halted their horses close enough to embrace each other from their saddles; then they dismounted, embraced each other again, and arm-in-arm entered the pavilion of cloth of gold.

There followed more than a fortnight of festivities—reciprocal visits and feasts, joustings, dances, masked carnivals and competitions with the sword and the bow. The grand tournament which was the centrepiece of the celebrations was to have begun on the Monday following the first meeting, but the day proved to be too windy, and its opening had to be postponed till the Thursday. Monday was not without its eventfulness however, for we are told that on that day Francis, presumably beginning to find things rather monotonous, rose very early, eluded his bodyguard, and paid an unofficial visit to Henry who was still in bed. The two exchanged gifts, Henry taking a golden collar from his neck to give to his 'captor' and Francis reciprocating with his bracelet. They talked of the joustings to come, and Francis insisted on remaining to help his 'royal brother' to dress. It seems to have been quite a human encounter—rare because it was spontaneous; but Francis's nobles, though relieved that he returned unscathed, were also scandalised. The only other spontaneous approach was less happy. After the grand tournament was over, Henry expressed a wish to wrestle with the French King. Francis acceded, and it took only a few minutes for him to throw his opponent. Henry rose, decidedly vexed and anxious to pursue his revenge, but the tactful intervention of French courtiers postponed the match— indefinitely.

On Saturday 23 June in an improvised tent, there was a service for which choirs were drawn from both France and England, and Cardinal Wolsey officiated. In the evening the bonfires were lit to celebrate St John's Eve. Next day came the leave-takings; the kings departed, the ephemeral golden city disappeared, and the French were left to consider what had been gained.

From the French point of view not much. In the first days at Guines, the ambassadors had confirmed an earlier treaty by which Henry returned Tournai[2] to France for a considerable sum of money, and agreed that his infant daughter Mary should marry the Dauphin; and that was all that there was to show. What did not show was even less advantageous. Before setting out from England, Henry had received the Emperor Charles at Canterbury, and had agreed to a further meeting after the Cloth of Gold. Now, with the French junketings behind them, Henry and Wolsey went on to Gravelines to meet the third of the young men who held the destinies of Europe in their hands. Charles was indeed the youngest of the three, being only just twenty, and there is in this very youthfulness a symbol of the changes that were coming over Europe. By this time it was clear that the ideas engendered by the Italian Renaissance were influencing countries beyond the Alps. They were penetrating all departments of life, and everywhere the old order, religious, social, economic and cultural was soon to be in the melting pot. Within ten years the death of old monarchs in Spain, England, France and the Empire had brought three young men—Charles, Henry and Francis—to the head of affairs. Older statesmen might look askance, but things were now going to be done differently. Youth was at the helm, and a different age was coming into being. The three young monarchs were all Renaissance men.

It was not that any of them consciously wished to upset the old order, especially not the old order of religion, but they were caught

2 Captured in the reign of Francis's predecessor Louis XII.

in a cross-current because among the developing conceptions was
that of nationalism, and to that they were all in thrall. It appealed
to their youth and their ambition; it gave hopes of power that
regional sovereignty had never implied before. The spirit of
nationality was to become the final sanction of the European
states; it was to acquire a moral force which previously only
religion had attained: it was to be strong enough to make the
Holy Roman Emperor fight against the Pope, to cause the Most
Christian Monarch of France to ally with the Turk, and to induce
Henry VIII to set up a national Church. Henceforth there was no
doubt what was the overriding concern of each European monarch.

Henry VIII well knew that as a ruler he was weaker and of less
European significance than either of his rivals. Economic and
political considerations alike made France the permanent enemy,
but he sometimes chose to see himself in the rôle of arbiter, and
his country as a makeweight in the precarious balance of Europe.
It would make him nearly worthless as an ally but it could give
England a transient disproportionate importance; it would inevitably lead to double-dealing, as on this occasion at Gravelines when
he virtually bound himself not to adhere to a French alliance
and to postpone his daughter's marriage with the Dauphin. Although Henry's friendship was now sought after by the two most
powerful monarchs, from the European point of view his position
would still be a humble one. It was for Francis to acquire magnificence, to become the Renaissance Monarch par excellence and
to make France the prototype of grandiose monarchy. Charles, in
terms of his possessions at any rate, was the most important: it is
necessary to give some consideration to his office and his personal
possessions.

Throughout the Middle Ages the agglomeration of German
states—counties, marks, duchies, petty kingdoms, estates of the
Church—which sprawled across the centre of Europe had been
loosely held together under the rule of the Holy Roman Emperor,
so called to suggest both the wide-spread rule of ancient Rome and
the fact that the later Emperor enjoyed his authority in partnership with the Head of the Universal Church. For some centuries
the Emperor was regarded as the temporal ruler of the whole of
Christendom, and even in the sixteenth century, long after the
Italian cities had attained a virtual freedom, and Spain, France

and England had come to ignore the imperial claims, there remained a general observance of the theory of the Emperor's supremacy. He was still, if only in a nominal way, the temporal head of Christendom. The vast possessions of the new young Emperor, Charles V, added to this theoretical pre-eminence a great deal that was substantial. The Emperor was elected by seven Electors who were in fact the rulers of seven particular German states, and they had shown in later centuries a tendency to prefer a member of the Austrian house of Habsburg. Recent Emperors had striven to make the office almost hereditary by having their successors elected in their own life time and designated King of the Romans. The Emperor Maximilian, who died in 1519, had been married to Mary of Burgundy, the heiress of Charles the Bold, whose inheritance comprised the Netherlands, Luxemburg, the County of Burgundy[3] and an area which is now part of north east France. Mary's son Philip had been married to Joanna, daughter of King Ferdinand of Spain, and Charles was their son. Philip was Duke of Burgundy and ruler of his mother's dominions after her death in 1482, and when Philip himself died in 1506 his young son Charles became Duke of Burgundy in his stead. In 1516 Ferdinand of Spain died, and as his daughter Joanna was incapacitated by insanity, Charles became King of Spain—with dominion over all the land in America that had been acquired following the discoveries of Columbus.[4] When the Emperor Maximilian died in 1519, Charles automatically became ruler of Austria and the Habsburg family possessions of the Upper Rhine, but the imperial office was elective, and Maximilian had died suddenly while still negotiating to have his grandson elected King of the

3 Also called Franche-Comté.

4

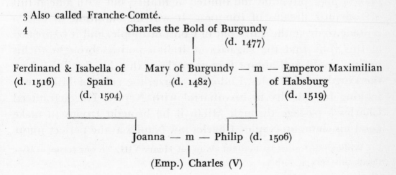

Charles the Bold of Burgundy
(d. 1477)

Ferdinand & Isabella of Spain (d. 1516) (d. 1504) — Mary of Burgundy (d. 1482) — m — Emperor Maximilian of Habsburg (d. 1519)

Joanna — m — Philip (d. 1506)

(Emp.) Charles (V)

Romans. The election as Emperor proved to be by no means automatic. Francis I, who had been four years on the French throne, put forward a strong challenge,[5] but after the most corrupt and hard-fought campaign on record, Charles became Emperor as Charles V with all the power—and all the immense difficulties— that the position held.

When we consider the dominions over which Charles would rule, it is easy to see that Francis I would feel his country encircled, but there was also another factor to stimulate the hostility of the two men: the claims which each made on parts of Italy. Francis's desire for dominions in Italy, which became a guiding principle in his life, may be said to have been originally something he inherited with his crown. His predecessor, Louis XII, had made war in Italy, and Louis's predecessor, another cousin, Charles VIII, had initiated this disastrous policy. Throughout Francis's life-time, French wars in the Italian peninsula were an accepted part of national life.

Charles VIII (1483-1498) had come to the throne as a boy of thirteen under the regency of his sister Anne of Beaujeu. Their father Louis XI (1462-1483) was the king who, by a policy more crafty than martial, had unified France, crushing many of the mighty feudal nobles and snatching the Duchy of Burgundy (as distinct from the more easterly County of Burgundy) from Mary and Maximilian. Anne of Beaujeu completed her father's work by incorporating the semi-independent Duchy of Brittany. Anne of Brittany, a young girl of seventeen, had succeeded to her father's dukedom in 1491, and Anne of Beaujeu compelled her by force of arms to marry Charles VIII. At twenty-one Charles was a young man of poor physique and limited mentality, but with a head full of romantic dreams of conquest. It was his ambition to lead a crusade to drive the Turk out of Constantinople, and it happened at this time that the vagaries of Italian politics brought to his notice an old and almost forgotten claim that his family had on the kingdom of Naples. Ludovico Sforza, the ruler of Milan, was looking for an ally in his quarrel with Naples. He guaranteed Charles a passage through Milan if he brought troops to make good his claim on Naples. Charles saw Naples as the perfect jump-

5 Wolsey put forward a hesitant claim for Henry VIII. No one seems to have taken this very seriously.

ing-off place for his projected crusade, and in 1494, he took the fateful decision and marched into Italy. It was the beginning of a new chapter of Italian history.

At first all went well for the invaders. Piero de' Medici allowed him to pass through Florentine territory (although this caused the enraged Florentines to drive the Medici from power), the Pope, Alexander VI also granted him free passage, the King of Naples abdicated, his successor fled and within a few days the kingdom had submitted to the French. The triumph was not to last however. The Italian states were now awake to the danger they had brought upon themselves by allowing the French into the peninsula. Even Sforza of Milan joined in forming a league against the invader. Charles had to act quickly to avoid being trapped; and he did move just in time to extricate his army, although with the loss of the greater part of their equipment. The dream of glory faded for Charles, but Italy was now a French aspiration that was to beckon and to betray his two successors.

Charles VIII had no children who survived infancy, and when he died in 1498 he was succeeded by a cousin, Louis XII. Louis had no ambition to go on a crusade, but to the French claim on Naples he added one on Milan itself which he derived from his grandmother, and in 1499 the French armies again crossed the Alps. Milan was conquered and reorganised as a French dependency, but before he went on to Naples Louis thought it advisable to enter into an agreement with the King of Spain to make a division of the territory. Naples was ruled by relatives of King Ferdinand of Spain and it was likely he would come to their aid if he were not appeased in this way. Naples fell to the invaders as easily as previously, but as might have been expected, the marauders fell out, and the next three years were spent in warfare between Spain and France in the south of Italy. It was the period when chivalry, on the wane as a whole,[6] was passing through a phase of sunset glory with the nobility of France. Fighting on the battlefields of Naples during these years were some of the greatest of French heroes, of whom the most famous was Bayard. But the French were doomed to defeat. Prodigies of valour by individual knights were not enough; the army leaders were quarrelling, plague was rife, and at the beginning of 1504 Naples

6 See Cervantes, p. 231.

had to be ceded to Spain. Seven years later Milan too was lost. Louis's health was failing, his spirit was broken, and in 1515 he died, leaving no son, so that the throne again passed to a cousin— Francis, Duke of Valois.

It is not surprising that Francis I came to the throne with thoughts of Italy in his mind. It had been an intense preoccupation with all the French nobility while he was growing up, although throughout that time he had had only a fluctuating hope of becoming King of France. That hope, so strongly nourished by his mother, Louise of Savoy, had grown stronger with the passing of the years, but for Louise, if not for Francis himself, the extraordinarily shifting family circumstances must have caused periods of suspense very hard to endure.

Francis sprang from the younger branch of the Orleans family, and the Orleans themselves were a younger branch of the royal family. The most recent common ancestor of Charles VIII, Louis XII and Francis I was Charles V (1364-1380).[7] Charles, Count of Angoulême, a cousin of the Duke of Orleans had married Louise of Savoy, a woman who proved to have not only ambition but also considerable strength of character and talent for government, as well as a genuine appreciation of the culture of her time. Her first child was a daughter, Marguerite, born in 1492, and then on 12 September 1494 at his father's estate of Cognac, her son Francis was born. At the beginning of 1496 his father died, and the infant Francis, now Count of Angoulême was placed under the guardianship of his cousin, Louis of Orleans, heir presump-

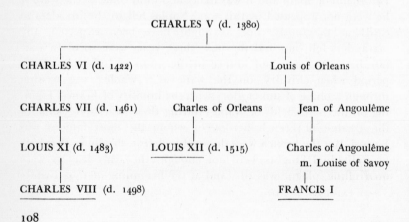

tive to the throne of France. Louise was perpetually conscious
that her son stood second in the line of succession; Louis of Orleans
was married to a cripple who could not hope for children,[8] and
the three sons so far born to Charles VIII and Anne of Brittany
had died in early infancy. There seemed, however, no reason why
more should not be born to them. Then two years after the death
of Francis's father, Charles VIII died suddenly at the age of
twenty-eight, and with the accession of Louis XII, Francis may be
said to have attained his first real sight of the throne. Not that
he was of an age to appreciate it, but Louise was alert to every
opportunity. After a suitable demonstration of grief for the passing
of the late king, she was ready with her family to obey immediately
the summons from Louis XII. They journeyed to his castle of
Chinon in the valley of the Loire. Francis must now be educated
as the Dauphin.

Louis offered Louise another Loire château at Blois as a residence, but she disliked it, and in December 1498 she and her
family were installed at Amboise which was to be Francis's childhood home. Francis was made Duke of Valois, a duchy intermittently associated with the Crown since the twelfth century. His
mother had asked that he should be Duke of Orleans as Louis XII
had been before his accession to the throne, but Louis had his own
reasons for not acceding to this request.

Life at Amboise for the next ten years was singularly pleasant
for a boy of Francis's birth and prospects. The château itself was
an ancient royal dwelling which had been renovated and extended
by Charles VIII. He had decided upon this before his Italian
expedition, and a number of French master masons were already
employed when he set out. He returned with many new ideas. In
Italy he had seen artistic marvels, and his extended plans for
Amboise may be said to mark the beginning of Renaissance influence on French architecture. Italian architects, masons, sculp-
tors and gardeners were brought to enlarge and decorate the
château and to lay out its grounds. The work had stopped with
the death of Charles VIII and it was still uncompleted when
Francis I's family went into residence; but it must have been one

8 She was a younger daughter of Louis XI and the marriage was arranged
by that king as part of a policy to prevent claimants to the throne from the
House of Orleans.

of the most attractive dwellings in France with its spacious courts and lofty towers, its extensive terraced gardens, the Loire flowing round it, and the deep wooded country stretching beyond.

Here the young Francis was surrounded with love and adulation. An adoring sister and an indulgent mother increasingly dedicated their lives to his happiness and his future. For most of his life we see Francis with Louise and Marguerite just in the background, a permanent chorus of admiration, but also firm and practical supports. The importance of these two women in his life can hardly be exaggerated. They influenced him more than either of his two wives or any of his numerous mistresses. Francis, Louise and Marguerite move as a trio through two decades of French history.

Louise indulged her son, but she also trained him. A succession of directors and tutors were appointed by Louis XII to attend to his education and Louise saw that lessons were not neglected. She herself was a cultivated woman with a great love of literature which she succeeded in communicating to her children. Marguerite became an accomplished poet and prose writer; Francis himself was to write a good deal of verse in a gallant vein. As a boy he studied history, Latin and Italian with his tutors, apparently effectively; and above all, he grew up with a genuine love of all the arts and a discriminating judgment in those of painting, sculpture and architecture.

For the time being, though, life was largely play at Amboise. Young scions of noble families were brought to live at the château and share the sports of the young duke. It was a time when, all over France, a great interest in games was developing: bowls, skittles, quoits and an elementary form of hockey, together with many rougher forms of contest would all probably have had a place at Amboise. Certainly there would have been tennis, for this game was immensely popular. Until Charles VIII's reign it was played by hitting the ball with the hand; then a special kind of glove was used and by the time of Francis's boyhood, racquets of various shapes were introduced and the modern method of scoring established, although the 'net' was still only a cord with a fringe that did not reach the ground. The tennis courts (jeux de paumes) were enclosed which allowed for the ball to be played as it ricochetted off the walls.[9] Francis became a skilful player, and soon courts were being built which provided galleries for spectators.

There were two physical activities more important than games. One was hunting, the pastime that was to be the passion of Francis's life, and the other comprised the contests that were quasi-military exercises. The boys' imaginations were nourished on the reports of the war in Naples where knights like Bayard and Gaston de Foix performed such doughty deeds. They were their heroes and from the moment the young nobles could mount a horse or wield a toy sword they were imitating them. They had their juvenile suits of armour; they learned to shoot with the long bow and the short bow, to joust and to tilt; in a word, they learned what knighthood meant, all the rules of the tournament— and war. For all this training of the body and of the imagination inevitably produced the warrior, and in none more markedly than in him who was later to be King of France.

Francis was already manifesting the character traits that were to be conspicuous in the king; he was happy-go-lucky and cheerful, good-tempered in the main, a generous opponent not inclined to bear a grudge. At the same time he was markedly pleasure-loving, thriving in sunshine and wishing to avoid all unpleasantness. Certainly he was courageous: his physical audacity caused his mother much anxiety. In Louise's journal are references to falls from his horse, blows from stones in rough play, and wounds of all kinds received in the hurly-burly of the youngsters' games. If Francis showed a tendency—which was to increase—to turn his back on life's awkward problems, he never avoided a physical risk.

If the days at Amboise were sunlit for Francis, they were not without shadows for Louise. Louis XII was not content to remain in his marriage with a crippled wife, and early in 1499 he negotiated for its annulment. The Pope's acquiescence was immediately followed by Louis's marriage to Charles VIII's widow, Anne of Brittany. His purpose was twofold: to keep Brittany united to France, and to provide himself with an heir. Louise again had to face the probability that Francis would not inherit the throne. By the end of 1499 a child was born to the King and Queen, but it

9 As the game was also played on outdoor courts, two separate forms developed: royal tennis, and lawn tennis. There is a royal tennis court of Henry VIII's time at Hampton Court.

was a girl, christened Claude. In the summer of 1508, as there was still no dauphin, Francis, then aged fourteen, left his mother to reside at the Court, usually either at Chinon or Blois. Here he could enjoy hunting in plenty, although he was not allowed to go to the wars however much he might chafe against the restriction. The following year his sister Marguerite married the Duke of Alençon, and Louise returned to her château at Cognac. The joyful days of Amboise were over.

In 1512, during the month before the loss of Milan, when France was being threatened on all sides by the league the Pope had raised against her, Francis, a young warrior of eighteen, saw his first military campaigns in Guienne and in Flanders. Louis had by this time decided that Francis should marry his daughter Claude; if he was to be denied a direct heir, he could at least keep Brittany firmly tied to France. In January 1514 Anne of Brittany died, and the marriage of Claude and Francis took place in May. It was not the wife Louise would have chosen for her son. Claude was short and fat and a little lame, but she seems to have been amiable, and to have been much loved by the French people. In any case, although she did her duty devotedly and bore Francis seven children in nine years, she was only a cipher in the affairs of the nation. Francis, Louise and Marguerite were to remain for a long time an effective triumvirate.

Louise could hardly have been other than relieved by the death of Anne of Brittany, but the alternation of her hopes and fears was not yet ended. In the October of 1514 Louis XII was married again—to Mary Tudor, sister of Henry VIII. England, since Spain and the Empire had deserted her, desired an alliance with France. Mary, who was only eighteen, was to be sacrificed by her marriage to Louis who was fifty-two at the time and very old for his years. The sacrifice was limited, however. On New Year's Day 1515 Louis XII died suddenly at his château at Tournelles. Mary was able to marry the man of her choice, Louise's fondest, most persistent dream came true and Francis entered upon his reign magnificently as befitted the prototype of Renaissance royalty.

On 25 January he was consecrated at Rheims, and in February he made his grand 'entry' into Paris. It was a foretaste of the vast number of entries, progresses and celebrations with which his reign was punctuated: they all took the form of magnificent public demonstrations of the pomp of the French King.

Francis further marked his accession by creating his mother Duchess of Angoulême, bestowing with the title large tracts of land in Anjou and Maine, and by establishing a number of his boyhood friends and advisers in high offices of state.

One project dominated the new king's mind—the recovery of Milan. His imagination had long been fired by the stories of knightly deeds in the peninsula, but also by the glory of the Italian Renaissance, and by the challenge presented by the failure of his two predecessors to hold their conquest. All these motives intertwined to urge him into Italy directly he had the opportunity. He secured his country as far as he was able by treaties with England and with the not yet very confident Charles of Burgundy; he made Louise regent for the period of his absence, and in June 1515 his Italian adventure began. It began characteristically with a series of 'entries', first into Blois and Amboise, and then more spectacularly into Lyons. They cost the citizens a good deal of money, but they enhanced the glory of the young warrior king, and it was a long time before there would be complaint.

From Lyons the French army, comprising a cavalry drawn from the nobility and an infantry largely mercenaries, streamed through the Alpine passes to encounter the combined resistance of Milan, Spain and the Empire. On 14 September 1515 the decisive battle was fought. By his complete victory at Marignano, Francis recovered the Milanese at a blow. It was the achievement of his most persistent ambition, the fulfilment of the chivalric longings of his boyhood, and he crowned it with a symbolic act. Fighting with Francis that day had been the greatest of all the French knights, Bayard—'le chevalier sans peur et sans reproche'—and since only one already a knight could confer knighthood on another, Francis was able to offer Bayard the honour of bestowing the accolade upon his sovereign. The Chevalier at first demurred; he was too humble a person to be thus honoured, but Francis overruled him. Bayard drew his sword, and the King knelt before him to arise a member of the old-fashioned order of Chivalry whose importance was already vanishing in the rapidly changing world. It is appropriate that before he left Italy, Francis had a short meeting with Castiglione,[10] the Italian writer who was to celebrate those virtues

10 See Philip Sidney, p. 192.

of chivalry that could yet shine with a fresh lustre in the courtier-knights of the Renaissance world.

For the next two or three months, Francis was organising the Milanese and celebrating its recovery with fêtes of customary splendour. He was also discovering the full elegance and sumptuousness of Italian Renaissance culture. Milan was artistically one of the most advanced cities; here Leonardo had worked after leaving Florence[11] in the service of the Ludovico Sforza who had first invited the French into the peninsula. Francis was stimulated to the greatest enthusiasm. The architecture, painting and sculpture of the city, all were admired; even the jewellery and the dresses. Francis sent back to his royal ladies a number of little dolls dressed to exemplify prevailing fashions.

Amidst all the junketings one serious piece of business was achieved which was to be of great importance to France and to Francis himself. On 11 December 1515 Francis went to Bologna to meet the Pope, Leo X (the son of Lorenzo de' Medici). Here he negotiated with him the Concordat which, while appearing to be a concession to the Papacy, greatly enhanced the power of the French king. For seventy-five years the French Church had had a special arrangement by which its Chapters elected their own archbishops, bishops and abbots instead of having them nominated by the Pope. It was also excused the payment of annates, the first year's revenues of each new bishop. Successive popes had wished to have this arrangement changed, and now Francis agreed to renew the payment of annates provided that he himself was accorded the right to appoint the ecclesiastics. It kept the French Church more independent of the Holy See than was customary in other countries, but it made it dependent on the King. Francis's right to fill these high offices with his own nominations was an important step towards the absolutism of the last two-thirds of his reign. It is not surprising that the Parlement[12] of Paris protested vigorously when asked to register the agreement, and it was only by browbeating the members that Francis enforced his decision on it in 1518.

11 Cf. Lorenzo de' Medici p. 19.

12 The Parlements of France were primarily judicial bodies whose duty it was to register royal edicts. The Parlement of Paris was the most important, but there were also twelve provincial ones.

On his return to his country in 1516, Francis was met at the border by Queen Claude, who had recently borne him a daughter, and his mother. There was the inevitable 'entry' into Marseilles, and a series of splendid welcomes at all the towns on the Rhône on his way back to Amboise. At Marseilles there was an interesting incident when the King boarded a galley that was coming from Africa, in order to see 'une merveilleuse bête appelée reynoceron' which was being sent by the King of Portugal as a present to the Pope. It was probably the first rhinoceros ever seen in Europe.[13] Animals were always of great interest to Francis. He kept innumerable pets—dogs, cats, and a variety of monkeys; he also had small menageries of wild beasts at some of his chateaux.

After the spectacular French victory at Marignano there was energetic diplomatic activity in all quarters, but as far as France was concerned from 1516 till 1521 there was peace, and Francis was able to abandon the rôle of warrior and take up that of Renaissance Monarch, Patron of the Arts. Throughout his reign these were his two alternations. After Marignano came a long period of unbroken royal splendour.

Francis was a sincere amateur of the arts; he had a vivid appreciation of all that was beautiful, and a discriminating taste. Among the French artists who worked exclusively for him were Jean Bourdichon and Jean Clouet; after Marignano he persuaded the great Leonardo to come to France, and established him at the little château of Cloux, near Amboise.[14] Later came Andrea del Sarto for 'his long festal year at Fontainebleau' and Jerome della Robbia, a member of the famous della Robbia family. Francis was extravagant by nature, and if he ignored the future, he could afford to indulge his tastes. His interest extended to jewellery, tapestries and fine clothes, but above all he was interested in architecture. It was as a builder that he made his outstanding contribution to French Renaissance culture. His was the age of the great châteaux of the Loire, and a host of castles and palaces in other parts of France. Already when Francis came to the throne, members of the French aristocracy had been seized with the fever of building. In the north Georges Amboise, Archbishop of Rouen,

13 King Manuel of Portugal used to parade with it in the streets of Lisbon. Dürër made an engraving of it.
14 He died there in 1519.

had built his château of Gaillon of which only ruins now remain; and Bohier, a Treasury official, had already undertaken the most spectacular of all the Loire châteaux—Chenonceaux—which came into Francis's hands twenty years later, and stands today, a joy to all who visit it.

In 1519 Francis began extensions at Blois. This had been the family property of Louis XII and he had made it the principal castle of the royal family. It was thus the childhood home of Queen Claude. Francis added to it the Renaissance wing with the famous exterior staircase in its octagonal tower projecting into the courtyard. But the most important project of that year was the immense château of Chambord. Francis knocked down a hunting lodge and on its somewhat unpropitious site caused to be built, by a team of French and Italian designers and masons, this monument to his own extravagance. It contains fourteen imposing staircases, to mention one feature alone, and it is not surprising that the work went on for the rest of the reign. Until Francis became enamoured of Fontainebleau in the later part of his life, Chambord was his pet project, intended as an enduring expression of his personality. On innumerable buttresses and arches can be seen repeated his salamander emblem and the letter F; but indeed its every feature seems to bear his signature.

This overpowering pile of architecture[15] does not give the impression of having been comfortable to live in, though one must never forget the size of Francis's household and court. The Household proper, comprising a multitude of officials and servants of all ranks, was divided into departments. Apart from the strictly domestic and secretarial sections there were the Military department, the Chaplain's department, the Kennels, the Stables and above all, the Hunt. For hunting, together with falconry, was the main occupation of the Court.

The Court was not synonymous with the Household; it composed a floating population of people, including both near and distant relatives of Francis, who did not live permanently with the monarch, but who came to render homage, to pay social visits, or to act as ambassadors. There had long been a royal court, of course, but Francis greatly increased the festivities, and added to their elegance by the special place he gave to women. For almost a

15 See Plate p. 2(b).

decade the life of the highest in the land was perpetual celebration.

Francis found plenty to celebrate in these years. In 1517 Queen Claude had her belated coronation, and in February 1518 her third child, and first son, was born. France had a Dauphin. In April the christening took place at Amboise amidst scenes of great splendour. Then there were the 'progresses'—long processional journeys to visit different parts of the realm which became a feature of Francis's reign. Perhaps the triumphal journey home after Marignano was the origin of the idea; it certainly set a pattern. In 1517 he visited the north-east section of his realm, in 1518 Anjou and Brittany and in 1520 he went to Angoulême and toured the region of his birthplace. The journeyings became great public demonstrations. The King, his family, a vast splendidly apparelled entourage of courtiers and officials, would be accompanied by men-at-arms, archers and bands, trains that frequently involved more than 6,000 horsemen and 12,000 pedestrians.

However it might be for the followers there must be luxury for the King, and all the necessary paraphernalia for his comfort had to be hauled along. The towns through which they passed or into which they were received would be lavishly decorated and the citizens would offer entertainment in the form of masquerades, pageants and tableaux, presenting religious and historical themes slanted to honour the House of Valois. Artists organised the pageants, poets wrote verses to be declaimed; the overall pattern was always very similar, although the towns competed keenly to supply detail that was original. It was all very expensive and as the reign wore on citizens of towns that might be in the path of a royal progress began to pray that they would after all escape.

There is something about all this pageantry that recalls the glory of the Renaissance in Medici Florence, but now that it had reached France it had begun to cloy. There was the extravagant pomp of Francis in contrast to the simple citizenship of Lorenzo, as there was the elaborate hierarchy of France that kept her ruler from mingling with the people in the way the Medici family had done. The Florence of the young Lorenzo has the freshness of springtime; in France, as soon as Francis is on the throne it is already high summer. In its time of flowering, Florence had a statesman to lead it; the King of France was at heart a playboy.

There are a number of portraits and busts of Francis that give us an impression of his personality.[16] The earlier ones show a face that at first glance seems genial, almost merry; the very long nose at first seems to lend a humorous quality, but when taken in conjunction with the eyes, it gives him a sardonic expression. The eyes themselves are not to be trusted; there is an inescapably crafty look. The mouth can be seen in an odd way as either good-humoured or cruel. The face as a whole is one that we can imagine changing rapidly from one expression to another. In the portraits of Francis in middle age, when in the line of the mouth cynicism had triumphed over good humour, it is certainly sensuality that predominates.

When Francis rode forth to the Field of the Cloth of Gold he was in his heyday. Physically he was at his most attractive and he radiated the glory acquired in Milan. In realistic terms, however, he knew that he had just met his first setback since coming to the throne; he had been defeated in the imperial election of 1519. He came knowing that the Valois—Habsburg struggle was inevitable, and he was intelligent enough to know when he left that the Cloth of Gold had achieved very little. War would certainly come soon.

In order to understand this struggle which was the background of the rest of the reign it is important to keep certain considerations in mind. An important factor is the implacable hostility of the two men, even when in appearance they are being drawn together, at a time when national rivalry was developing so sharply. This is reinforced on Francis's side by the lure of Italian conquest; whatever were the outward appearances, privately he never brought himself to accept the surrender of Milan. It is also important to remember that neither side was as strong as it appeared to be in its periods of dominance. Both were short of money; Charles was perpetually harassed by the dissensions of the Reformation within his German realm, and by the advance of the Turks on his eastern border. Hence, both often desperately needed

16 The best are: Portrait by Titian (Louvre); portrait by Clouet (Louvre); bust from the Château of Sansac; wood painting and drawing by Clouet (Musée Condé, Chantilly).

. The Medici-Riccardi Palace built in 1430 for Cosimo de' Medici

2a. The Monastery of La Rábida, near Palos, where the room occupied by Columbus can still be seen

2b. Chambord. A part of the château Francis I began to build in 1519 on the site of an old hunting lodge. The photograph shows the Porte Royale from the south-east

The hall in the Prinsenhof Delft where William the Silent was assassinated. The plaque marks the spot where the bullet struck the wall

Lorenzo de' Medici

Sir Thomas More

Erasmus

Columbus

Plate 4.

Francis I

Montaigne

Sir Philip Sidney

William the Silent

Plate 5.

6. The tomb of Columbus in Seville Cathedral. The pall-bearers represent the sovereigns of Castile, Aragon, Leon and Navarre

7. Montaigne's Tower. The only part of the present château remaining from his time

8.  The statue of Don Quixote and Sancho Panza in Madrid

a truce. Auxiliary to the main conflict was Henry VIII's policy which he implemented sometimes by seeking to arbitrate, sometimes by crafty double-dealing and sometimes by open warfare against the side that his interests decided was the enemy of the moment. When we remember that the Pope and rulers of other Italian states were also engaged in striking one antagonist off against the other, we realise how complicated the alliances would necessarily be. The combination of all these factors explains the oddly shifting partnerships, the vicissitudes of fortune and the unexpected lulls which make the struggle so difficult to follow.

War broke out again in January 1521 because of a feudal squabble in the Netherlands, and France found ranged against her an alliance of Pope and Emperor which was soon to include England. She was beset on all sides. Towards the end of the year Milan revolted against its French government and by April 1522 it was lost. To Francis its recovery seemed more important than the security of the homeland, and he proceeded to Lyons to plan the offensive in North Italy which he himself would lead. But fortune was to strike two hard blows before he himself could go to Italy. In August 1523 it was discovered that Charles Bourbon, Constable of France, was plotting against his king. He was the most powerful noble of France; the old feudal pretensions had not yet been submerged in national loyalty and Bourbon had several grudges against Francis. After the discovery of the plot, he managed to escape to Italy, and he became, until his death in 1527, a leader on the side of the Emperor.

Eleven months later, Queen Claude died. Francis was surprisingly affected by her passing. Two women, at any rate, had, at different times, meant more to him than his wife: earlier in his life, Françoise de Foix, Countess of Chateaubriand, a member of the famous military family; and, about this time, Anne de Heilly (de Pisseleu) who, as the Duchess of Etampes, was to be an important influence in the last years of the reign. But his mourning for Claude seems to have been genuine. ' If I thought,' he said, ' I could bring her back by giving my own life, I would gladly do so. I would never have thought that the marriage tie would be so strong and so difficult to break.'

Meanwhile the French armies were failing in their attempt to recover Milan, and at last, in October 1524, Francis personally led his army to the region of his successes in 1515. But notwithstanding some initial success there was no Marignano awaiting him this time; instead, on 24 February 1525, the French were utterly defeated at the Battle of Pavia, the King's horse was shot under him and Francis himself was taken prisoner by the Commander of the Spanish troops. The next day he wrote to his mother: 'Nothing remains to me but my honour and my life.' He sent a letter to the Emperor pleading for magnanimity. He assumed his captivity would be honourable; he was, after all, a knight. There would doubtless be a substantial ransom to pay, but meanwhile. . . . With his easy-going capacity for refusing to look unpleasant facts in the face, he set himself to extract what entertainment he could from the situation. He was allowed visits from his friends who played games with him, and he spent hours writing verses for Anne de Heilly, some of them love poems, and some, more usefully, his account of what had happened at Pavia.

The Emperor did not reply to the letter, but in May Francis was taken to Spain. At first he was accorded more than the treatment due to a knight; he was fêted for two months at Valencia and Barcelona before his journey to Madrid; but once arrived there he was confined to one room, barred and guarded in the Alcazar, and for the next six months that was his sole habitation. He was, after all, the Emperor's prisoner.

Francis deeply desired an interview with Charles, but for a month the Emperor did not respond to this wish. Then Francis fell desperately ill with fever, and it was only when it seemed that his prisoner would die, thus removing a most valuable hostage, that Charles came to his prisoner's room and the two rulers met for the first time in their lives.

Charles was all friendship, provided Francis would accept his terms for a treaty. Marguerite came too on a safe-conduct demanded by Louise who was dealing with the difficulties at home with great energy and acumen. Marguerite came partly, doubtless, because her brother was critically ill, partly to attempt to soften the Emperor's terms. After nearly a fortnight's suspense, it was clear that Francis was going to recover, but Marguerite was failing to make any impression on Charles. Her safe-conduct was running out; she and her brother made one bizarre attempt to effect his escape. One of his attendants was a tall negro, and it was arranged that this man should lie covered in the King's bed while Francis, with his face blacked and wearing the attendant's clothes should walk out carrying the fuel box. Unfortunately a servant with a grudge against a French officer revealed the plot, and the negro was not allowed to enter the King's room again.

There was nothing left to do but accept the Emperor's terms, and they were very unpalatable. His principal demands were that Francis should renounce his claims in Italy, that he should rein-state the renegade Bourbon in his domains, and that he should surrender the Duchy of Burgundy to the Empire. It was this last proviso that had held up the negotiations so long. Italy might per-petually fascinate Francis, but it was not identified with his realm, nor so close to his people's hearts as Burgundy was. Charles added to his territorial terms a request that his sister Eleanor should become Francis's second wife.

Francis signed the Treaty of Madrid in January 1526, and he swore upon the gospels to abide by it, but the evening before he had gathered together all the French plenipotentiaries in his room. He declared to them that whatever promises he might make on the morrow would be wrung from him by force, and that, how-ever firmly sworn to, they would be without validity. He called upon God to witness that as he would not be taking an oath as a free man, any agreement he made would from the outset be null and void.

Charles still had one more demand to make. It was that Francis's two eldest sons, then aged eight and seven, should be sent to Spain to remain as hostages till the fulfilment of the treaty. Knowing he did not intend to fulfil it, aware that the means of averting the consequences of disavowal were not at all clear, the King assented to this inhuman proposition. He was then freed.

On 17 March 1526, Francis arrived at the River Bidassoa on the borders of Spain and France. On the French bank were his two small sons. In the middle of the river was an anchored raft. Two boats, one from each side, then put off at the same time, one bear-ing the King accompanied by Lannoy of Spain, the other the little princes and Lautrec of France. At the raft the King exchanged boats with his sons, blessing them briefly as they passed. Francis himself, once landed in his own country, went on to Bayonne to be rapturously received by members of the royal family and the populace. The whole episode is an eloquent comment on Francis's character. He rarely committed acts of cruelty that would be before his own eyes; he was adept at looking the other way. He had returned to France to repudiate the Treaty of Madrid, and the two small boys went into more than four years of exile and harsh surveillance.

The truly majestic period of Francis's reign commences after his return from captivity. The war continued, with intermittent truces, for the rest of his life—sometimes so desperately for Francis that he was forced to shock Christendom by an alliance with the Turk—but in the years between 1527 and 1540 he embellished the notion of kingship. He achieved an absolutism surrounded with splendour which was the foundation of the monarchy of Louis XIV, and which was to continue till its inevitable downfall in the French Revolution. He also renewed with greater zest his patronage of the arts. Absolutism; splendour; the arts; those are the key words to the domestic activities of Francis during these years.

French society, passing out of its feudal period, was still clearly divided into Clergy, Nobility and the Third Estate—the last group comprising everybody who did not qualify for the first two. The nobility had not yet all been drawn to the Court; the majority were still country-dwelling, and under their supervision and that of the country gentlemen, estates prospered and the soil of France was well cultivated. Town life was flourishing too, and a rising bourgeois class was making progress towards social importance. In spite of constant war there was a spirit of hopefulness in the land. The condition of the peasantry ranged from comparative ease to wretchedness, but everywhere was tremendous loyalty to the King personally, and pride in the monarchy.

At the same time, it was inevitable that there should be some restiveness. There had been enormous increases of taxation of all kinds, both to finance the wars and to support the royal magnificence. The steady increase in absolutism itself made the Parlement fractious. If Francis was ready after his return from Madrid to plunge into fresh building projects and let the war take its course, his mother realised the urgent need for a spell of peace. Louise negotiated with Margaret of Austria, the Emperor's aunt who acted as Regent of the Netherlands, and between them in the summer of 1529 they managed to persuade the two monarchs to subscribe to the Treaty of Cambrai (known later as the Ladies' Peace). Neither Francis nor Charles really had the means to continue the struggle. It was a sensible treaty, and although no more than others did it make peace permanent, it cleared up many of the problems still unsettled after Madrid. Charles agreed to give up his demand for Burgundy, and Francis to waive all Italian claims. The princes were to return, although in exchange for a huge ransom levied on the long-suffering people of France, and the marriage previously arranged between Francis and Eleanor was to take place. By 1 July 1530 the money was paid over; the Dauphin and his brother (wan and listless as a result of their experiences) came back to France accompanied by their future stepmother. Francis met them between Bordeaux and Bayonne and at the little abbey of Saint Laurent-de-Beyrie the marriage was solemnised. It was celebrated by an 'entry' into Bordeaux, followed by a grand coronation of the new Queen in the following March.

It would be unjust to Francis to say he had given no thought to his exiled children. It was probably Louise who had missed them most, and who had been moved to struggle for the Peace of Cambrai partly by her love for them, but their father had been striving to get the boys returned against a ransom ever since he had renounced the Treaty of Madrid. His main preoccupation during these years, however, was undoubtedly his building schemes. Besides the earlier Chambord, Francis built or reconstructed eight other châteaux and palaces during his reign. In 1528 he had work under way on five châteaux in the Paris region besides that continuing on Chambord. This included pulling down the old remaining tower of the fortress of the Louvre, and making there a palace which would be a fit habitation for the Court. But his great new love was Fontainebleau.

In the midst of forests which would provide hunting, in place of an old castle, there arose a curiously designed palace, an agglomeration of loosely connected parts which is a strange mixture of old Gothic confusion and new Renaissance form. The whole, however, is imposing, and Fontainebleau was one of the great joys of Francis's later life. The work, begun originally by French master masons, was continued increasingly by Italians throughout the rest of the reign. By 1534 it was ready to be occupied; henceforth the King returned to it at least once a year. Whenever he said 'I am going home' he meant to Fontainebleau. Even while he resided there, workmen from Italy continued their work of sumptuous internal decoration. Francis showed unabated interest in every detail of ornamentation. Besides being 'home' Fontainebleau became the treasure house of all that he valued most. There were special galleries for the famous pictures and tapestries he acquired, special niches for small objets d'art; there were even specially designed chests for his collection of gems. Whenever the King was seeking a particularly valuable piece, it was for Fontainebleau.

There too he built up a library of books and precious manuscripts in various languages[17] supervised by a permanent librarian who was at one time the famous hellenist Guillaume Budé. Francis had close contacts with scholars and savants, and at this stage of his life it was his custom to summon them daily to give him a reading from some classical work. He encouraged translation and printing, and was generous in his endowments to schools and colleges; above all, in 1529, he founded the Collège de France. It was in some respects in opposition to the Sorbonne which was very much governed by its theological faculty, and always inclined to reaction.

The new college was based on the teaching of Greek, Latin and Hebrew; it was to be a monument to the new learning. Professors were appointed, and their salaries—often overdue, alas—were paid from a royal allocation. Francis never got so far as providing the buildings he had promised, and the lectures had to be given in the class rooms of various other institutions; but the Collège de France was to survive, an institution of intellectual independence, and a permanent tribute to its royal founder.

Francis was not totally preoccupied with learning. He had always been restless and could not remain long without travelling. Towards the end of 1531 he decided to make a grand tour of France, and the journeyings took up much of his time until early in 1534. In September 1531 his mother had died. Perhaps that brought on a new fit of restlessness. In November the great cavalcade set out on travels which, before they ended, had

17 Origin of present Bibliothèque Nationale.

covered Picardy, Normandy and Brittany in the north; the central regions of Berry and Auvergne; Champagne, Burgundy, and the Lyonnais in the east; and the southern provinces of Languedoc, Dauphiné and Provence.

Meanwhile, shadows were falling. However much Francis might concentrate his interests on his humanistic schemes, he was to receive some blows, both private and public, that were too painful to ignore. In August 1536 the Dauphin died suddenly at the age of eighteen. Francis had taken great pride in his eldest son while for his second son, Henry, now Dauphin, he had little affection; he had been the dreamy sulky type of child that was repellent to the gaiety-loving monarch.

In the public sphere, the war had started again, and with it came another wave of unrest. France had made great strides economically during the reign of Louis XII and was fundamentally a prosperous country, but the extravagances of Francis were of an order that no state could sustain. Throughout the reign he had steadily increased both direct taxation and duties. He mortgaged royal domains, forced loans from towns and the clergy and invented new offices in order to sell them to the highest bidders. At the same time the very improvement in the economic position of the bourgeoisie made them more inclined to voice their discontent. Public finances were inextricably mixed with the personal expenses of the king, and an attempt at monetary and financial reform early in the reign had come to nothing.

There was, too, another source of unrest, always present, but manifesting itself critically during the last fourteen years or so of Francis's life. This was religion. The papal struggle with Luther and the revolt of the German Protestant princes fell within Francis's reign. France was not exempt from the impact of the reform movement. There was in France a group of Catholic reformers who held views similar to those of Erasmus. They collected round Brissonnet, Bishop of Meaux, and included eminent humanists and literary men. Their activity also attracted the sympathy of Francis's sister, Marguerite. The Biblists, as they were called, had little sympathy with the breakaway movement of Luther and still less with the extreme views being preached in France by Calvin just before his departure from the country in 1534; but as the Sorbonne hardened in intolerance, other, more heterodox groups, sought to express themselves in more rebellious terms.

Francis himself probably never gave very deep thought to religious questions. His sister had interested him in the views of the moderate reformers, and he had always disliked the intense conservatism of the Sorbonne which seemed to him to obstruct the progress of the new learning. In any case, there were certain factors to modify his official Catholicism. In the first place, he was naturally a tolerant person; it was part of his sunny easy-going nature, and on more than one occasion he intervened to save a scholar from persecution. Besides this, he needed the alliance of the German Protestant princes who could be very use-fully stirred up against the Emperor; and he was occasionally forced into alliance with Henry VIII who had been excommuni-cated by the Pope. But his desire for the unity of his realm and his own absolutism was paramount. In October 1534 came the affair of the placards; in Paris, Amboise and Orleans there appeared posters expressing approval of Luther and denying the doctrine of transubstantiation. Francis connected the agitation, probably correctly, with other signs of unrest. He saw in the protests a challenge to the position of the king. Repression and persecution, which had always occurred intermittently, now became a con-sistent policy. All printing was subjected to severe restriction; heretics were burned; and for the increasing number of des-peradoes, partly recruited from unpaid soldiers, a hideous new torture was devised by which they were stretched and broken on a wheel.[18] The religious persecution culminated in 1545 in the wholesale massacre of a community of French peasants in Provence who lived under some unorthodox variation of the faith.

After the suppression of the placards Francis organised a great cleansing ceremony in the course of which representatives of all religious orders, citizens of Paris, members of the University, officials of Court and State went with the royal family in pro-cession to Notre Dame to ask God's forgiveness for the national lapse. Queen Eleanor rode on a white horse, surrounded by her household, but the King himself went on foot, bare-headed and clad in black. The monks bore banners and crosses and some of

18 Wheel = *Roue*. It gave the French language the word *roué* (for an evil liver) which also became used in English.

the most precious relics of Christendom which had never left their sanctuaries since the days of St Louis.[19] Everyone else, including the King, carried a torch or candle, and the whole procession passed through streets hung with black. It was a pageant of a different kind.

Later in the day, Francis made a speech at the University in which he emphasised his royal duty to defend the Catholic faith and his determination to banish 'errors' from his kingdom. 'Those who are justly accused shall be punished, but I promise punishment no less to all false accusers.' While he was speaking six heretics were being committed to the flames.

Beneath the gathering clouds of his closing years Francis continued his lavish patronage of the arts. In 1540 Cellini, the great Italian sculptor and goldsmith, came into his service. He executed for Francis some of his finest works: the gold salt-cellar (now in the Vienna Museum), a six-foot silver model of Jupiter (which was intended to be the first of a series of statues of Greek gods to stand as candelabra round the table at Fontainebleau), and a bronze nymph (now in the Louvre) to surmount the entrance hall to the same palace. Cellini has left in his lively *Memoirs* a vivid account of Francis in his later years. He brings out clearly his generosity towards artists, his deep interest in all aspects of their work which caused him frequently to visit their workshops, and his genuine respect for their calling which, in spite of occasional tempestuous interludes, led him to meet them on terms of equality or sometimes even with deference.

We do not know why Cellini removed himself from Francis's service after four years (he always spoke nostalgically afterwards of his days in France) but there is a hint of the reason in his difficult relations with Anne de Heilly, now the dominating Duchess of Etampes. She never liked Cellini and did her best to turn the King against him. It was difficult, even for his mistress, to turn Francis against favourite artists, at any rate for long, but she was much more successful in influencing him against rival court factions which emerged during these years of incessant intrigue. Francis's mother was dead; his sister had married as her second husband, the King of Navarre, and was no longer at his side. Queen Eleanor hardly counted in his life, and without the two

19 King Louis IX (1226-1270).

women who had moulded his career, he was more directed
by his mistress than previously. The Dauphin, Henry was
married (for political reasons) to Catherine de Médicis,[20] but a
far stronger influence was that of his mistress Diane de Poitiers.
Francis's dislike of his second son did not extend to his daughter-
in-law; he found Catherine amusing, but she, in her early twenties,
was already revealing the capacity for intrigue for which she was
later to become notorious. She, her husband and his mistress
formed a bloc in opposition to the King, and inevitably to the
Duchess of Etampes. They represented the future, and the
Duchess was frightened. She made a counteralliance with Francis's
youngest son Charles of Orleans; high officers of state became
involved, and the Court was rent by faction.

Francis himself was losing touch. He was ageing, and since 1540
it had been apparent he was in failing health. His interest in the
arts, his mania for hunting, both persisted; occasionally he made
a stroke in the interminable war, but he was of a generation
that was passing, and he had little prescience of the future. It
had been an age of sharp transition, and during his reign France
had been changing more quickly than the King realised. It had
passed out of its feudal phase into full nationhood; and it had
emerged to find itself confronted with all the problems posed by
the Protestant Reformation. There was no escaping them. Francis
had moulded the nation; he had inaugurated its first national
army, he had given the people a patriotic pride. He may be said to
have been the founder of the monarchy of France as it has stamped
itself on the imagination of Europe. Above all, he had made that
association between the name of France and all that is finest in
human culture that was to endure until our own time. But he
was handing on to his successor a depleted exchequer, an unfinished war and a religious situation too explosive to be
contained.

If Francis could not envisage his country's future tribulations,
he could no longer avoid disagreeable thoughts about his
personal life. Still in his early fifties, he had become an old man,
worn with disease. The one inescapable experience loomed ahead.

The death of Henry VIII in January 1547 was a severe shock.

20 Daughter of Duke Lorenzo de' Medici and great-grand-daughter of
Lorenzo the Magnificent. This is the form of her name used in France.

Francis felt deep grief, springing from his consciousness of how much they had in common. He ordered an elaborate memorial service to be held in Notre Dame.

For the next two months all was restlessness. With his unwieldy household and his crowd of courtiers he trailed from château to château, spending a few days at each in hunting for as much of the day as his health would stand. Towards the end of February he arrived at Rambouillet. For one more month his life dragged on amidst all his accustomed luxury, and he continued to hunt almost to the end. On 31 March 1547 he died.

The obsequies lasted for three weeks, and the procession that bore him to his elaborate tomb at St Denis surpassed in its length any that had ever been accorded to a predecessor. In his death Francis offered to his subjects a final spectacle. Perhaps they watched it with appreciation of the show rather than regret for the King who had cost them so much. Perhaps, on the other hand, since they could not foresee the sequel, their predominant feeling was pride in the grandeur of the reign.


## FURTHER READING

C. A. H. GUIGNEBERT. *A Short History of the French People,* trans. F. G. Richmond. Allen & Unwin 1930. Part II (First four chapters).

*The New Cambridge Modern History, Vol II: The Reformation.* Cambridge University Press. Chapter XI.

W. L. MC.ELWEE. *The Reign of Charles V.* Macmillan 1936.

ROYALL TYLER. *The Emperor Charles V.* Allen & Unwin 1956.

# Jean Bodin

## (1530-1596)

*A Commonwealth may be defined as the rightly ordered
government of a number of families and of those things
which are their common concern by a sovereign power.*

IT WAS INEVITABLE that the Renaissance should produce a new kind of political awareness. Medieval Christendom, for centuries the accepted organisation of Europe, was passing away, and the rebellion against a universal Papacy which had long been linked with feudal overlordship was accompanied by corresponding political and social disturbances. In the German states the peasants' revolts which had been sporadic in the last century, increased in violence, and baronial conflicts were intensified. The existing economic conditions which these earlier outbreaks implied were doubtless of assistance to the religious revolt itself; later the overt discussion inspired by the reformers could be transferred to the secular sphere. Men who had learned to question religious authority were apt to ask why their overlords—whether the barons who ruled the peasants or the princes who ruled the barons—should have control over their material lives any more than the Catholic Church should dictate their theological beliefs.

Outside the German empire, compact national states—Spain, France and England—had come into being, and within them the establishment of order had necessitated a strong central government of a despotic nature. Once the concept of a 'nation' under a firm secular authority had established itself with an appearance of permanence, it is not surprising that, under the accepted order of monarchy, questioning began among those who wished for some share in the power of kings. Philosophers, lawyers and statesmen began to ask themselves: 'What does the government of a state really consist of? Who actually wields the power? Who ought to wield it?' And going further, 'What is the nature of a state? What brings it into being?'

Jean Bodin, a Frenchman who lived from 1530 to 1596, was the first political thinker of the modern world to provide answers to these questions in the form of definitions which would serve as a starting point for clear thinking and so be useful to men in understanding the nature of their future society. He was, in fact, the first philosopher of the new national state. He was not the first modern writer on politics if by that we simply mean one who addresses himself to the practical problems of his time rather than to the abstract and metaphysical theories which preoccupied the thinkers of the Middle Ages. Machiavelli, a Florentine official, writing in the time of the grandson of the great Lorenzo, had already discussed some of these questions in terms of the six-teenth-century Italian City-state, and his book *The Prince* has had a fame—or more exactly a notoriety—which has outlived that of Bodin's much more comprehensive work; but although men's political actions have perhaps all too often been based on the more cynical precepts of Machiavelli, their capacity to analyse social problems, and to develop an historical philosophy, was nourished by the ideas of Bodin.

Machiavelli, abandoning both the methods and morals of medi-eval thinkers, had adopted a completely realistic approach. He did not conjure up ideal states, nor indicate ways to the 'good life'. His book was in the form of a manual of active statecraft, and purports only to give advice to him who would succeed as a ruler. Looking at man and society as he saw them and not accord-ing to some pre-conceived ideal, he remarked what succeeded, and in the Italy of the late fifteenth and early sixteenth centuries this hardly encouraged a premium on morality. His advice is quite unscrupulous, even if pre-eminently practical, and *The Prince* has usually been seen by posterity as a shocking work. This impact of the book is unfair to Machiavelli because it is actually only the best known fragment of his extensive political writings which taken as a whole show a unique awareness of the historical developments of his time. It may be that his lack of idealism should be deplored, but his severance of politics from ethics did assist him to a scientific analysis of the concept 'state'. He intro-duced a new approach, that of genuine investigation into existing circumstances and future possibilities.

Bodin, who like Machiavelli had a close-up view of practical affairs of state, was not unaffected by his great Italian predecessor. Though he is generally influenced by moral considerations, occa-sionally a tinge of Machiavellianism creeps into his proposals, but more pronounced is the similarity of his method. Both men believed that through the study of history and examination of existing institutions, guidance could be obtained for dealing with the problems of the contemporary state.

It is at first surprising to learn that in spite of these sensible modern ideas, Bodin, in another part of his work, places considerable reliance on astrology, and that a few years after the publication of *The Republic*, he was writing a most repulsive book on the methods of hunting down and punishing those suspected of witchcraft. Surprising, that is, until we remember that Bodin was a man of the Renaissance standing on the bridge between the Middle Ages and the modern world, and that it is characteristic of so many men of his time that they harboured this kind of inconsistency. Our own age, doubtless, entertains a variety of ideas and beliefs that will look as strangely in conflict to generations that come after us. It is much easier to be wise about times we can look back upon.

We are not much concerned with the facts of Bodin's life except in so far as his vocations affected his practical thinking; we do need to concern ourselves rather more with the conditions of the time in which he lived. Jean Bodin was born at Angers in the west of France in 1530 into a little known family. He studied law at Toulouse and then lectured there before going to Paris to work as an advocate. He was always interested in literature, producing books steadily from the age of twenty-five. First came translations, and then works on a range of subjects which included economics, law, philosophy, theology and (in 1576) the great work in six books on political theory, known as *The Republic*.[1]

In 1571 Bodin had obtained a post in the household of the Duke of Alençon, the younger brother of the King, and ten years later, when Alençon had become Duke of Anjou and a suitor of Queen Elizabeth, Bodin accompanied him to England. By this time Bodin's views, which were anti-feminist and particularly strong on the subject of women rulers, were well known and the English Queen seems to have treated him rather coolly: she always insisted on referring to him as Monsieur Badin. At least he must have been gratified to find that his fame had travelled so far, though he was shocked by the bad Latin translation of *The Republic* that was being studied both in London and Cambridge. The discovery of this led him later to make his own translation into Latin.

1 Also called in English ' The Commonwealth '.

Some time before the visit to England Bodin had found favour with Henry III himself and was made King's Attorney at Laon. He was also elected by the Third Estate[2] of the Vermandois district to the Estates-General (or Parliament of France) which met at Blois in 1576. The times were very turbulent and the King extremely vacillating, so that it is not surprising that a man of intellectual integrity—which Bodin was—did not remain long in royal favour. He did, however, obtain a post in the magistracy at Laon, and the latter part of his life, after the death of the Duke of Anjou with whom he had visited the Netherlands[3] in 1582, was spent in virtual retirement in that city. There he wrote his last works, and there he died of the plague in 1596.

Bodin's work on political theory was inevitably influenced by the fact that he had studied law. His juristic temperament reveals itself both in his love of exact definition and in the stress he puts on analysing systems of law when studying history. For him it is essential first to draw conclusions about law—divine and natural, as well as human—in order to determine the best form of government for any society. But an equally important influence on his conclusions was the alarming condition of sixteenth century France.

During the reign of Henry II (1547-1559) the reformed religion, which had begun to penetrate France during the reign of his father Francis I, gained considerable ground in spite of fierce persecution. The French Protestants (Huguenots), inspired by the teaching of Calvin, began to claim not only tolerance but supremacy: the Catholics resisted the claim with all the passion of a rooted faith, and France, more than any other country, became the scene of violent collision and protracted civil wars. All countries where a considerable number wished to renounce the Papacy were having to face concomitant political and social problems as well as the basic problem of toleration, but whereas the countries of northern and southern Europe were to declare definitely for Protestantism and Catholicism respectively, while the German states paused in an uneasy compromise, in France the two sides were more even, more bigoted and more belligerent than elsewhere

---

2 That is, those electors who were neither nobles nor clergy.
3 Cf. William the Silent. p. 184.

K

and the struggle between them was to persist throughout the rest of the century.

One striking feature of the French Reformation was the number of nobles who embraced Calvinism. This was to be a complicating factor because these noble families were closely related to the reigning house and were ambitious for power whenever circumstances should be favourable. The circumstances were provided by an unexpected period of regency government. Henry II was killed in an accident in a tournament in 1559 and his widow, Catherine de Médicis[4] was left with four young sons aged fifteen, nine, eight and five.[5] Francis II (who was married to Mary Queen of Scots) ascended the throne only to die within eighteen months, and in December 1560 Catherine became regent for her second son Charles IX. It was a signal for the various factions, religious and political, to break into armed conflict, and from 1562 till 1598 France was rent by civil wars relieved only by occasional brief truces. The confusion throughout the country was such as to be an open invitation to all who wished to fish in troubled waters. Although nominally the point at issue was the degree of toleration to be allowed to the Huguenots, motives were intertwined and it is impossible to tell how much individuals were fighting for a religious cause and how much for personal ambition. The Guise family of Lorraine, to whom Mary Queen of Scots was related, were the leaders of the Catholic faction, and the Bourbon family, the head of which was Antony, husband of the Queen of Navarre,[6] provided the rallying point for the Protestants. Antony himself was a waverer, but his wife was staunchly Huguenot and she was supported by his younger brother Condé, and the Châtillon family of whom the best known is Admiral[7] Coligny.

Charles IX died in May 1574, having reigned till he was twenty-four, but two years before his death the bitterness of the struggle had been intensified by the grim massacre of St Bartholomew. Charles, seeking to heal the breach in France, had swung to the

4 Great-grand-daughter of Lorenzo the Magnificent.
5 There were also three daughters.
6 She was the daughter of Francis I's sister Marguerite who had married Henry II, King of Navarre.
7 At this time a military title.

policies of Coligny, and this roused the jealous hostility of the Queen Mother. Motives are obscure but, at a time when Paris was full of Huguenots come to celebrate the marriage of the King's sister to young Prince Henry of Navarre, the King seems to have been won over by threats to give consent to a planned assassination of the Huguenot leaders. The attack quickly developed into a wholesale massacre in which the pro-Catholic Paris population joined, and it was in the aftermath of turmoil and suspicion that Henry III came to the throne. The Catholic League, which was formed in 1576, favoured strenuous persecution of the reformed religion, and looked to Henry to be its leader. When the King tried instead to pursue a policy that would avoid war, the League became anti-royalist, and the nobles who chiefly composed it began to hanker after their lost feudal powers, so that Henry, a vacillating person by temperament, was caught in hopeless uncertainty between the Huguenots and the Catholic League. In such circumstances, Bodin wrote his famous work.

There was no lack of humanist scholars in the France of this time who tried to put forward a sane middle view which would allow for toleration of both religions. Their political counterparts were a group called the 'Politiques' composed of moderate men from each side, and between 1560 and 1567 Catherine de Médicis's chancellor, Michel de l'Hôpital, himself a humanist, had ably bridged the views of liberal politicians and scholars. If we can say Bodin had lasting affinities with any ideological group it was with this one; he certainly shared their view that French nationality could be held together without the necessity of strict religious uniformity.

In order to find a centre for a power which could unify France, Bodin seems first to have asked himself what the ultimate power in the state—or in any state—really was. Did that power lie with the so-called sovereign, the King? Was his sovereignty real? If not, where was sovereignty placed? What was the final sanction which everyone in a state accepted? In terms of political theory it would be useful to know: for Bodin's France it was essential for preservation. But even prior to the question of ultimate power was the problem of what the state itself actually was. How did one know that these new 'nations' were states—larger versions of the City-states of medieval Italy? These are some of the questions discussed in *The Republic*.

Bodin's book is badly planned, the language is often confused, it has a major weakness in that some of the most outstanding ideas are not clearly related to others, and there are palpable inconsistencies; but for all that, from it emerges a number of clear-cut ideas which were a fruitful addition to the data of political thinkers. Of these the statement on the nature of the state and the concept of sovereignty are the two most important.

For Bodin, the family is the basis of the state, for he holds that a family of father, mother and children together with their property is a natural unit, and that within this original group, the father should have complete authority. In this connection we find Bodin looking back even further than the Middle Ages for he goes so far as to say that in a rightly ordered state a father would have the power of life and death over his children. However, his assumption is that generally family discipline will be based on love and respect, and following from this, man's social instinct will cause him to make contacts of friendship outside the circle of purely 'natural affection'. Families may, and do, join together in wider associations as, for example, colleges based on their common calling, and corporations for various ends, but these unions have no real power and cannot compel their members to remain permanently within them. The association which is different from all others in that it possesses sovereign power is the State in which families have been united. The State is not a natural unit like the family. It does not exist because the people speak the same language, hold the same religion or are living within certain natural geographical boundaries; it has come into being simply because the sovereignty that resides in it is recognised and accepted by certain groups of families, and the fact of their acceptance constitutes them a State. The fathers, so powerful within their families, have become citizens under the superior government of another. The State may often originate in force, but once its sovereignty is accepted and expresses itself in the form of laws which all obey, it has become a permanent institution, and its members cannot contract out of it. Although the State has commonly originated in force (as, for example, the emergence of a victorious chieftain) its ends are not merely material. Its basis may be economic, but its aim should be virtue. This implies the happiness of its members as an aim, for this is a result of the satisfaction of morality and reason.

Where one can recognise sovereignty—that is a power which is subordinate to no other, and which all who are grouped under it obey—there one recognises the State. What is the nature of this sovereignty and where may it be located? Sovereignty (says Bodin) is really an unlimited right to make laws without the sovereign himself being bound by them. It is perpetual although it could be transferred to an individual for life provided the transfer was free of all conditions. Having stated this, Bodin proceeds to hint at some conditions of his own. He recognises the existence of a rather vaguely defined natural law, and this the sovereign (exempt from man-made laws) must obey. Also the sovereign cannot destroy the basis of the State itself—that is, the family and the property rights of citizens. It is worth noting in this connection that the chief reason for Bodin's losing the favour of Henry III was that he opposed the King's demand that he should be allowed to alienate (i.e. sell) public lands which the Crown held in trust. A sovereign monarch who transgresses the Law of Nature must not however, be resisted on this account; he has turned himself into a tyrant and tyranny can be punished only by God, although Bodin concedes that conscience may impel an individual to disobey and take the consequences.

This brings us to the point where we can see that for Bodin sovereignty should reside in an absolute monarchy. He saw the problem in terms of the constitution of sixteenth-century France. Frenchmen were disputing where sovereignty lay, but they had not clearly grasped what it involved. Bodin's aim was to assist in clarification. Temperamentally he also preferred absolute monarchy, although his justification of it is different from the theory of the Divine Right of Kings which was widely accepted and was to be so much debated in seventeenth-century England. To begin with he did not see the absolute monarchy as ordained by God, or at least only so far as everything on earth was created by Him. He never even suggests that it had more divine approval than any other form of government. For him it was a matter of expediency and he advocated the system he believed to work best. Indeed, one of Bodin's contributions to political theory was that he cut it away from the entanglement with theology, and except for the mention of God as the final judge of a tyrant's conduct, he speaks of constitutional questions entirely in terms of man-made arrangements. He did believe that some generally accepted form of religion should be upheld by the State, but that persecution should be avoided as far as possible since belief is essentially an expression of the individual mind. His approval of absolute monarchs which did not extend to tyrants, did so even less to dictators who, being temporary, could never be said to be in possession of sovereignty at all. He used the term 'Royal Monarchy' to describe his ideal State where natural and divine laws were respected, and the succession was hereditary by primogeniture, with enforcement of the Salic Law which prohibited the succession of females, or of claimants through the female line.

Bodin recognised other constitutional forms. Although there was only one form of State (the union of families) there could be different forms of government. An aristocracy was one in which sovereignty was vested in a selected few; a democracy one where it was vested in a numerical majority of the people. A democracy, he thought, might be the best ideally, but it was always tainted with fickleness and venality, and in practice became a mere fiction; in any case, he regarded equality as against nature. He conceded that absolute monarchy might not suit all states, but he seems to have regarded democracies as being on a lower plane and there is a confusing hint that in them perhaps true sovereignty could not exist.[8]

In considering these views of Bodin—and also for that matter those of Machiavelli—we must be careful not to take a hind-sight view from our position in twentieth-century democracy. Bodin could judge only on what had happened up to 1576. In the City-states of Italy, the tentative democracies had all been replaced by despotisms before the end of the Middle Ages; the new nation states were all absolutist, and perhaps it was a condition of their very existence. The point that is important is not that Bodin believed in a form of government that men have since outgrown, but that he had isolated the conception of sovereignty, so that

8 Presumably because 'in a popular State rulers and ruled form a single (sovereign) body and so cannot bind themselves by their own laws'. Thus such States would always be in danger of dissolution.

thinkers who came after him could see that its existence was not dependent on a particular form. Where someone (or some group) has sovereignty over a number of families there the State exists.

Bodin put his own characteristically inconsistent limitation on his conception of absolute government. He was so keen on the rights of private property and so sure that to interfere with them was an infringement of a natural law that his sovereign was not even allowed to tax his citizens, except as a temporary measure in an emergency, and even then he regarded a forced loan as preferable. It is not, of course, simply a question of taxing them without their consent. Taxation was always an unquestionable evil. This seems a shattering limitation to us who have come to think that the most important branch of government is that which controls the purse, and that those who accord it the right to tax are the sovereign people.

Although Bodin's thought had weaknesses and inconsistencies, and the fame that he won in his day barely survived the seventeenth century, he has proved to be a fruitful thinker. It would be wrong to claim that even his important ideas are completely original. Most of them had been touched on, and many elaborated, by ancient Greek thinkers, notably Aristotle. But these ideas had been lost sight of in the very different conditions of the Middle Ages, and when the Renaissance brought a revival of Greek thought many of them did not exactly apply to the new conditions. Men needed to learn their political grammar again in the context of their own times.

The analysis of the origin of states and the definition of sovereignty are the contributions by which Bodin is most frequently remembered, but amidst a wealth of other political ideas there are two which stand out as pointers to later labourers in the same fields. The first is his theory of climate[9] and the effect it had on political and social institutions, which although unscientific, and in some parts nonsensical, did draw attention to the fact that geographical conditions influence national character. The second, and more important, is his conception of the significance of change and the emphasis he places on its processes. Firmly as he believed that political science could only be founded on a permanent moral law, he also recognised the transience of all

9 For Bodin the term covers the totality of physical conditions.

human institutions. He was deeply imbued with the historical spirit. As early as 1566 he had written a book called *The Method for the Easy Comprehension of History* in which he stated that observed facts must be the basis of all conclusions. Philosophy, for him, could never be merely a defence of views that were acceptable. He sought truth first by careful observation of existing and past societies with particular attention to their laws, and then by reviewing his findings in the light of the philosophy of history which he had evolved. He saw quite clearly—more clearly that is than many historians and statesmen were doing at the end of the nineteenth century—that all political forms are necessarily temporary. Change is the one thing certain. Perhaps it is easier to see this in revolutionary times than it is in more stable periods; but, in any case, it is an important historical concept. From it Bodin developed his theory of revolutions.

For him a revolution could be simply defined as a change in the location of sovereignty. It could not be said to have occurred if sovereignty still remained in the same place. Since change was inevitable and revolution undesirable, we should be prepared to accept the slow peaceful decline of a State and its gradual transmutation into a different form as preferable to sudden and violent upheavals. It is now a truism that the reform movement of yesterday is the conservative acceptance of today, but are communities, taken as a whole, not inclined still to rest in that acceptance? Are we yet sufficiently forward looking to be able to develop our societies intelligently and peacefully into the next stage?

It is unlikely that there has ever been anyone able to accept as a whole the views set out in Bodin's book. Apart from his obscure inconsistencies and what has come to seem the nonsense of the astrological section, he is essentially a writer that gave to all his readers something to accept and something to reject; and because it is not possible to extract coherent theory from Bodin's writings, people have, even more than usual, taken the suggestions they needed and ignored the rest. With the passing of time his *Republic* has ceased to be a very necessary piece of political reading, but some of the most important ideas contained in it, worked over since by a host of later writers, still serve as useful starting points for serious political thinking.

## FURTHER READING

J. E. NEALE. *The Age of Catherine de Medici.* Cape 1943.

R. H. MURRAY. *The History of Political Science.* Heffer 1926. Chapter IV and VI.

J. W. ALLEN. *A History of Political Thought in the Sixteenth Century.* Rev. edn. Methuen 1957. Part III, Chap. VIII, Part IV, Chap. II.

A recommended edition of Machiavelli's *The Prince* is that translated by Luigi Ricci and published in the World's Classics, Oxford University Press 1960.

There is an abridged edition of *The Commonwealth* translated by M. J. Tooley (Blackwell).

# Montaigne

*(1533-1592)*

*Our great and glorious masterpiece is to live appropriately.*

WE HAVE SEEN that the dazzling radiance of the French high Renaissance swiftly faded into the sombre atmosphere of the civil wars. The latter part of the sixteenth century was indeed one of the blackest periods in the history of France, but it was a period that was to make great contributions to literature and one voice[1] in particular rings out to claim the attention of succeeding generations and to reaffirm the values and attitudes which contemporary agitation was trampling underfoot. It is a voice which is distinctively French, but which speaks—as much as any ever has done—for all mankind. It is the voice of Michel de Montaigne. We honour ourselves by making his acquaintance early.

Montaigne is, perhaps, not an author for the young. Most of his thought derives from his basic belief that there is not an argument in the world that cannot be matched by another argument on the other side, and when we are young we wish passionately to take sides. Yet our very freedom to do this flows from an accepted toleration of whose principles Montaigne was the first modern exponent. Sometime or other everyone who would be educated should encounter this civilised mind, but it may be well to know something of the man even before we are ready to read his book.

One says his ' book '—he refers to his literary work as ' my book ' so often—because he is essentially a man of one vast work, and one reason for his enduring influence (although not the most important) is that he invented, however unintentionally, a new literary form. The work, which is actually composed of three books using the word in the sense of a ' part ' or a ' section ', is entitled *Essays*, and its chapters have the sort of titles, and their subjects the sort of treatment that we have come to associate with that word. But we use it derivatively: Montaigne meant something a little different. He was, he says, by writing, making trials

1 The other writer of comparable stature is Rabelais.

146

or tests[2] of his judgement ('I essay my judgement'), and what he wished to judge was life itself in all its many sidedness, and man's relation to his universe; he was indeed the first since the Greeks to attempt a critique of the human situation.

Since he believed that 'Each man bears the entire form of man's estate' where could he better study his subject than in his own thoughts, moods and actions? This he did, and so it comes about that the book, in spite of the different subjects of its chapters (or essays) has in fact a unity—the picture it presents of Montaigne himself, and, because of the crystalline honesty of his thought, of all his readers too. It is true that we can with profit dip in at any place and read an individual essay, but it is also true that those who read more deeply in Montaigne find that there is a development of his personality, and hence of his theme, as the book proceeds.

Since his innovation the essay has become one of the most widely recognised forms of literature, but the importance of the *Essays* rests on something greater than that. Their author is of permanent significance because of the spirit of humanism and reason that emanates from his writing; the spirit of Ancient Greece which animated the Renaissance world was epitomised in Montaigne; he absorbed all that was best in the great intellectual heritage of his time, and recast it in a form so distinctively modern that it has influenced the best minds of every generation since. Europe's greatest tragedies have come when western man has denied that spirit. Montaigne set out in his easy discursive fashion —for he could be doctrinaire no more in manner than in matter— the great liberal truths acclaimed by all who would travel the sane middle way; a belief in tolerance, the right to freedom of thought and speech, the importance of the search for objective truth and the courage to utter the truth we find even when it happens not to suit our book, and, above all, the value of the individual with his strengths and weaknesses and all his awkwardnesses and oddities which make him a distinct human being, albeit one who can find a great deal of his happiness in co-operation with his fellows. 'If our faces were not similar we could not distinguish man from beast; if they were not dissimilar we could not distinguish man

2 *O.E.D.* Essay: 'The action or process of trying or testing; an attempt endeavour '. The word was new with Montaigne in the literary sense.

from man.' And he believed that these virtues flourished best in an atmosphere of relaxed good-humour; no one could be less censorious, less kill-joy or less rigid. 'I love a gay and sociable wisdom, and shun harshness and austerity in behaviour, holding every surly countenance suspect.'

Montaigne's study was life, and his philosophy (although he would have rejected the word) is composed of his observations of living. It is as well, therefore, to know something of the circumstances in which his lot was cast. Much of what is known comes to us direct from his own book. He was born to Pierre and Antoinette Eyquem in 1533 at the château of Montaigne in the Dordogne region of south-west France, and was the first of their numerous family to survive infancy. His immediate ancestors had been merchants, but his great-grandfather had purchased this property and his father had been born there. The possession of the estate ennobled the family, and Michel later dropped the Eyquem from his name. His father seems to have been a remarkable man with definite and original ideas on education, and an attitude to religion which was strikingly liberal if we consider the time at which he was living. His wife was, in fact, a Protestant, partly of Jewish race, and their family seem to have been Catholic or Protestant according to individual inclination. Michel was, and remained, a Catholic.

The atmosphere surrounding the boy in his earliest years was one of kindness and good humour. In an age when not much thought was given to the emotional needs of the young, his father insisted that there must be no physical punishment, and that all shocks must be avoided. He also instituted an original method of teaching his son Latin, which he naturally accepted as the basis of education. He put him in the charge of a German tutor whose Latin was so proficient that he had no need to use any other language, and the young Montaigne learnt it as his mother tongue. There were two assistants who also spoke only in Latin, and Montaigne tells us that even the valets and housemaids picked up enough of it for it to be an inviolable rule that he was never addressed in any other language. He goes on, 'Altogether we Latinised ourselves so much that it overflowed all the way to our villages on every side, where there still remain several Latin names for artisans and tools that have taken root by usage.'

It is not surprising that when he went to the College of Guy-
enne at the age of six, he knew more Latin than his teachers,
nor that his Greek, most of which was learnt at school
by more conventional methods, never reached a similar
standard.

Few subsequent details of Montaigne's boyhood are known to
us, but in 1553 we find him, a youth of twenty, finishing a law
course at Toulouse. On returning home, he took up a post at
Perigueux in the Cour des Aides, a court recently established by
King Henry II to deal with special taxes. That is, he became a
kind of judge. His father had held the office, but had recently
been elected Mayor of Bordeaux, and the young Montaigne was
allowed to succeed him in the judgeship at the age of twenty-one
although the regulation age was thirty. This new type of court,
however, was exceedingly unpopular and in 1557 Henry had to
dissolve it, and its officers were transferred to be members of the
Parlement of Bordeaux. This was primarily a judicial body, which
promulgated the King's edicts applying to its particular region,
and Montaigne remained a member of it for thirteen years. He
seems to have performed his duties conscientiously, if without
immense enthusiasm, but the chief importance of his membership
of the Parlement is that there he met as a colleague, and embraced
as a friend, Etienne de la Boétie.

Montaigne, at this stage of his life, was a lively pleasure-seeking
young man, somewhat undisciplined and often indolent. He had,
however, a genuine enthusiasm for the thought of the ancient
(particularly Latin) writers, and a keen desire for discussion of
their philosophy. La Boétie, two years older and a good deal
steadier, was an entirely beneficial influence on the younger man;
he was happily married and had a mature sense of responsibility
both to his household and to his public duties. He was also of a
calm and even temperament, 'yet as ardent' Montaigne somewhere observes 'as if he were not'. Unfortunately the friendship,
begun under such happy auspices, was not to last; six years later
La Boétie died, leaving Montaigne with a sense of loss from
which he never wholly recovered. Some ten years later in one of
his finest essays, 'Of Friendship', Montaigne is telling us, 'If you
press me to tell why I loved him, I feel that this cannot be expressed, except by answering: Because it was he, because it was

I. . . . . Our friendship has no other model than itself, and can be compared only with itself.'

Montaigne seems to have sought frivolous distractions from his grief for two years, and then in 1565 he married Françoise de la Chassaigne, the daughter of a fellow member of the Parlement, almost, it would seem, because he regarded it as his social duty. He appears never to have brought much warmth to his relationship with his wife, nor to have showered a great deal of paternal affection on Lénor, the only daughter who survived out of the six that were born to him. Some of Montaigne's feeling was numbed after the death of La Boétie, and one cannot escape the impression that the natural affections were rather weak with him. On more than one occasion he mentions his freedom from emotional ties. There are several hints in the *Essays*, however, that Montaigne would have responded more warmly to a son, and there is perhaps one piece of evidence that his dormant affection could have been roused by a more lively-minded daughter. Poor Lénor does come through as rather dull and colourless; but when, towards the end of Montaigne's life, a young girl called Marie le Jars de Gournay became a kind of adopted daughter to him, he appreciated her superior intellect and was grateful for her intelligent estimation of his work.

Of his father too he speaks frequently with affection and admiration, and when Pierre Eyquem died in 1568 he felt his loss keenly. He inherited the estate of Montaigne, and with it the guardianship of a much younger brother. He improved and extended his house, building on to it for his private use a tower, in which he was later to spend most of his days. In the years since La Boétie's death public worries as well as private griefs had come upon him. The quarrels which rent the nation at large were reflected in the Parlement of Bordeaux. Moderate Catholics (the Politiques[3]) quarrelled with the extremists who, as supporters of Guise, were to form the Catholic League,[4] and after the moderate de L'Hôpital had been dismissed from the service of the Court in 1568, Montaigne seems to have felt that his time too had come to turn his back on public life. In July 1570 he resigned his seat in the Bordeaux Parlement and retired to his estates, there to spend

3 and 4. See Bodin p. 137.

most of his time in his tower reading and culling quotations from his favourite authors, meditating, and at length writing the three books of *Essays*. Literary occupations were not new to him; he had already done some translation and had been busy with the publication of La Boétie's last work; but the writing he now undertook sprang from his loneliness, from the loss of like-minded friends, and his sense of isolation in a country torn by factions where so few wished to walk with him the middle way. The fall of L'Hôpital seemed to him like the defeat of reason; public life was distasteful; his father and La Boétie were dead. It was with La Boétie that he had shared his mental life, and discussed all his philosophical ideas and personal problems. In a sense, the reader comes to take the place of the dead friend. The book, begun apparently as a compilation of thoughts from great authors in the fashion of his time, became largely a discursive conversation with the reader; it should be read in that spirit.

The tower[5] in which Montaigne was to spend most of his time for the next ten years was not simply a study. It had three storeys of which the ground floor was a chapel, and the next his bed-room, but it was the top floor that was the most important. There he had his library, and opening out of it a smaller warmer room where he could also work, and where on his first retirement to it, he had caused to be inscribed on the wall in Latin: ' In the year of Christ 1571, at the age of thirty-eight, on the last day of February, his birthday, Michel de Montaigne, long weary of the servi-tude of the court and public offices, while still fully vigorous has come to rest in the bosom of the Muses where in calm and free-dom from all cares he may pass what little remains of his life, now more than half run out. He hopes the fates will permit him to complete this sweet ancestral retreat, and he has dedicated it to his freedom, tranquillity and leisure.'

There were inscriptions in the library too. Carved on the beams of the ceiling were some fifty quotations which reflect the cast of Montaigne's mind. They are taken from the ancient authors, Greek and Latin, and from the Old and the New Testaments; and the majority of them point out the limitations of man's under-

5 It still stands in the village of St. Michel de Montaigne about fifty kilo-metres east of Bordeaux just north of the main road to Bergerac. (St. Michel is the name of the church.) See plate 7.

standing and the vanity of his pretence to any final knowledge. This vein of scepticism is an essential part of Montaigne's make-up, and during the years he was writing the first two books it was particularly strong. Perhaps three quotations selected from the inscriptions may sum up his mental outlook at this time, and, with some change of emphasis, throughout his life.

' I determine nothing. I do not comprehend things. I suspend judgement, I examine.'
' The for and the against are both possible.'
' I am a man, and nothing human is alien to me.'

In his library he was at peace. 'There is my throne. I try to make my authority over it absolute, and to withdraw this one corner from all society, conjugal, filial and civil. . . . Sorry the man, to my mind, who has not in his own home a place to be all by himself, to pay his court privately to himself, to hide.'

Although literary activities occupied most of Montaigne's time for ten years, he did pay some visits to Paris, either for the purpose of superintending the printing of La Boétie's work or on semi-political missions. In 1571 he was made a Chevalier of the Order of St Michael and a little later an Honorary Gentleman of the King's Bedchamber; in 1574 he was in Paris for the funeral of Charles IX. By 1579 he had finished Books I and II of the *Essays* and in the spring of 1580 the work was published. It was received with a variety of opinion, which would perhaps have pleased Montaigne who always gloried in human diversity, but on balance, there is no doubt it was a success, sealed by the royal approval of Henry III. As a result, Book III which was published eight years later displayed a new confidence and authority replacing the diffidence about his undertaking which was intermittently apparent in the earlier parts. Not that Montaigne ever had any doubt about the purpose of his book. It was a study of human nature in which he treated man in general through the examination of one individual: 'Others form man; I tell of him, and portray a particular one, very ill-formed, whom I should really make very different from what he is if I had to fashion him over again.' He told his readers squarely in a short preface to the first edition, ' I am myself the matter of my book ', and ' I want to be seen here in my simple natural ordinary fashion without straining or artifice; for it is myself that I portray'. No such extensive and honest study of human nature had been given to the world before. As he was to say himself in Book III, 'It is not my deeds that I write down; it is myself, it is my essence'. And, lest anyone should regard this as a vainglorious occupation, he added, 'No particular quality will make a man proud who balances it against the many weaknesses and imperfections that are also in him, and in the end, against the nullity of man's estate'.

From the outset he was aware both of his limitations and his changeability. 'These are my humours and my opinions: I offer them as what I believe, not what is to be believed. I aim here only at revealing myself who will perhaps be different tomorrow if I learn something new which changes me. I have no authority to be believed, nor do I want it, feeling myself too ill-instructed to instruct others.' And there is no pompous self-righteousness. The book is shot through with gentle irony and humour. 'No one is exempt from saying silly things. The misfortune is to say them with earnest effort.' Montaigne had need of a sense of proportion for before the publication of Books I and II he had been attacked by the disease of the kidneys that was to plague him with periods of excruciating pain for the rest of his life.

In June 1580, the book safely launched, he set out on extensive travels to take various foreign waters in relief of his ailment. Accompanied by his younger brother, a brother-in-law, secretaries and the usual retinue of servants, he travelled through the Vosges into Switzerland and Germany and then through the Brenner Pass into Italy, visiting Verona, Venice, Florence and Siena on his way to Rome, where he passed the winter of 1580-81. He then spent four months near Lucca taking the waters. Montaigne was an excellent traveller, and he has left us an entertaining travel journal describing this most extensive of his journeyings. He was an eager, interested tourist, and everywhere he went he tried to live the life of the people he was among, and to appreciate each country, and even city, for its own particular qualities. Even from the *Essays* we should know that he had the unbiassed cosmopolitan outlook that one would expect from a man of his liberal views. He comments on the great variety of customs in the world, and their different usefulness for different nations. He recommends travel for the young as part of their education, and declares: 'I am ashamed to see my countrymen besotted with that stupid disposition to shy away from ways contrary to their own; they think they are out of their element when they are out of their village.' Not so Montaigne. 'The diversity in fashions from one nation to another affects me only with the pleasure of variety.' And most important of all: 'I consider all men my compatriots and embrace a Pole as I do a Frenchman, setting this national bond after the universal and common one.' While in Rome he had been granted the title of Roman Citizen. He tells us that he deliberately sought this honour, and he was so proud of it that he printed the bull of citizenship in full at the end of his essay 'Of Vanity', remarking characteristically that of all Fortune's empty favours there is none that so pleases his 'silly humour'. Perhaps the little boy whose first stories had been by Latin authors had become a man who found in Rome his spiritual home.

While he was in Italy he received news that he had been elected Mayor of Bordeaux. At first he was going to decline—had he not finished with public work?—but on hearing that Henry III was urging it, he accepted and at the beginning of October 1581 he began the journey home. On arrival at Montaigne, he recommended himself to the electors with quaint candour, 'exactly such as I feel myself to be: without memory, without vigilance, without experience, and without vigour: also without hate, without ambition, without avarice and without violence so that they should be informed and instructed about what they were to expect of my service. And because their knowledge of my late father had alone incited them to this . . . I added very clearly that I should be very sorry if anything whatsoever were to weigh so heavily on my will as their affairs and their city had formerly done on his.' Too much earnestness was contrary to Montaigne's firm belief in moderation. He seems, in the event, to have performed his duties conscientiously enough, and at the end of two years he was elected for a second term. It was an honorary office concerned mainly with keeping the town in touch with the monarch, and organising ceremonies.

By this time the south-west of France was heavily disturbed by the political and religious commotions and Bordeaux, 'situated at the very hub of all the turmoil of the civil wars', was in a difficult position, caught between the importunities of those who remained loyal to Henry III and the supporters of Henry of Navarre. Montaigne had always remained loyal to his sovereign, and had on occasion fought on his side; but he was also as friendly with Navarre as circumstances permitted, and after the death of the Duke of Anjou[6] made him heir to the throne, the position became easier and their relations still more cordial. In 1584, Navarre visited Montaigne's château and joined a hunting party there. Montaigne was consistently hostile to the Catholic League; they represented the uncompromising extreme with which he could never come to terms.

In 1585 he laid down his office—thankfully, for the plague was raging at the time—and retired again to his tower to complete the third and last book of *Essays*. Besides writing the third book, he also made between five hundred and six hundred additions to the other two: he was careful to explain, ' I add, but I do not correct . . . because when a man has mortgaged his work to the world it seems to me that he has no further right to it.' The changes are ' only to vary, not to delete '. A new edition containing all three books—the completed work—was published in June 1588. During the years of his mayoralty he had made one friend of considerable interest to us. Francis Bacon's brother Anthony, who lived for twelve years in France, spent a good deal of time at Bordeaux and came to know Montaigne well. They corresponded after Anthony Bacon's return to England, and so there was established a direct link between the first essayist and the first English writer in that form.

Montaigne had not much longer to live. The dislike he felt for the perpetual violence of his times must have been increased by the assassination of Guise in 1588 and that of Henry III the following year. But he could rejoice in the accession of Henry IV, and his own last years were cheered by the admiration of the young Marie de Gournay in whom he at last found a friend with whom he could discuss his writing. After his death from quinsy in 1592 at the age of fifty-nine, she remained in touch with his wife and daughter and prepared a new edition of his work.

It is all too easy to see Montaigne as a meditative scholar with-

6 Cf. Bodin p. 135.

drawn into an ivory tower, although certainly for the last twenty
years of his life the man and his book are almost inseparable; but
it would be wrong to think of him as a recluse, and even more
wrong to regard him as some of his critics were to do, as a destruc-
tive sceptic who 'put all things in doubt'.[7] He was not defeatist—
he believed pessimism cowardly; he was not negative—no-one who
could say in what must have seemed like France's darkest hour,
'The most difficult and important branch of human knowledge
seems to be that which deals with the rearing and education of
children', could possibly be that; and he was not merely
theoretical—as Mayor of Bordeaux he founded a home for
destitute children. He was, quite simply, a many-sided man,
and he produced a book that has proved to be one of the most
living things of the Renaissance, in style, in method and in
thought.

The *Essays* is a huge work; by its nature it is more to dip into
than to read through, and it is inevitable that one part should
contradict another. Throughout his book, Montaigne was not
building up a thesis, he was portraying a man; and man is a very
contradictory creature. He wrote down just what he happened to
be thinking at the time, and what human being has ever thought
consistently? Thus we find him in one place extolling learning as
'a great ornament and a wonderfully serviceable tool', and
declaring books 'the best provisions I have found for this human
journey'; and in another place announcing that 'we need hardly
any learning to live at ease', for practical capacities are more to be
desired than bookishness and 'how tedious is the proficiency that is
purely bookish'. Occasionally he almost rejects his book itself:
'Whatever I may be I want to be elsewhere than on paper. . . . I
have put all my efforts into forming my life. That is my trade and
my work. I am less a maker of books than of anything else.' We
sometimes find him deploring the stupidity of war, and another
time thrilling with martial ardour. On one occasion he is 'of the
opinion that the most honourable occupation is to serve the public
and to be useful to many', and on another, public service is merely
masked ambition for power, and we are advised to flee from our
gregarious instincts and try to repossess ourselves. It is all this

7 Pascal (1623-1662).

that makes him so human. We do feel drawn different ways at different times, and if we are by temperament of those who like to look at both sides of a question, we steer an erratic course. 'Those who make a practice of comparing human actions are never so perplexed as when they try to see them as a whole and in the same light; for they commonly contradict each other so strangely that it seems impossible that they have come from the same shop.'

There is in Montaigne what may seem a basic contradiction. This most liberal of thinkers was also a conservative. He was quite temperately on the side of the established Catholic religion, and the established institutions of France. He disliked innovations, and deplored the activities of the Huguenots. He was conservative in the same fashion as Shakespeare, who often echoes him, sometimes deliberately. A large-minded acceptance of things as they are—and humanity as it is—freed him by the very security of its acceptance to be unconventional and flexible about all lesser things, as well as charitable and uncensorious towards his fellow-men.

At the end of all the contradictions it is a definite impression that emerges, the impression of a mind that has a positive message for mankind. For anyone who reads the book through, there is also to be observed a kind of development. The writer of Book III has enriched his personality by more than the confidence springing from success. It is not easy, of course, to trace the development of Montaigne's thought. We know that everything in Book III was written between 1580 and 1588, and therefore represents a later phase of his thought, but as during this time he also made his large number of additions to Books I and II we are not always sure of the date of what we are reading.[8] All the same, each Book has its distinctive quality. The early essays, as we might expect from the circumstances which led him into writing, give much attention to the subject of death. It appears in the titles of three of them. They are, however, noble rather than depressing. He combats the horror of death with the teaching of the old Greek and Roman Stoics in whom he was so well versed, and 'philosophy is learning how to die'. 'I want death to find me planting my

8 This problem has been largely solved now that we have the splendid edition translated and arranged by the American scholar D. M. Frame.

cabbages, but careless of death and still more of my unfinished garden.'

Book II strikes a more sceptical note. A large part of it is taken up by one very long essay based on the thought of a book by one Raymond Sebond which he had translated from the Latin. The dominant idea is the vanity of all human knowledge, and the impossibility of our ever really knowing anything as truth. Montaigne sees that if we cannot really know anything, then even our moral judgements are in doubt. He writes at length about customs which are regarded as immoral in one society and yet are acceptable in another. Yet he sees that if we say nothing is always right or always wrong, we are on a slippery slope. He seems to conclude that we must conscientiously try to learn what we are, and then follow our own nature, providing we do not confuse this with giving in to our baser instincts. Beyond this we are dependent on the grace of God. The implications of this discussion were,[9] of course, of immense importance in a fast-moving age which had produced great social upheaval.

With Book III where the essays are in general longer, we pass into a more serene and bracing atmosphere. Montaigne's is the unusual case of a man who became more optimistic as he got older, and not only as he got older, but as the troubles of his time thickened round him, and he was himself subjected increasingly to illness and pain. We are told that happiness can result from our very incapacity to change our fate, and more and more he comes to terms with himself. Physical pain, which he had feared so much in anticipation, has proved to be supportable—even with cheerfulness: 'it is in us, if not to annihilate it, at least to lessen it by patience, and even should the body be disturbed by it, to maintain nevertheless our soul and reason in good trim'. Profound self-knowledge is revealed, and in these last chapters he both exalts the uniqueness and freedom of the individual while finding a new purpose and point in human co-operation. For on some questions Montaigne does seem simply to have changed his mind, or at any rate, his attitude. Although we are told Montaigne's father had him put out to nurse with simple people and let a peasant hold him at the font in order that he should start his life in association with common men, he seems in the earlier essays to display some

8 And are.

contempt for 'people of humble means', and (like Shakespeare again) to distrust 'the mob, the mother of ignorance, injustice and inconsistency'. By Book III he has mellowed; there is free acknowledgement that we are all members one of another—'the administrations which admit the least disparity between servants and masters seem to me the most equitable'—and a new respect for what simple people have to teach us: 'The least contemptible class of people seem to me to be those who through their simplicity occupy the lowest rank. . . . The morals and the talk of peasants I find commonly more obedient to the prescriptions of true philosophy than are those of our philosophers.' Above all the emphasis in the last Book is on the art of living well.

Montaigne always remains open to the criticism that can be levelled against those who take up a middle position. He is no fervent reformer, he is no saint, he is not heroic in any spectacular way. Some or other of his views are certain to be repellent to most of his readers, but he could not have portrayed the human mind, nor have been loyal to his first great principle of absolute sincerity, if he were not occasionally as repellent to us as we are sometimes to ourselves.

From this vast sprawling work in which almost every *opinion* is at some point contradicted, there does emerge not only one of the most civilised and conciliatory of human beings, but a body of *values* which are as definite as they are humane and never meet with any contradiction whatsoever.

The most eminent of all Montaigne's qualities, his balanced outlook, embraces all that the Greeks meant by the Golden Mean. His respect for objective truth induces in him an open-minded approach to controversial questions, 'for all those predispositions that are born in us without reason are bad; they are a kind of disease that we must combat'. This does not excuse us from decision, for to stand aloof from problems is 'not a middle way, but no way at all', but he would never wish to be so involved with one party as to fail completely to see the point of view of the other.

A balanced attitude emanates, of course, from moderation and self-control. These Montaigne esteemed as classic virtues. 'The worst condition of man is when he loses knowledge and control of himself.' He has, he tells us, 'taken the moderate measure as the most perfect', and since 'wisdom has its excesses and has no less

need of moderation than does folly', he has no use for the attitudes of rigid puritanism. The good things of life are there to be
enjoyed, and there is no more virtue in turning one's back on
them than in indulging oneself to excess. 'I do not consider the
philosopher Arcesilaus less virtuous because I know that he used
gold and silver vessels as much as his fortune allowed him to; and I
esteem him more highly for having used them moderately and
liberally than if he had given them up.' For Montaigne a tee-
totaller is almost as far off temperance as a drunkard.

His humanism derives from this—his cheerful acceptance of the
human lot with all its pains and pleasures, its failings and its virtues: 'I rarely repent, and my conscience is content with itself—
not as the conscience of an angel or a horse, but as the conscience
of a man.' And from his honouring of the human being springs his
intense conviction of the value of the individual and his right to
freedom. 'We owe ourselves in part to society, but in the best part
to ourselves.' He glories in the great variety that exists among men.
'I do not share the common error of judging another by myself. I
easily believe that another man may have qualities different from
mine. . . . I have a singular desire that we should each be judged
in ourselves apart, and that I may not be measured in con-
formity with the common pattern.'

By temperament he hated restrictions. 'I flee command, obligation and restraint. What I do easily and naturally I can no longer
do if I order myself to do it by strict and express command.' His
passion for freedom was real; it had to be the very sensation of
liberty. 'I am so sick for freedom that if anyone should forbid me
access to some corner of the Indies, I should live distinctly less
comfortably.' Thus he is shy of too much legislation, being
sceptical as to how far men may be made more moral by statutes.
'If the action does not have something of the splendour of freedom, it has neither grace nor honour.'

Tolerance was for him the greatest necessity of human intercourse, and he had to live at a time when it was being totally
rejected by large numbers of his compatriots. He made no concessions to the standards of his age, and he castigates its vices freely;
but, not to be too self-righteous, he comments, 'It is good to be
born in a very depraved time; for by comparison with others you
are considered virtuous for a cheap price'. He is fully aware that

as people grow older the state of society is apt to seem worse than it was formerly—no one saw straighter about old age than Montaigne—but he is also aware that since history runs through good times and bad, it is sometimes true that it is worse. No one who has lived since has attempted to deny the turpitude of sixteenth-century France. Montaigne tells us he can hardly admit what he has suffered in beholding the ruin of his country; in his essay on 'Education of Children' he explicitly states that a boy must be hardened to bear pain, perhaps even to face torture since bigotry is attacking good men equally with bad; but still there is the emphasis on the need for a sense of proportion. 'Seeing our civil wars who does not cry out that this mechanism is being turned topsy-turvy, and that the Judgement Day has us by the throat, without reflecting that many worse things have happened and that ten thousand parts of the world to our one are meanwhile having a gay time?' And fortunately, 'Pure naturalness and truth in whatever age, still find their time and place'. Meanwhile 'We may regret better times, but not escape the present; we may wish for different magistrates, but we must nevertheless obey those that are here'.

He has sufficient confidence in the future to give a good deal of thought to education, and as we should expect from his interests and his background, he has plenty of ideas on the subject, partly in consonance with those of other Renaissance educationists, but for the most part in advance of his time. As would seem likely, he puts more emphasis on personality than on scholarship, and stoutly avers 'that a well-bred man is an all-round man'. Body and mind must both be educated, and the aim of the teacher should be to stimulate curiosity, and to train the judgement. The child should not be stuffed with learning that he may use to show off. 'We should inquire who knows *best*, not who knows *most*.' There should be no brutal punishments, and it is essential that the teacher should admit his own errors as an example to his pupils. Above all the entire programme should be shaped so that the children may deduce some philosophy suitable to their years. As things were, people were taught how to live after they had already made their mistakes.

Whatever opinions Montaigne may be airing, certain qualities of his mind are constantly apparent. There is always what one may describe as a respect for his reader, one is never harangued; he is the perfect host: ' I think it ugly to talk to your guests about the way you are treating them, whether to excuse it or to boast of it.' There is, especially in the late chapters, the refreshment of his dignified optimism, his conviction that things never turn out to be quite as bad as we have feared, and that 'the surest sign of wisdom is constant cheerfulness '. Even about the state of France he can be optimistic. ' Perhaps we are not on our last legs. . . . The preservation of states is a thing that probably surpasses our understanding. . . . Our government is in bad health; yet some have been sicker without dying.' And throughout the whole we glimpse the sense of humour which always forbade him to take himself too seriously.

Above all stand the qualities of sincerity, integrity and undeviating intellectual honesty which more than anything give the book its unique value. For all his easy-going tolerance there are certain virtues Montaigne expressly recommends and they are all of this class. He reminds us that only we ourselves know how we really behave, and it is by this knowledge that we must judge our actions; philosophy should train us to be, not to seem. He exalts truthfulness and loyalty to friends, and insists that he always tried to avoid both deviousness and the taint of treachery even in the politics of his difficult times. He asserts repeatedly his hatred of lying as the vice one should combat before all others, and not only direct lying but any form of evasion or conveying false impressions. He was determined that his book should be a perfectly true account of himself: that was, after all, the whole reason for its existence. ' I expose myself entire. . . . It is not my deeds that I write down; it is myself, it is my essence.' There are other writers renowned for their candour, the very luridness of whose confessions make one suspect their motives. What emerges is exhibitionism. Montaigne, with more courage and less sensationalism, reveals the petty meannesses to which we all have to admit we are liable, as well as the grosser misdeeds.

It is his rare and unselfconscious sincerity that makes it true to say that in Montaigne's case the style is the man. He revealed himself truly in the only manner he could: to have brought more artifice to his writing would have destroyed his purpose. It may seem to some that he is a difficult author to read—presented as he often is in rather fusty volumes—and one may at first recoil from the length of his periods or the profusion of learned names which besprinkle his pages. It is true that he sometimes wrote long tortuous sentences, but these are usually broken down in modern translations; he was also somewhat addicted to going back to remote origins to illustrate a point, and then working his way through all the examples of history, but this is not the important part of his work. Generally, it is a beguiling style, simple and conversational for all its striking metaphors, a style of easy good manners which, once we have been captured by its spirit, carries us along. He is a rambling writer and we must ramble with him; the last thing we should do is to try to follow the 'plan' of the essay. At any rate no one has made it easier for his book to be picked up and put down at will.

Montaigne's originality lies in the form of his work and his approach to his subject. His ideas, taken severally, are not often in themselves original; he was, as he himself put it, out to portray 'the common sort' not the savant or the pioneer. He carried his learning lightly, as he did also his virtues; he did not feel too guilty about his sins. He was, for all his careful equipoise, a positive person, and it is not surprising that he has had power over so many different kinds of mind. Any impression one gives of him can easily be a wrong one; any attempt to claim him for our 'side' is certain to be defeated. But constantly there is his generous forbearance, and, above all, he has pride. He was proud to be a man, and he set the human standard high just because he did not set it too high. He observed on more than one occasion that those who set out to behave like angels are apt to end by behaving like beasts; better simply try to be a man. To read Montaigne is to gain more courage to face mankind's predicament. He is Europe's greatest exponent of all that we mean by humanism.

## FURTHER READING

Montaigne's *Essays*. A useful selection is published by Penguin Books. Introduced and translated by J. M. Cohen.

DONALD FRAME. *Montaigne's Discovery of Man*. Columbia University Press 1955.

EDITH SICHEL. *Michel de Montaigne*. Constable 1911.

# William the Silent

*(1533-1584)*

*Je maintiendrai.*

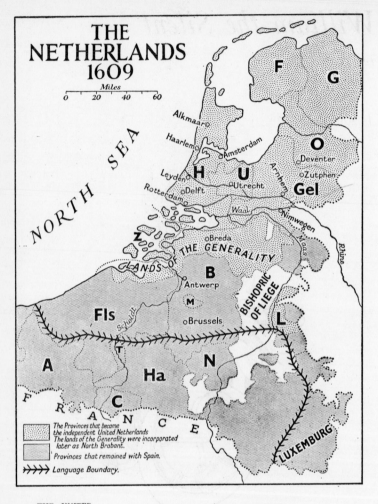

# THE NETHERLANDS 1609

Miles
0      20    40    60

NORTH SEA

Alkmaar
Haarlem
Amsterdam
**F**
**G**
**O**
Deventer
Zutphen
**H**
**U**
Leyden
Utrecht
Arnhem
Nimwegen
Rotterdam
Delft
**Gel**
Waal
Maas
Rhine
**Z**
Breda
*LANDS OF THE GENERALITY*
*ISLANDS OF*
**B**
Antwerp
**BISHOPRIC OF LIEGE**
**Fls**
Scheldt
**M**
Brussels
**L**
**A**
**T**
**N**
**Ha**
F
R
A
C
N
**C**
C
E
**LUXEMBURG**

The Provinces that became
the independent United Netherlands
The lands of the Generality were incorporated
later as North Brabant.

Provinces that remained with Spain.

>>>>>  Language Boundary.

| THE UNITED NETHERLANDS (1609) | | REMAINED SPANISH | |
|---|---|---|---|
| G | Groningen | B | Brabant |
| F | Friesland | M | Mechlin |
| O | Overyssel | Fls | Flanders |
| H | Holland | T | Tournai |
| U | Utrecht | A | Artois |
| Gel | Gelderland | C | Cambrai |
| Z | Zeeland | Ha | Hainault |
| L | Limburg | N | Namur |

WHEN ELIZABETH OF England, after some twenty years of indecision, sent an expedition to the Low Countries under the Earl of Leicester in 1585, she was intervening in a revolt which had by then run half its course, of which the pattern of the final outcome was plain, and the greatest hero already dead. The people of the Netherlands—provinces occupying the area which is now divided between Holland, Belgium and Luxemburg—had been struggling for more than two decades against their tyrannical Spanish masters, and by the time of William the Silent's death in 1584 it was certain (or so it seems as we look back) that there would be a partial victory. The freedom and unity of all the provinces would not be obtained, but the leadership of William and the spirit of the people had made it certain that in the north a new nation— which today we call Holland—would be born. Not that this was clear to William's young son, Maurice of Nassau, who was continuing to fight for his father's cause; he was still striving to recover the lost lands of the south, and at the same time desperately searching for an ally lest the north itself could not stand. It was natural that he should think of all seventeen provinces as essentially united; they had all equally suffered the exactions of Philip II, and it must have been difficult to detect clearly the various strands, religious, historical and military, whose entanglement was pulling the community asunder.

The provinces were part of the Emperor Charles V's inheritance from his Burgundian grandmother.[1] Separated from Burgundy itself by the Duchy of Lorraine, and with different economic interests from those of their German neighbours, this confusing collection of counties, duchies and free cities known as the Netherlands had, by the time they passed to Charles, already developed a spirit of communal interest and flickering signs of national consciousness. There were considerable forces against unity, one of the strongest being that the people of the most southerly pro-

1 See Francis I p. 105. The provinces of the extreme north were added—by force—during Charles V's régime.

vinces spoke French while the rest used various Low German
dialects later to be welded into official Dutch. It is not surprising
therefore that the central government was not strong, and that the
Regent and Council of State appointed by the monarch had to
leave local affairs largely to the provincial governments. The
central authority did, however, select for each province its Stadtholder, a person of considerable importance, chosen from among
the noblemen, who usually did not hold office in the region of his
own lands. Each province had its own Estates (or Parliament) of
which the Stadtholder was chairman, and they sent their delegates
to the Estates-General (or Central Parliament) in Brussels. Altogether there was much less uniformity than Charles would have
wished, but neither did he like to offend his Netherlandish subjects, partly because he had been brought up among them, and
also because they were, at this time, the most prosperous people
in Europe.

In 1555 Charles V decided to abdicate. He was worn out with
his life time of struggle—against France, against the Reformation
in Germany, against the encroachments of the Turks—and he
wished to spend his remaining days in religious meditation. His
vast dominions he divided, arranging for the German lands to pass
to his brother, while his son Philip inherited Spain, the New
World, the Italian possessions and the Netherlands. The change
of overlord came at a difficult point in the history of the Netherlands, for there as elsewhere the vast upheavals of the times were
making themselves felt. The Protestant belief to which Charles
was opposed not only as a devout Catholic, but also because of the
division it had caused among his German subjects, had penetrated
there. The great majority of Netherlanders were sincere Roman
Catholics, but they had developed an easy-going attitude towards
their religious observances, and undoubtedly their bishops were
somewhat slack in recalling them to their duties. With the
appearance of heresy, mainly in the south, Charles had early in
his reign set up the Inquisition, but the objections of the nobility
had hampered its working in many parts of the country and persecution although oppressive was never thorough. Towards the
end of Charles's reign there were ominous signs. Protestantism,
besides spreading to the northern provinces, began to take the
form of Calvinism instead of the earlier Lutheranism, and al-

though its adherents were still a minority of the population, they were a more assertive, not to say fanatical, minority. Charles replied to their demands by augmenting the power of the Inquisition and publishing a series of increasingly severe edicts against heresy.

If, by the time of the abdication, Charles's subjects were getting restive both on account of his religious policy and because so much of their substance was wasted in his war against France, their sincere attachment to their overlord kept them in check. Philip had neither the personality nor the aptitude to cope with the situation he inherited. A religious bigot who had been brought up in Spain with no knowledge of either the French or Dutch tongues, he appeared to the Netherlanders as a foreign ruler without tact or charm, and his determination to amplify and enforce the plans of his father made it certain that the gathering storm would break.

The basic causes of the revolt of the Netherlands, all emerging clearly in the first three years of Philip's reign, fall into three categories. In the sphere of religion, the King's decision to make fourteen new bishoprics, thus providing eighteen for a population previously served by four, and his early affirmation of his father's last Edict, both met with heavy opposition. Some increase in bishoprics was undoubtedly necessary for the efficient working of the Church, but the announcement that the bishops would be nominated by the Crown (and not by the Chapters as formerly) caused the Netherlanders to see the whole religious policy as the subordination of their Church to the state—the state of Spain. The second group of causes was constitutional and affected the ancient privileges of the Netherlands. Philip had appointed his half-sister, Margaret, Duchess of Parma, to be his Regent and it soon became clear that she was to be primarily assisted, not by the old Council of State on which the Stadtholders sat, but by an inner circle of three who could be relied on to support the King and of whom the most important was Granvelle, Bishop of Arras, soon to be Archbishop of Mechlin and Primate of the newly organised Church. The third group of causes was financial. Charles had left the country heavily burdened with debt, and Philip had to demand increased funds from his Estates-General. He tactlessly asked for them in the form of a nine-years' subsidy which looked to the

Estates like the suspension of their own power for that length of time. They opposed the demand and complained of the Spanish troops which were still quartered upon the country although Philip was at this time at peace with France. It was in this connection that William the Silent first appeared in public opposition to the new king. He was already Stadtholder of Holland, Zealand and Utrecht[2] and a considerable influence on the other nobles. He now came forward with the suggestion that subsidies should be granted to the King (and they could hardly be refused altogether) only on the condition that the Spanish troops should be removed. The King consented, but how much he was impressed by the statement of ancient constitutional rights which accompanied the voting of the subsidy was far from clear. The incident had, however, revealed the man who was to be Philip's untiring opponent. It is time to see something of his background.

William, Prince of Orange, called the Silent, was born on 24 April 1533 at Dillenburg in the German province of Nassau, the first son of the Count of Nassau-Dillenburg, who already had two daughters by a previous marriage. His mother had been a widow with four children when she married the Count, and as brothers and sisters followed William in rapid succession there were eventually seventeen children in all at the Dillenburg estate. The family was not rich by the standards of even the lesser nobility. The Count was a younger son and inherited only the German part of the family possessions. His elder brother Henry, Count of Nassau, had inherited the bulk of the property which was situated in the Netherlands, and there he came to be a person of considerable importance.

The life of the Dillenburg children seems to have been simple and pleasant. Shortly after William's birth, his parents embraced the reformed faith, so the children were brought up as Lutherans. The Count was a moderate man, however, who managed to keep out of the religious quarrels of the time, and the family life was as peaceful as it was unpretentious. Part of the castle had been made into a school and a resident Head Master appointed so that the large brood of children, joined by some of those of the neighbouring nobility, could receive their education at home. William's

2 It was constitutionally possible for different provinces to have the same Stadtholder.

young life, therefore, was set on very domestic lines when, just after his eleventh birthday, an event occurred which changed fundamentally the pattern of his existence.

William's Uncle Henry, in the Netherlands, had married a sister of the Prince of Orange—a small principality in the south of France—and had an only son René. The Prince died childless so that in time his nephew René became both Prince of Orange and Count of Nassau. In 1544 René was killed in battle at the age of twenty-six, and it was found that he had bequeathed his titles and possessions to his cousin William of Nassau-Dillenburg. It was a condition of the will that the boy should go to live in Brussels and be brought up in the Roman Catholic faith. These stipulations were accepted by the parents—with what misgivings we do not know. At any rate it must have been a staggering change to the little boy who was taken by his father from the simple family life of Dillenburg to the elegant and formal court of Brussels.

He was put in charge of the Regent of the Netherlands, at that time Charles's sister, Mary of Hungary, and thenceforward his education proceeded on very different lines from formerly. Probably his parents, if somewhat overawed, felt that it was an amazing piece of good fortune that had befallen their son. He had inherited vast territories stretched across the southern Netherlands, as well as estates in the provinces of Holland and Zealand, France and Italy, and the petty principality of Orange. He was, in fact one of the wealthiest noblemen in Europe. The material value of Orange itself was slight, but his succession to it made him a sovereign prince—a status that was to prove useful to him later on.

Meanwhile William, who was an attractive friendly boy, won the favour of Charles V. The Emperor saw to it that besides his religious and courtly instruction, he also received the right military training and experience; and when he was eighteen, he found him a suitable bride in Anne, the young daughter of the Count of Buren, and with her he set up his first household at the castle of Breda. Two years later he received his first military command, and he was a central figure in the magnificent and emotional scene in the hall of the palace of Brussels where in 1555 Charles V's abdication was so dramatically staged. After the illustrious company had been assembled in the body of the hall,

Charles came on to the specially prepared platform leaning on the shoulder of a sumptuously arrayed Prince of Orange, followed by his son and the Regent. Throughout the ceremony it was William's office to support the gout-ridden Emperor and it was he that finally assisted him from the hall.

Within three years of the imperial abdication William lost his wife who died of some vaguely diagnosed illness leaving him with a son Philip (named after the King of Spain whom William regarded as his rightful sovereign) and a daughter, Marie. His grief was submerged by new activity, for in September 1558 he went as a delegate to negotiate the treaty of Câteau-Cambrésis with the French, and subsequently proceeded to Paris as one of the hostages required of King Philip by the preliminary terms. William's colleagues at Câteau-Cambrésis had included the Duke of Alva and Granvelle, Bishop of Arras, and in Paris he learned by accident that they had planned with their ex-enemy Henry II of France a policy of intensive persecution for the Netherlands. The revelation filled him with horror. His personal life so far had been easy-going enough, but he was compassionate by nature, his early years had been passed in Lutheran surroundings, and he had come to love the friendly independent people of his adopted country. The essential tolerance, based on equal respect for all men, which is the key to the character of William the Silent forced him to awareness of the coming struggle. But even at the age of twenty-six the statesman in William caused him to keep his own counsel for the time being. It was from habitual discretion of this kind that he got his name 'Le Taciturne'. Silent in the sense the English word conveys he certainly was not, rather was he genial and friendly by nature, with a great capacity for adapting himself to the changing times. His strong conviction that individuals were more important than the political community into which they were organised made him a man of the future rather than of that feudal Europe which Renaissance and Reformation were breaking up.

William was no revolutionary, however. He honoured his King, even though his conscience required that the King should also honour the traditional rights of the Netherlands. In 1563 William and two other leading noblemen, Egmont and Horn, demanded that Granvelle should be recalled, and when this was not done, they withdrew from the Council of State of which, they complained, they were only nominal members. The Regent, with a more realistic view of the situation than that of her brother, was alarmed about the possible effect, and at last, in 1564 persuaded Philip to remove Granvelle after much complicated face-saving. On the question of religion the King would make no compromise; indeed, he ordered sterner enforcement of the Edict, and both persecution and agitation against the Inquisition correspondingly increased.

Meanwhile, in August 1561 William had married again. The bride was Princess Anna of Saxony, daughter of the great Elector Maurice and niece of the reigning Elector. The marriage was difficult to arrange and did not turn out happily. The bride's Lutheran grandfather objected to her marrying a Catholic; Philip II objected to William's involvement with the Reformers; but William, who realised his growing importance in the struggle against Philip's tyranny, felt that the Lutheran alliance was just what he wanted. He arranged that his wife should follow her own religion privately, but that she would publicly conform to Catholic practices. Anna, unfortunately, was a self-centred neurotic who, during the next seven years, passed through phases of hysteria to a condition of insanity, and the best memory the world has of her is that she was the mother of William's famous son Maurice.

During these years of domestic unhappiness, political events moved quickly. William's brother Louis was now in the Netherlands, and in 1566 he joined with some of the lesser nobility in forming a Confederation. They drew up what is known as the ' Compromise '—in effect a petition to Philip—protesting against the King's Inquisition policy; it is noteworthy that this was signed by Catholics as well as Protestants. It was not only the heretics who felt that the constitution of the Netherlands was being undermined.[3] Also noteworthy is the fact that William did not openly associate himself with the Confederation, probably because the other nobles would not come with him. In any case his method was as far as possible one of conciliation and he may have

3 It is probable that the Catholics would not have protested against the Papal Inquisition, but all feared the introduction of the Spanish Inquisition which, besides being more terrible, was used by Spain as an instrument of royal absolutism.

feared that this was the way of extremism. The tide, however, was running more strongly than he thought.

Early in April the Compromise, in the form of a 'Request' was presented to the Regent's Council. When one of Margaret's councillors, attempting to calm her agitation, remarked 'What! Can Your Highness be afraid of these beggars [ces gueux]?' the confederates clutched the contemptuous term to their bosoms; it provided them with a popular title, a symbol and a rallying cry. Throughout the provinces for years to come men would respond to the shout of 'Vivent les Gueux'. At an uproarious banquet held a few days later in Brussels the Confederates were drinking toasts from the wooden bowls of beggars, and hanging mendicants' wallets round each other's necks, and the next morning numbers of them were seen riding away dressed in coarse grey cloaks with wooden bowls at their sides. The bowl was now the emblem of the Confederate movement, and in the form of trinkets and badges it was worn by increasing numbers of people in all parts of the Netherlands.

In the summer a wave of religious fanaticism swept the country with such violence that William came to feel that association with the Confederates would be the more prudent course. Calvinism was now making converts in great numbers, and it was becoming increasingly aggressive and more strenuously opposed to all the observances of Catholicism. The first disorders were at Antwerp, but the trouble rapidly spread to other parts of the country and there was a week's orgy of image breaking which culminated in the desecration of Antwerp Cathedral. William was by this time admitting, at any rate privately, that he had been re-converted to his original Lutheran faith, but he did not want openly to identify himself with the Calvinist opposition to Philip. He was sufficiently tolerant—and how much ahead of his time it places him—to be able to co-operate with men of different beliefs; but he was still trying to steer a course of moderation. Extreme Calvinists were as intolerant as Philip himself, and their excesses had already alienated the liberal Catholics who opposed the King on constitutional grounds.

The Regent, fearful and hard-pressed, was herself suggesting concessions to the Protestants, but she was insincere and merely playing for time until Philip should act. She seems to have assumed, quite wrongly, that William was encouraging the extremists, though his success in calming the rioters at Antwerp at the time of the first disorders should have convinced her of his conciliatory policy.

Philip's response was the decision to send a Spanish army to the Netherlands. When William learned this he recognised that events were hurrying forward to disaster, and he wanted the greater nobles to join in organising effective opposition. Egmont and Horn were not, however, ready to co-operate. Much as William disliked some aspects of the Calvinist policy, he did his best to strengthen their anti-Government attitude; he had to recognise that the real opposition to the Spanish tyranny would inevitably take a religious form. Liberal Catholics were already dissociating themselves from the ' Beggars ' and probably only intense religious conviction could animate enough people for enough time to endure what was to come.

In February 1567 the Regent demanded a new oath from Stadt-holders and other functionaries, requiring them to swear to act against anyone the King might indicate without restriction. This William refused to do. Egmont felt that he could continue to serve the cause while in full allegiance to Philip, and accordingly took the oath, but for William it was the parting of the ways. Having refused to be drawn into plans for premature revolt by either the lesser nobles or the Calvinists he left the country for his family home in Nassau, there to plan the liberation of the Nether-lands. This may be said to mark the end of his full loyalty to Philip. William was still sufficiently influenced by Europe's feudal past to accept that a group of small states such as the Seventeen Provinces should have an overlord, and to endorse the accident of history that had made that overlord King Philip II. He still recognised him as the legitimate sovereign, but he was a sovereign who had violated the liberties of his subjects and his actions must be resisted. In fact William, always in advance of his age, was adopting the dawning view that a king was party to a contract, and not a divinely placed ruler.

Events rapidly proved William's estimate of the situation to be a just one. In August the terrible Duke of Alva arrived at the head of troops which included the first musketeers ever organised for war. He immediately had Egmont and Horn arrested and set up what was officially called the 'Council of Troubles' but was soon known throughout the country as the 'Blood Council'. With Alva as its President, and powers to override all other tribunals, this special court inaugurated a veritable reign of terror and was soon claiming its victims by hundreds. It was more than the Duchess Margaret could stand. She resigned her office and left the country; in any case Alva now had all the authority. One cannot but feel some pity for Margaret of Parma; constantly pressed by the arbitrary and unrealistic commands of her brother and harassed on all sides by the rising discontent of the Netherlands people, she was not a strong enough personality to pursue the moderate course which she seems occasionally to have envisaged. She had at least been in a position to see when Philip's policy could be pushed no further, but her attempts to stand for her people's last scraps of liberty had never been acceptable in Spain.

At the beginning of 1568 the Blood Council summoned William to answer a charge of high treason, and on his non-appearance proceeded to seize all his estates. His eldest son Philip, Count of Buren, at this time a boy of thirteen studying at the University of Louvain, was kidnapped and sent by boat to Spain—an exile from which he was only to return, transformed into a Spaniard, twenty years later. William himself, amidst all his anxieties, went on building up his army in Germany where he was able to acquire mercenaries released by a temporary lull in the French civil war. Before his troops took the field, he published and had distributed all over the Netherlands, the document known as the 'Justification'. Part of its purpose was to show that he still regarded himself as the King's loyal subject, and to place the blame on agents and advisers from whose evil counsel he hoped his sovereign might be delivered. William wanted to conciliate moderate opinion and in the eyes of Europe at large he did not wish to appear simply as a rebel against royal authority. Such people were still held in horror in all countries by those who counted most, and William was hoping for the support of other sovereigns who had their own quarrels with Philip of Spain.

In April 1568 the military attempt to expel Alva's forces began. William's own invasion was preceded by a three-pronged attack from the south, from the east and from the north-east. Louis of Nassau, attacking in Friesland, came nearest to success, but Alva,

having secured the defeat of the other two armies, decided to go
north in person to avenge Louis's initial victory. Before leaving
Brussels the Duke ordered the execution of Egmont and Horn,
and on 5 June the two noblemen went bravely to the scaffold. Alva
then felt free to march against Louis, and within six weeks the
patriot army was in full retreat, Louis only saving his own life
by swimming across the Ems.

William himself had not been ready to take advantage of
Louis's temporary ascendancy, but in September, ignoring his
brother's defeat, he began his attack from the east. He penetrated
the southern provinces, and managed to cross the Maas, but was
then forced to retreat into French territory. The campaign had
ended disastrously. The Netherlanders had not risen to support
him as he had hoped, his army degenerated, and since he could not
satisfy their claims for payment, he was reduced to fleeing from
his own troops. Too ill to ride, and suffering from the effects of
days without food, he made his way to Strassburg whence he was
able to return to Nassau secretly by barge.

It was the low-water mark of his career. Since the confiscation of
his estates, money had been an increasing problem, so that he and
his brothers had been reduced to mortgaging family property and
selling plate and jewellery to equip the armies which were now
defeated and disbanded. William had travelled far from the
opulent pleasure-seeking days of his early manhood, but he had
so far achieved nothing he could look back on with satisfaction.
His immediate situation looked hopeless. There was nothing left
except his own stubborn will to persevere.

Dawn duly followed the darkest hour, and in the new year
(1569) occurred the first of two events which changed the outlook.
Elizabeth of England in one of the more aggressive phases of her
long-drawn struggle with Philip, had seized the Spanish treasure
ships lying off Plymouth. The result was an urgent need to raise
compensatory funds, and Alva proposed a tax which he hoped
would serve the further purpose of making him independent of the
Estates-General. It was called the 'Tenth Penny' and would put a
five per cent tax on all land sold and a ten per cent purchase
tax on all goods sold, perpetually. It was greeted by a roar of protest throughout the land. North and south, Catholic and Protestant, were united as they had never been before in opposition to a

measure which was likely to strangle the economic life of the country. So unanimous was the resistance that Alva was forced to postpone the application of the tax for two years, and by then much had happened to encourage the rebels.

Further stimulus to resistance was provided by an important sea victory. Around the coasts swarmed ships manned by rough and ready crews known as the Sea Beggars. Most of them were, in fact, privateers, but their hostility to Spain was well attested and since the disbanding of William's army they had been joined by a number of noblemen. William recognised the usefulness of this force and in an attempt to discipline them, he issued them, in 1571, with letters of marque (which his status as sovereign Prince of Orange entitled him to do) so that henceforth they flew the flag of Nassau. By 1572 another swing in Elizabeth's policy caused her to forbid the English ports to the Beggars, and they were thus sorely in need of a base in the Netherlands itself. On 1 April while the Spanish force were occupied with a minor insurrection in Utrecht, the Nassau fleet captured Brill in the west of the province of Holland, and held it in William's name. Immediately the towns of Holland and Zealand rose in revolt. It was a turning point. Henceforth these two provinces were the hard core of the unceasing resistance, as they were also the germ of a new nation.

William was to have further reverses in the south. He tried another invasion that failed; the Massacre of St Bartholomew extinguished his hopes of help from the French Huguenots; he narrowly escaped death in a raid on his camp; but he was animated by a new hope. In October 1572 he dissolved his army and went himself to Holland: he was never to leave the Netherlands again. Enough people of the northern provinces were determined now on the fight for freedom, and William was the accepted leader. Everywhere they were singing the newly published war song, 'William of Nassau', the song that was to become the national anthem of the Netherlands.

William made his permanent home at Delft. He was at the head of a state now, a state which comprised Zealand and considerable parts of Holland, Utrecht and Friesland, the parts of the country where Calvinist zeal burned most fiercely. The Calvinists were not a religious majority, but with the control passing to the rebels, the Government was of their persuasion. Against a sombre background of atrocities committed by both sides, two of William's qualities shine out as gold. He strove consistently for freedom for both religions; particularly he tried to mitigate the intolerant cruelty of the Sea Beggars towards Catholics who came into their power. And he withstood all temptation to be a dictator. Although his prestige was such that he could have possessed himself of absolute power, he continued to work through the clumsy and often insufficient democratic machinery that was available.

A new spirit was abroad but danger did not diminish. Alva's troops swept northwards as far as the area of the distributaries of the Rhine and Maas, capturing the town of Nymwegen and passing on, by way of Amsterdam[4] to lay siege to Haarlem in December 1572. The siege lasted for seven bitter months and was marked by deeds of savage cruelty on both sides. Only when the population was reduced to eating rats and shoe leather did the town surrender. Then its submission did not, as Alva expected, herald a general collapse; rather had its stubborn defence served as an example which other cities in Holland were prepared to follow. When Alkmaar, further to the north, was besieged in its turn the inhabitants saved the town by cutting some of the dykes and allowing the sea to flood the countryside. These tactics were repeated on a grander scale at the siege—or more accurately, blockade—of Leyden in 1574.

The defence of this town is one of the epics of European history. The two phases of its ordeal lasted throughout a year, during the latter months of which the starving, pestilence-stricken population were only induced to endure by the exhortations of their heroic Burgomaster and his immediate colleagues within the city, and the efforts of William to bring relief from without. The patriots had to contend with every conceivable difficulty, including a mutiny of the despairing, and disaffection among partisans. For the conditions of siege brought out the worst as well as the best in the citizens; the spirit of faction, and downright selfishness frequently weakened the will to resist. At one point the Governor had a gallows erected in the centre of the town as a warning to flagging loyalty. But the heart of Leyden was sound, and the Civic Guards

4 Amsterdam was a chartered city, and at this time was not on the side of the rebels.

reliable: the frequent overtures of the Spaniards for capitulation were all rejected.

Communication with those organising relief gradually broke down, and the messengers who frequently failed to get through had to be supplemented by carrier pigeons and a system of gun salvoes and flash signals. It was a pigeon that at length brought the news, four days before the end, of the near approach of the relieving force. The defenders already knew that the dykes of the great rivers had been breached. They were pierced at sixteen places and the water flowed painfully slowly, but aided by the autumn gales, in the end, sufficiently over the surrounding country. A fleet of flat-bottomed boats was able to sail to the rescue, the panic-stricken Spaniards fled, and Leyden was relieved. One can say that with it Holland was saved, and William's policy in its next stages was tremendously strengthened. He had himself passed through a grave illness while the siege was in progress, and he had directed the closing stages of the relief operations during his convalescence.

The day after the successful issue William entered the town to thank its people for their share in what was the most significant victory since the armed struggle had begun. He commemorated it by a noble memorial—the foundation of Leyden University.

During these hectic years William's personal life had not been uneventful. In 1571 he had divorced the wretched Anna who had long made his private life a misery; and in 1573 he had taken the decision to join the Reformed (i.e. Calvinist) Church. Obviously there was a good deal that was politic in thus identifying himself with the official Church of his state, but certainly there was nothing of bigotry. The attribution of motives must always be in part guesswork, but William does seem to have been a man to whom religion was greater than dogma, and he always believed that men of different faiths could work together in tolerance of one another. Family sorrow came to him too at this time, for in April 1574, his favourite brother Louis and a younger brother Henry had both been killed in a battle intended as a diversion to relieve Leyden.

In 1575 William married again. His third bride was a daughter of the Duke of Montpensier, who had been a nun until, embracing the reformed faith, she had fled from the convent and taken refuge in Germany at the Court of the Elector Palatine. The marriage met with a good deal of opposition from various quarters and for various reasons, but it turned out to be very happy. Charlotte was a great support to William during the many trials that were still ahead of him, and he at last established a home which, although it could be to him only a place of occasional refuge and refreshment, was cheerful and well ordered. Six daughters were born of this marriage in as many years, and as Charlotte also took charge of William's children by his former marriages, her life, among the alarms and excursions of continual warfare can hardly have been one of repose.

Between the siege of Haarlem and that of Leyden, Alva, who had long been asking for his recall, was replaced by Don Luis de Requesens. The relief of Leyden was followed by a brief period of futile negotiations before Requesens went over to the attack and caused the patriot forces to suffer some heavy reverses in Zealand. In the following March (1576), Requesens died of fever and during the period that the Netherlands were without a Spanish Governor, Holland and Zealand took the opportunity to enter into a formal Union, William becoming its interim sovereign until the question of the monarchy should be finally settled. His aims remained the same; toleration for different faiths within the state, and support from outside power in the unequal struggle which a few small provinces could not wage indefinitely.

An unpleasant event now occurred to emphasise the need for union. The Spanish troops, long discontented owing to lack of pay, rose in mutiny, and, first in Zealand and then in Flanders, towns were seized and terrorised. This revived the anti-Spanish feeling among southern Catholics and provided an opportunity for an unauthorised meeting of the Estates-General of the whole Netherlands. Representatives of sixteen of the provinces met at Ghent, and although all were agreed on the desirability of expelling the Spaniards, the question of toleration was, as usual, a more difficult one. Another spur was provided. In November came the news of the sacking of Antwerp by its Spanish garrison. This was the real 'Spanish fury' and some seven or eight thousand citizens are thought to have lost their lives.

In these circumstances the Pacification of Ghent—which was essentially a treaty between the Union of Holland and Zealand on the one hand and the provinces still under the Spanish-controlled

181

Estates-General on the other—was drawn up somewhat hurriedly. It united all the provinces to expel the Spaniards but it put off the final settlement of the religious question until an extraordinary assembly of the Estates-General should be called, meanwhile suspending everywhere the Edict against heresy and recognising the Calvinist religion in Holland and Zealand. It confirmed William in his original Stadtholderships and as Governor of Holland and Zealand, and promised restoration of his estates.

While the ordeal of Antwerp was at its height, there arrived the new Spanish Governor in the person of Don John of Austria, half-brother of Philip. Efforts were immediately made to get him to honour the Pacification and although he at first made it appear that he would do this, he was aggrieved by his somewhat hostile reception, quickly lost patience, and called upon his troops to suppress the revolting provinces by force. So war began again, but in circumstances more favourable to William. The north was consolidated; Brabant was anxious to continue resistance and had chosen William as Stadtholder. His state entry into Brussels marks the highest point of his popularity. In the extreme south, however, more trouble loomed. The Catholics in the French-speaking provinces were more determined to defend their religion than their constitutional rights, and to add to the general restlessness, various outside governments and factions were fishing in the troubled waters.

William had one overriding problem. In terms of sheer military necessity he had to get outside aid. He was prepared to take it from Elizabeth of England (but she was unpredictable), from French Huguenots (but they were unstable) or from a French Catholic prince if, on anti-Spanish grounds, he would offer himself. In a way, William rather preferred a Catholic, for it was Catholic opinion he had to conciliate, but whichever ally he acquired it was certain that some section of Netherlands opinion would be bitterly offended.

In October 1578 Don John died and he was succeeded by the Duke of Parma, son of the Duchess Margaret. He was a more subtle diplomatist than his predecessor, and exploited the religious differences to such effect that in January 1579 the French-speaking provinces of the south formed themselves into the League of Arras for the defence of the Catholic faith. The League at once made peace with Philip. The northern provinces must continue the struggle alone, but by this time there was no doubt that they would continue. By the end of January five of them (Holland, Zealand, Utrecht, Gelderland and Friesland) had joined together in the Union of Utrecht. The northern (i.e. Dutch-speaking) sections of Flanders and Brabant agreed to co-operate. Neither the members of the League nor those who formed the Union of Utrecht intended to make a permanent division; they each saw themselves as a nucleus for a future union of the whole country. They were, in fact, defining the communities which, with modified boundaries, were eventually to be Belgium and Holland.

Meanwhile the military situation was still critical, and the need for outside help imperative. William was now facing a painful dilemma. As a practical statesman (and if ever anyone has deserved that name it is William the Silent) he had to act; his critics were able to reject all the possible courses because they were not responsible for the choice. There were three possibilities. The provinces could capitulate, but that was unthinkable; they could fight on alone, but they would certainly be beaten; or they could accept whatever ally would bring them aid, but he would almost certainly be objectionable. William was realist enough to recognise that the very nature of a dilemma implies the choice of something unpleasant and his grasping the nettle much reduced his former popularity. He negotiated with the only ally then possible, the Duke of Anjou, brother of Henry III of France who, even though a Catholic, was prepared to support Protestants if he could harass the Spanish enemy.

Before the treaty with Anjou was signed the rising feeling against William was mitigated by a grim action on the part of Philip. He declared William an outlaw, forbade all his subjects to associate with him and offered a reward of 25,000 golden crowns to anyone who would 'deliver him dead or alive or deprive him at once of life'. The natural effect of this was to swing popular feeling in the Netherlands back to William's side; to William himself it was now clear that he must renounce his allegiance to Philip and sever Spain's connection with the Netherlands. In December 1580 he published his famous 'Apology', which was translated into four languages and circulated throughout Europe. In this statement he replied to Philip's ban by justifying his own

N

activities, hoping to make other governments understand that he was not an irresponsible rebel, but the leader of a people morally bound to reject a king who had failed in his obligations. It expressed a view of the relations between kings and their subjects that was only to be generally accepted in later centuries, and it ended by renewing his loyal support of the cause with the words taken from his family coat of arms that were to become the motto of the Netherlands: 'Je maintiendrai' (I will keep on).

On 26 July 1581 Philip was formally deposed at a meeting of the Estates-General held at the Hague. In February 1582, the Duke of Anjou arrived from England[5] and the majority of the provinces rendered homage to him as Sovereign of the entire Netherlands. The majority did not include Holland and Zealand which by the treaty of alliance had a special status under William as their Count, and with their existing religious arrangements guaranteed. Although there was widespread misgiving about the Duke of Anjou, the country as a whole did not contest the desirability of having a powerful outsider as sovereign of their country. So much were men's minds still conditioned to previous ideas of overlordship. The misgiving, which was to be rapidly justified, was due to the personality of Anjou himself. The Calvinists, of course, disliked him simply because he was a Catholic, but he was soon even more detested by his co-religionists in the south amongst whom he lived. Indeed there was little to recommend Catherine de Médicis's youngest son—a degenerate fop, fickle and unprincipled whose arrival with his retinue of time-serving debauchees only intensified the atmosphere of suspicion and treachery in the ever-restless south. Even the troops he brought with him achieved only a temporary improvement in the military situation. Certainly he did little to ease William's burden.

William had long regarded himself as dedicated to the cause of the Netherlands; he had accepted that his life would be one of unremitting toil and hazards. Since the price had been put upon his head, he must have known that his life was forfeit. Time was short and there was much to be accomplished. In March 1582 came the first attempt to win the assassin's reward. William was at

5 He was there to press his suit on Queen Elizabeth, cf. Bodin p. 134 and Sidney p. 206.

his own house in Antwerp, and as he was leading his guests out from dinner a merchant's clerk, at the instigation of an avaricious master, pushed his way through a crowd of petitioners and shot William in the face at short range. Everyone, including the victim himself, at first thought that the murder was accomplished, and the wretched assailant swiftly fell to the swords of the guard. The wound though serious was not fatal, and after lying five weeks in bed and surmounting at least one crisis in which his life was despaired of, William was able at first slowly, and then with full vigour, to resume his active life. His recovery was largely due to the patient nursing of his wife, but if Charlotte had saved her husband's life, her exertions had probably shortened her own. Enfeebled by years of heavy demands both physical and spiritual, she died of a fever within a few weeks of William's recovery. It was the greatest personal loss he had ever sustained.

William was now nearing fifty, and his days were obviously numbered. How far in his loneliness could he console himself with the thought of a task well done? His goal was still not certain of attainment, but something of his inflexible determination was already shown by his young son Maurice, and realistic optimism was part of William's nature. He had been involved in an enterprise of the greatest complexity. It was not simply the fight of a small people for liberty; it was the struggle of a people basically of two different races distributed through a heterogeneous collection of feudal states and free cities, divided into three different religions and producing leaders—feudal nobles and successful burghers—whose interests were apt to be at variance. Neither were the divisions clear-cut; even the language line dividing the Dutch-speaking north from the French-speaking south ran through the provinces of Flanders and Brabant. Through all the manœuvring these complications made necessary William held firmly to his two avowed aims; a free United Netherlands and religious toleration.

He had endured years of lonely internal struggle over the question of his public and private loyalties, and if by this time he had emerged from the strife with considerable obstinacy and some vanity those traits could always be transmuted into self-control and confidence. Cautious by nature, he always pursued unspectacular long-term policies that he thought would succeed, rather than win popularity by more dramatic action; his was the courage of persistence, of the refusal to be either daunted or embittered. Je maintiendrai. Withal he was a man of action who placed little reliance on dogmas; people were always more important to him than theories. Through all his rough and busy life he kept his essential gentleness and consideration for others, for the lowliest of his troops, for the tenants on his estates, for the pages that served in his household. If he was occasionally disingenuous, some excuse lies in the complexities of the situation. It was part of his quality that he was realistic enough to make concessions while preserving his own standards of loyalty and tolerance; it was part of his greatness that he avoided dictatorship. He probably came as near as anyone has ever done to being uncorrupted by power: his heart remained in the right place. Whatever his or his contemporaries' estimate of his success at this time, an example had been given to the world.

The unflinching realism that had compelled William to accept alliance with Anjou equally made him aware of possible treachery. Even so he was taken by surprise when in January 1583 the French prince let loose his troops in Antwerp in an attempt to make himself the arbitrary sovereign of the Netherlands. The attempt failed, and Anjou retired to France,[6] but irreparable harm had been done. The south (which had seen the worst of the French allies) swung away from William again, and he felt it necessary to move to the north to ensure that resistance there remained firm. It is probable that William did not intend to live permanently in the north; but before his final intentions were clear death intervened and the south chose to regard it as desertion. In less than three years the southern provinces were to resume full obedience to Philip.

In 1583, while still at Antwerp, William married for the fourth time. His choice of Louise de Coligny, daughter of the prominent Huguenot leader may perhaps be regarded unromantically as 'defence in depth'. If it were necessary for the time being still to keep in with Henry III and the Catholic party in France, there was no telling when a Huguenot alliance might be useful. William took his new wife to Delft in the province of Holland, and there

6 He died in June 1584.

they took up residence in an old convent taken over by the Calvinist Government, and put at the disposal of Stadtholders as the Prinsenhof—the name by which it is still known.

It was again a dark period of the war, for William had to see a number of his erstwhile supporters change sides, seduced by the guile of Parma. It looked more and more likely that the religious gulf was too wide to be bridged, and that the south had been lost to the cause of freedom. In December 1583, William's Countship of Holland and Zealand was made hereditary and in January 1584, at the Prinsenhof, was born Frederick Henry, the son who, since Maurice died unmarried, was destined to carry on the house of Orange.[7] Within a few months the infant prince was fatherless.

William the Silent's assassin was a young Burgundian named Balthasar Gérard who had a fanatical loyalty to King Philip. He first got contact with William by pretending that he was the son of a persecuted Huguenot, and that he wished to serve the Protestant cause. William found him a messenger's employment and gave him some money which he, in fact, used to buy the pistol with which he committed the murder. On the morning of 10 July 1584 Gérard obtained entrance to the Prinsenhof on the pretext of needing a pass. As William, accompanied by his family and some army officers, was leaving the dining-hall after the midday meal, Gérard took up a premeditated position among the group of petitioners who were waiting in the hall. William walked across to the stairs and had just placed his foot on the first step to go up to his study when Gérard fired. Three bullets entered William's body, one passing right through and striking the staircase wall where its mark can still be seen today.[8] The Prince tottered into the arms of an equerry who laid him on the stairs. He was already dying; but his last words show that his thoughts were still with the cause he had served. 'Oh God have pity on my soul: oh God have pity on this poor people.' They carried him back into the dining room, but he was already unconscious and died before medical help could reach him, and before he could say anything

7 Frederick Henry's son, William, married Mary, daughter of Charles I of England and their son, William married Mary, daughter of James II and became William III of England. The Orange family in the Netherlands only assumed the title of King after the fall of Napoleon.

8 See Plate 3.

to soften the hideous rites of revenge which accompanied his murderer's execution.

William the Silent died when all his faculties were still unimpaired and with his great task unfinished. The loss was irreparable but the work he had done was not wasted. It remained as the foundation of the Dutch Republic. The Estates of Holland, on the very day of the murder, announced their intention of continuing the struggle, and although the provinces collectively were still without any sovereign in the place of Philip II, those that fought on found a great military leader in William's son, Maurice of Nassau, who, although only seventeen, succeeded his father as Stadtholder of Holland and Zealand as well as being appointed to that office by several other provinces. More important still, in August 1588, he became Captain-General of the Netherlands forces. Maurice had no bent for politics but he found an admirable partner for that branch of the work in John Van Oldenbarneveldt, a leading member of the all-important Estates of Holland who became Advocate of the province. Their task was no easy one. Parma was a commander of outstanding ability and unquenchable spirit who might well have succeeded in subduing the Netherlands but for Philip's determination to divert his resources to support the Spanish Armada. As it was, his troops swept north as far as the rivers besides making conquests in the extreme northeast. Although Maurice recovered the north-east section and pushed the enemy back from the river area, the main division had to be accepted as permanent. Maurice and Oldenbarneveldt produced a Republic of the United Netherlands composed of the seven northern provinces. The ill-starred intervention of Leicester and his unsuccessful period of governor-generalship between 1585 and 1587 did as much as anything to rid the Dutch of the notion that they needed a sovereign from outside to unify their provinces. After Leicester's departure, the sovereignty of the new republic was vested, somewhat vaguely, in the Estates-General itself.

By 1595 both England and France had allied with the Dutch Republic thus recognising it as an independent power. Spain still refused to do so, but it was already obvious that this was only a matter of time. Spanish confidence had been badly shaken by the defeat of the Armada in 1588 and the following year the accession of Henry IV (of Navarre) to the French throne had ended the possibilities of intrigue among religious factions in France. In 1598 King Philip died, and in 1609 his successor entered into the Twelve Years Truce with the United Netherlands which recognised them as a sovereign state. Thus there came into being the country we are accustomed to call Holland from the name of its leading province. The southern part of the country was to remain under Habsburg rule until the time of the French Revolution.

The Revolt of the Netherlands and the work of William the Silent—the two are inextricably bound together—were of immense significance for Europe. The emergence of this new young nation underlines the fact that the Renaissance had worked its way out of the medieval world into the modern one. The concept of nationality was a sign of the times, but other nations had been able to achieve unity and independence because they were large and powerful enough to ignore the theories of the Holy Roman Empire. Now a small nation had asserted its right to self-government and freedom because it seemed just that these things should be. The revolt began in feudal fashion, encumbered by deeply-rooted medieval beliefs, but it grew to embody a theory of government which would challenge and destroy that of the divine right of kings. William's judgement and self-control had ensured that the state which was born should have at any rate the potentialities of democracy. The western world may owe him a greater debt, for he was the first statesman in the Christian era to conceive of toleration in any modern sense. In this he was ahead of his contemporaries, and the subsequent history of his people was to show grave defections from his ideal. The battle is of course, never finally won. The twentieth century, feeling less passionately on religious issues, has its own ghastly record of bigotry and persecution in other spheres: nevertheless, tolerance has remained an aspiration of the western mind since the epoch when it received early tentative expression in the work of William the Silent.

### FURTHER READING

PIETER GEYL. *The Revolt of the Netherlands*. Benn 1932.
C. V. WEDGWOOD. *William the Silent*. Cape 1944.
G. N. CLARK. *The Birth of the Dutch Republic* (Raleigh Lecture). Oxford University Press 1947.

# Sir Philip Sidney

*(1554-1586)*

*All thought exists for the sake of action.*

IT IS AN evening in March 1507. At the Court of the Duke
Guidobaldo di Montefeltro in the little Italian duchy of Urbino
a group of some dozen men and women have gathered to entertain
themselves, not as more frequently with music and dancing, but
with a discussion that is almost a formalised debate, after the
fashion of the time. It is a gentle after-supper pastime to round
off a day filled with more active amusements, for it is a period of
festivity in Urbino. The duchy has just been freed from Papal
dominance, and although it is to prove to be a freedom of only a
decade, the Court at present is animated with a new spirit of
confidence and intellectual curiosity. The company that is assembled in the presence of the Lady Elizabeth, wife of Duke
Guidobaldo, is a distinguished one, including kinsmen of the
Duke, famous scholars and churchmen. Among them, we notice
with interest Guiliano the youngest son of Lorenzo de' Medici
whose family is at this moment exiled from Florence.

The topic that has been chosen for discussion is what makes
a man a perfect courtier, and the conversations will have to go on
for several more evenings before the speakers have finished
'specifying all such conditions and particular qualities as of
necessity must be in him that deserveth that name'. In the end
there will emerge a pattern of nobility that stamps itself indelibly
on the mind of at least one listener who in his turn will instil it
into the consciousness of the western world.

The picture of the group and the matter of the discourse
have been given to posterity by Baldassare Castiglione who was
at the time in the diplomatic service of the court, and who
wrote his account of the conversations as a treatise on manners
in 1508. The book, called *The Courtier* was not published
until 1528, but within half a century of that date it was available in Spanish and French. In 1561 it was translated into
English.

Castiglione's setting may be imaginary: the historical personages were in fact present in Urbino at that time.[1] The conversations may not have taken place quite as reported, but the views
put forward in the book certainly reflect those held by a highly
civilised section of sixteenth-century society.

*The Courtier* is the best known example of the 'courtesy'
literature which was a characteristic product of the age. Most of
it came from Italy, the country which was regarded as the furthest
advanced in 'civilisation', but English writers also made a contribution both to the theories of courtly breeding and to the more
general conceptions of education which were being radically
overhauled.

Societies which accepted hierarchical structures and looked to
the courts surrounding their sovereigns for the pattern of ideal
conduct, offer us more literature concerned with the training of a
courtier and a gentleman[2] than educational manuals of more
general application.[3] Both types were there, however, and while
today we can immediately appreciate the importance of the
works that have helped to build up our present attitude to education[4] it may be necessary to ask ourselves why the age which marks
the beginning of the modern era placed so much emphasis on the
training of the courtier, and felt it necessary to provide young
aristocrats with a formulated ideal. It is easy enough to see why
the Courts themselves would take such works seriously, but why
did educated men and women everywhere, and to a large extent
their posterity, value a work like *The Courtier* and feel it to be a
contribution to the civility of man?

The basis of all courtesy literature is an awareness of the need
for training the crude human being. How much his fundamental
character could be altered was then, as now, a matter for debate—
*The Courtier* puts considerable stress on heredity while at the
same time pointing out the possibilities of moral improvement—
but he could at least be given manners and deportment that made
him an acceptable member of society. He could be trained to see

1 The Duke himself was absent from the conversations as he was an invalid.
2 Elyot's *The Governour*; Spenser's *Faerie Queene*; Lyly's *Euphues*.
3 Mulcaster's *The Positions* and *The Elementaire*; Ascham's *The Scholemaster* (in part).
4 Cf. Montaigne, p. 161

that his behaviour affected other people, and in an age that was still close enough to the turbulent end of the Middle Ages to give order a supreme value, he could be taught a disciplined respect for what had so far been established. There was in the late fifteenth and early sixteenth centuries, a constant awareness of the precariousness of civilisation, a realisation that man's advance from the coarse brutality of his ancestors was neither immensely far nor very firmly consolidated, and that the precious gains must not be jeopardised.[5] Manners were not superficial adornments. The educated classes believed with Wykeham that manners 'makyth man' from what, otherwise, is a mere animal.

Reading these treatises we are often surprised by the elementary nature of the instructions, while, on another plane, we find it difficult to adjust ourselves to the social assumptions. When we read the advice on matters like table manners we have to remind ourselves that everything has to be learnt for the first time and in an age that was only just beginning to use forks, much in this way was obviously still necessary. From the overall picture we realise how much all civility was grounded on 'deference to those above and duties to those below'. This was implicit in all training: it was an obvious deduction from the hierarchical order of things.

It was, then, natural that Castiglione in framing his ideal of manhood, should take a courtier as his model. The obligation was to see that he was not a mere courtier but also a man of action and a man of learning, a man of sensibility, manners and integrity. To such a person all could look for inspiration, and his influence would permeate the whole of society.

From the discourse of the four chief speakers in *The Courtier* emanates a picture of one who should fulfil completely the humanists' conditions. He is first of all a warrior with the essential qualities of courage and loyalty, and with skill in all manly exercises and sports: these attributes to be balanced by gentleness and self-control. Castiglione already accepts the Renaissance idea that Arms and Letters far from being inimical are necessary partners, and the courtier must have a deep respect for learning.

5 It is another aspect of Erasmus's intellectual struggle against what he considered the barbarism of the Middle Ages as compared with the dignified view of life of the Ancients.

He should speak and write well both in his own language and in those of several foreign countries, he should be well grounded in Latin and Greek, and should have some knowledge of music and art.

The moral qualities for which he is constantly to strive include truthfulness and modesty; he is to be unaffected in speech, manners and dress. This emphasis on self-effacement was something that perhaps the contemporary Italian (certainly something of an exhibitionist) much needed. In a practical way it was incorporated more successfully into the educational methods of the northern countries. Quite obviously it was to influence English education for a very long time.

The main impression one gathers from Castiglione's treatise is that his ideal gentleman will be a balanced personality, pursuing a constant course of moderation, able in the shifting scenes of life to respond sincerely to both the grave and the gay. He will have a genuineness which makes him always value the reality above the appearance. His friends are thus carefully chosen and he affirms a lofty conception of love.

Castiglione's ideas, taken severally, were not original; in England such courtesy practices were current before his book was known, but it helped to establish a standard which was to be accepted by several generations and to influence many more. In the later sixteenth century a new notion of chivalry arose to replace the waning ideals of the Middle Ages and to supplement the immature attitudes of the Bayard tradition; at least some of its attributes were sufficiently valuable to survive the satire of Cervantes and quickening social change.

For Englishmen this conception has become embodied in the person of Sir Philip Sidney.

*The Courtier*, translated by Sir Thomas Hoby and published in England in 1561, became a very well known work at the Court of Queen Elizabeth. As Philip Sidney was much at Court, and as Lady Hoby was a friend of his mother, it is extremely unlikely that the book was unknown to him. He had most likely read the translation before he went abroad in 1572. This is not to suggest that Sidney self-consciously modelled himself on *The Courtier*. Spontaneity was a strong element in his character, manifest in both his faults and his virtues, but from his early boyhood his was a personality striving for moral attainment. Castiglione's work may well have helped him to define his ideal.

The Court which Sidney began to attend when he returned in 1575 from three years of travel on the Continent was the most brilliant England had ever known. The Queen, who appeared to the twenty-year-old Sidney as 'somewhat advanced in years' was in fact forty-one, and in the eighteenth year of her reign. She had succeeded in making herself the focus of the entire national life and the symbol of England's rising power. She received the extravagant respect and adulation of her subjects as her divinely appointed right, and from her personality radiated the confidence that was animating the new age.

It is difficult to retain a balanced picture of the Court of Queen Elizabeth. From one angle it is splendid. Around the central figure of Gloriana throng the glittering personalities who have been impressed indelibly on the English imagination, symbolising a triumphant epoch in our national history. Niggardly as Elizabeth was in all departments of State expenditure—and few had felt this more than Philip's father, Sir Henry—there was no stinting of money for clothes, jewellery and all the furnishings that sustained her magnificence.

Courtly entertainment was sumptuous. The Office of Revels, which had assumed a new importance, impressed scholars to provide a constant stream of plays and masques and to devise themes for jousts and tournaments. The scholars themselves might chafe against the courtier's life and occasionally feel humiliated at having to petition for such employment, but since humanism had invaded the Court its devotees must needs follow it. Whether Elizabeth held court at Greenwich (as most frequently) or at one of her other palaces of Windsor, Richmond, Nonsuch and White-hall, its life presented the same dazzling spectacle of immense formality and lavish entertainment.

There were also the summer 'progresses', a custom that the Queen continued although her Court was more firmly domiciled in London than those of her predecessors. Elaborately organised visits would be paid to different parts of the realm and the sovereign, arriving in an open litter drawn by mules caparisoned in scarlet and gold, would be received and entertained by city authorities and great noblemen, and provincial England given a glimpse of the splendour usually reserved for the capital.

From another angle Elizabeth's Court is less glorious. One sees it centred on a despotic woman of uncertain temper, with false hair and blackened teeth, adorned to give a simulacrum of a past beauty, and demanding that all who came into her presence should subscribe to the fiction by which she fed her vanity. The whole fantastically artificial code of manners which made it necessary for her appearance at an ordinary meal to involve a procession of some seventy people and to oblige the servitors who laid the tables to kneel on entering the room even though no one was yet present, seems to be merely the prop of a gigantic sham.

Neither angle of vision would present us with reality. The Court, like most human institutions, embraced contradictions. It existed, after all, at a time when new attitudes were everywhere being forged out of traditions and innovation: it was a curious mixture of petrified forms and the new humanist spirit. If on one hand it used the humanistic training for its entertainment without much profiting by its wisdom, on the other hand there was at Elizabeth's Court some genuine regard for scholarship. The Queen herself was no mean scholar, a learned élite had begun to be seen as necessary to the state, and the nobility were made to feel that a university education was necessary for their children. Nor must we lose sight of the fact that behind the glittering façade much statesmanlike business was transacted between a sovereign of high intelligence and her councillors whom she always had the good sense to distinguish from mere favourites.

Finally, what is most historically important is how the Queen's court looked to the age itself. And of this there is little doubt. One cannot imagine the England of the latter part of the sixteenth century as anything but Elizabethan England. Elizabeth seemed to her contemporaries to be representative of a divine order, and they perhaps idealised her queenly office rather than the actual woman. The certainty is she commanded loyalty and inspired chivalry in the hearts of men whose judgement we cannot despise, and whatever vicissitudes her image may have undergone during four hundred years—sometimes tarnished and sometimes recovering its glowing colours—the testimony of her more articulate subjects compels us to accept her as the force that was welding the nation, truly representing her people in her single-

197

hearted devotion to England and its determined struggle against Spain. Despotic she might be, but her subjects recognised that she had brought them strong and stable government and in spite of all the alarms and excursions of the reign and the storms through which she (or her ministers) successfully piloted them they counted her reign as one of peace.

A man such as Philip Sidney—talented, many-sided, ambitious and idealistic—mentally chafed against the obligations of court life. Its social demands hindered what he regarded as his serious political duties; devising masques only distracted him from more congenial literary pursuits; jousting was no substitute for the service in arms which he craved. He hated the atmosphere of petty intrigue by which courtiers sought advancement. During the eleven years he was attached to the court he was never in high favour with the Queen, in spite of the fact that he made his début under the aegis of his brilliant uncle, the Earl of Leicester, at the time prime favourite, and that he derived from two families long accustomed to move in court circles.

Philip, the eldest of the seven children of Sir Henry Sidney, was born at Penshurst, Kent, the great house which had been bestowed on his grandfather by Edward VI. Both his father who was related to the Dukes of Suffolk, and his mother who was the elder daughter of the Duke of Northumberland[6] were of impressive lineage, and the high obligations of his birth were early enjoined on the boy. He was sent to the recently refounded grammar school of Shrewsbury, entering at the same time as his lifelong friend and biographer Fulke Greville.[7] When Sidney first went to school in 1564, his father was Lord President of the Council of Wales, residing nearby at Ludlow, but in 1565 Sir Henry was appointed Deputy of Ireland and for this reason Philip spent his holidays in the care of the Earl of Leicester or in the homes of his father's friends.

6 The Duke of Northumberland and one of his sons died on the scaffold in 1553 for their complicity in the Lady Jane Grey plot. Sidney's remaining uncles on his mother's side were Lord Ambrose Dudley (later Earl of Warwick) and Lord Robert Dudley (later Earl of Leicester).

7 Fulke Greville (1554-1628). Author of plays and poems, and much interested in the new learning. He was at court with Sidney, and was also a Member of Parliament.

He seems to have been an over-conscientious schoolboy, for his father wrote to him anxiously, advising him not to exceed the sufficient hours of study set by his masters. His life, however, held some excitements unknown to the great majority of his fellow pupils. In 1566, when the Queen was visiting Oxford, Philip then aged twelve, bravely apparelled in a doublet of crimson with a damask gown and carnation coloured hose, went under the guardianship of his uncle, Leicester, to take his first small part in royal festivities.

In 1568 he went again to Oxford, this time to take up residence as an undergraduate of Christ Church, and to be, as it turned out, contemporary with many who were to become famous. Sir Walter Raleigh, the dramatists Peele and Lyly, the theologian Hooker, the later Jesuit missionaries Campion and Parsons, were all at the University at this time, and Sidney seems to have been on terms of some intimacy with Camden the antiquarian, and Hakluyt, who was later renowned as a writer on English exploration. It was his friendship with Hakluyt, perhaps, that inspired Sidney with an interest he afterwards developed.

On coming down from Oxford in 1572 Philip obtained a licence to travel for two years to learn foreign languages, and at the age of seventeen he set out on a tour which in fact occupied the next three years. He went first to Paris, and there, from the house of Sir Francis Walsingham, the English ambassador, he witnessed the massacre of St Bartholomew when the vacillating policy of King Charles IX[8] and his mother Catherine de Médicis found at last a definite expression in the slaughter of hundreds of Protestants gathered in Paris for the marriage of King Henry of Navarre to the King's sister. It was an experience that made a profound impression on the horrified Sidney. Two years before he left England, Pope Pius V had pronounced his bull of excommunication against Elizabeth, thus making Roman Catholics virtually enemies of the crown. Sidney's English antipathy to the Roman faith was deepened and he demonstrated his abhorrence of the atrocities by renouncing the barony that Charles IX had just conferred upon him.

8 Francis I 1515-1547　　Francis II 1559-1560 ⎫　Regency of Catherine de
　Henry II 1547-1559　　Charles IX 1560-1574 ⎭　Médicis till 1563.
　　　　　　　　　　　　Henry III 1574-1589

o

After leaving Paris, Sidney travelled by way of Frankfurt, Heidelberg and Strassburg to Vienna, and passed a good deal of the following year in Venice. Almost half of his time however was spent in Vienna—with short trips to Hungary and Poland—and for this there was a strong reason. At Frankfurt he had met Hubert Languet, a Protestant scholar, Burgundian by birth, and at this time envoy of the Elector of Saxony at the Imperial Court. Languet, a man in his fifties, was much impressed by the qualities of the young Englishman and for the rest of his life (that is until 1581) he maintained a close and fatherly relationship with Sidney, corresponding with him regularly and advising him on his studies, his morals, his career, and providing a stimulating commentary on worldly affairs. Sidney was later to acknowledge his indebtedness in verse, cast in the contemporary pastoral fashion.

> ' For clerkly rede, and hating what is nought,
>   His faithful heart, clean mouth and hands as true
>   With his sweet skill, my skilless youth he drew,
>   To have a feeling taste of Him that sits
>   Beyond the Heaven, far more beyond our wits.
>
>   He liked me, but pitied lustful youth,
>   His good strong staff my slippery years upbore:
>   He still hop'd well, because I loved truth.'

On his return to England in May 1575, Sidney, as we have seen, entered court life, and he was soon participating fully in its rituals and festivities. In July he was present at the most elaborate and famous of all the Queen's receptions, that given by Leicester at Kenilworth when Elizabeth was on progress through the midland counties. At the same time he began to give his mind seriously to political questions. If the next ten years were to him a period of frustration, to us, looking back, they seem of the greatest significance. For it was during this time that he developed his interests and talents in such a way that his personality was to become, for no single outstanding reason, one of the most vivid in our national history. Certainly this development did not get its chief nourishment in courtly circles; and yet Sidney would not have been the representative Elizabethan he was if he had not had acquaintance with Elizabeth's Court.

He had returned from his European tour a cultured man. Encouraged by Languet he had continued his personal studies while abroad, acquiring a knowledge of international affairs, and exchanging ideas with influential men. For some reason he had come down from Oxford without taking his degree, but he continued his own education purposefully. He was competent in both Italian and French although he was impervious to Languet's repeated advice to learn German, declaring that he found that language unattractive.

The physical side of his education had not been neglected. He played tennis and engaged in field sports and his horsemanship, which he had practised under the Master of the Emperor's Stable when he was in Vienna in 1574, is highly praised by his contemporaries.

He was enthusiastic for all the arts. In a letter to his brother he urges the study of music as essential to a rounded education, but we do not know how skilful a musician he was. He seems to have had some technical knowledge, as he certainly had of painting. He had personal acquaintance with some of the great painters of his day.

Above all, of course, was his interest in literature, expressing itself not only in patronage of young writers and in illuminating contributions to the literary debates of his time, but also in his own works which have lived. Two of them particularly, *The Apology for Poetry* and *Astrophel and Stella* have won increased regard as the years have passed.

Like many sixteenth-century gentlemen Sidney regarded his writings as products of his leisure not to be taken as a serious part of his life's work. He said he only 'slipped into the title of poet'; none of his 'toyful books' was printed during his lifetime —as Fulke Greville said 'his end was not writing even when he wrote'—but they were known to his friends who regarded him as a courtier poet from the time he devised a pastoral masque called *The Lady of May* to entertain the Queen on a visit to Leicester at Wanstead in 1578. He was twenty-four at this time and two years later, when he was staying at Wilton, the Wiltshire home of his sister the Countess of Pembroke, he wrote the long prose romance *Arcadia* to entertain her. This is not a work readily acceptable to modern taste, but when it was published

shortly after his death, first by Fulke Greville and a little later in
a revised version by his sister, it was immensely popular, and was
soon the first English literary work to be translated into French
and Italian. It is the earliest prose work to be written in the
standard English into which the old regional dialects were being
welded and it spoke directly to its own age by the nature of its
idealism: what seems to us its mannered style would not have
been a barrier. Now, its ingenious allegory, the wealth of rhetori-
cal figures, and the fact that in it we can see the first shoots of
much that was to become great in English fiction make it
something of a connoisseur's piece.

Sidney's other two outstanding works have retained their
freshness. The sonnet sequence *Astrophel and Stella* still charms
us with its poetry and moves us with its passion. It tells the story
of Sidney's frustrated love for Penelope Devereux, the daughter of
the Earl of Essex. It had been the wish of her father, who died in
1576, when Sidney was in Ireland with him, that she should marry
Philip, but he seems not to have been moved in this way until
after 1581 when she had married a worthless nobleman, Lord
Rich and then Sidney realised his loss:

> 'I might—unhappy word—O me, I might,
> And then would not, or could not, see my bliss;
> Till now wrapt in a most infernal night,
> I find how heav'nly day, wretch! I did miss.'

The 108 sonnets and eleven songs record the progress of Astrophel's passion, his struggle to win Stella, and his own inner
struggle for the self-mastery which he finally attains.

Occasionally his anger at Lord Rich's treatment of his wife
expresses itself in bitterness, as in the punning lines:

> 'But that rich fool, who by blind fortune's lot
> The richest gem of love and life enjoys,
> And can with foul abuse such beauties blot,
> Let him, depriv'd of sweet but unfelt joys,
> Exil'd for aye from those high treasures which
> He knows not, grow in only folly Rich! '

Sidney did not regard this poem as matter for publication: only some of the songs circulated among his friends during his lifetime. But after its publication in 1591 it was to have great influence. The early sonnets are still governed by prevailing Italian conventions, and have direct kinship with the poems interspersed in the *Arcadia*, but as they become more personal and more passionate they exhibit a wide range of metre and diction, and the poet experiments freely and interestingly with his chosen form. Sidney was indeed the first of that generation which brought the sonnet to perfection and *Astrophel and Stella* was the forerunner of a long line of sonnet sequences.

Sidney's critical prose work *The Apology for Poetry*[9] remains important, as it is also a delight to read. It was written in reply to *The School of Abuse*, a pamphlet in which one Stephen Gosson, writing from the extreme Puritan point of view had attacked poetry as a vicious influence. For Sidney, poetry essentially ' intends the winning of the mind from wickedness to virtue '; but the book was more than a defence on these lines. It stands as the first English exposition of Renaissance critical principles. *The Apology* is both dignified and entertaining; Sidney argues his case with moderation and good humour, and often with ingenuity. He recognises the poor state of contemporary poetry, but he is obviously excited by signs of a coming revival, and writes with a prescience of the great flowering he was not to live to see. It is true that Shakespeare, as well as lesser men, were to prove abundantly that Elizabethan drama need not be shackled by the classical rules that Sidney would have imposed upon it, but there is much in other branches of his criticism (that of diction for example) that is both salutary and enduring.

Sidney would have been surprised could he have known that for a century after his death he would be the most read and admired poet of his generation, as he would also have been by the permanent place *The Apology* has had in English criticism. His interest in literature, genuine enough, was something he would have seen as becoming a courtier at a time when a new conception of his function was rapidly gaining ground. The new courtier, like Castiglione's, was required to be a man of culture, versed in the new learning as well as accomplished in the field of martial

9 Sometimes called *The Defence of Poetry*. By poetry Sidney meant the whole field of imaginative writing.

activity; at the same time he was now coming to be seen, by virtue of his learning, as a counsellor of his Government in worldly affairs. Literature could be only a small part of life in a new age which demanded breadth of interest before all else.

There was much to be interested in during this period of transition from medieval to modern times, and Sidney was connected with the Court at an intensely exciting period of English history. That he was not early called upon to play a more vigorous part was no fault of his, and his untimely death made impossible the full development of his powers; but he had conscientiously informed himself, and actively prepared to take a leading part in England's expanding concerns.

Within two years of his return home he was sent on a mission to Europe to congratulate the newly elected Emperor, Rudolf II, and to visit the Counts of the Palatinate in the interest of the Protestant cause, a visit which enabled him to meet both Don John of Austria and William the Silent.[10] The Queen must have been satisfied with the way he had carried out his embassy for Walsingham wrote to Sir Henry Sidney on her behalf praising his son's conduct: but after that date Philip made little progress as a courtier in the more restricted sense of the term. He fretted for action and responsibility; the Queen denied him both. Her policy did not allow of the decisiveness which would give him employment in the Netherlands. To Sidney, strongly under the influence of William the Silent, this seemed the obvious place to fight the battles both of England and of Protestantism.

Sidney had, of course, been brought up as a Protestant[11] and after the St Bartholomew massacre he had developed a deep repugnance to the Roman Catholic faith. His own religious views inclined—perhaps a little more than the Queen approved—to the Puritanism that had been the atmosphere of his schooling, although the keynote of his personal life was tolerance. To organised Catholicism Sidney was hostile, but to individuals of the Roman persuasion he was courteous and actively friendly. This was an attitude not always readily understood in his time. Languet seems to have been fearful that he might be won over if he

10 See William the Silent, p. 182.

11 Sir Henry Sidney, a counsellor of Edward VI, had 'conformed' to the religious arrangements under Mary.

travelled much in Catholic lands, and Campion so far misunderstood his friendliness when he met him in Prague during his embassy of 1577, as to give his opinion that Sidney was 'ripe for conversion'.

Some years later, after the Jesuit mission to England had begun, and Campion himself had been executed, Sidney was offered a grant from the forfeitures of the Papist recusants. He may even have made suit for it. If he did, he must have been very much in two minds about the matter, for he later expressed his distaste for the idea of mending his fortune by other men's suffering; all the same the probability is that he accepted the grant.

England's alliance with France had not been broken by the events of St Bartholomew. Elizabeth recognised Spain as a much graver menace. She intended, for the time at any rate, to pursue the middle way in her policy abroad as much as in religious affairs at home. France and Spain were, as far as possible, to be played off against each other.

Philip Sidney, younger, more direct and idealistic, influenced by what he had seen abroad and by his conversations with Languet, arrived at court in 1575 fired already with enthusiasm for a Protestant crusade and with a desire to help the Netherlands in their revolt against Spanish domination. After his embassy to Europe in 1577 he was more confirmed in these views. On his way to the Imperial Court he had visited the new Counts Palatine—Lewis, the new Elector who was a Lutheran and his younger brother Casimir, Count of the Lower Palatinate, who was a Calvinist. Casimir was keen to form a Protestant League, and from this time Sidney seems to have felt it was England's duty to place herself at the head of it—a feeling that must have been strengthened by his contact with William the Silent on the same occasion.

It was during the following year he began to complain of the 'ignoble ease' of his life at court, and at frequent intervals he was glad to slip away to Wilton, where, if he still had ease rather than action, he could at any rate use it to develop his increasing interest in literature. Still he was a member of the Court. Punctually at the New Year he would present the customary personal offering to the Queen, on one occasion 'a smock of cambric, sleeves and collar edged with small bone lace of gold and silver', on another, a crystal cup—gifts which Sidney could ill afford but which were, all the same, an obligation.

In any case his 'ease' was becoming increasingly ruffled by the agitation that was spreading through the Court on account of the marriage project of the Queen. Elizabeth—although we can see now, never quite in earnest—had for some years entertained the proposal of marriage to the Duke of Anjou, brother of King Henry III of France.[12] In spite of the existence of a group of advisers who wished her to accept it, the proposal was unpopular in the country as a whole. Feeling rose high between the different factions at Court, and disagreement on the question was the reason that a notorious quarrel about a tennis court between Sidney and the Earl of Oxford developed the importance of an affair of state.

More mature judges than Sidney were deeply concerned about the question, and it was in this matter that Sidney found himself obliged to fulfil one specific injunction of Castiglione to his courtier, who should have earned, Castiglione wrote, 'in such wise the good will and favour of the Prince he is in service withal, that he may break his mind to him and always inform him frankly of the truth of every matter meet for him to understand, without fear or peril to displease him. And when he knoweth his Prince's mind is bent to commit anything unseemly for him, to be bold to oppose him in it and to take courage after an honest sort at the favour which he hath gotten him through his good qualities, to dissuade him from every ill purpose.'

A group of statesmen which included Walsingham and Leicester, decided that Sidney was the best person to draw up a statement of their party's objections to the marriage both because the Queen had recently favoured him with discussions on the subject, and also on account of his ability as a writer. Some years earlier Sidney had addressed to the Queen a very able defence of his father's policy in Ireland—it is the first piece of his formal writing we have—and although this does not seem to have been very well

12 She had, at one time, briefly considered a proposal from Henry III himself when he was Duke of Anjou (1572). When he was elected King of Poland in 1573, his younger brother the Duke of Alençon was substituted as a suitor. In 1574 Henry III ascended the French throne, and his brother Alençon became Duke of Anjou in his place.

received, he was courageous enough to accept this new assign-
ment. The letter that he now wrote at the behest of his elders is a
lucid and cogent statement of the opposition's case. It was both
bold and tactful. How much Elizabeth was moved by it would be
difficult to guess. She probably knew her own mind more than
she had allowed it to appear, in any case. Sidney seems to have
suffered some disfavour—he spent most of the following spring
and summer away from the Court, at Wilton—but the letter was
no ground of permanent offence. After Anjou's last visit to
England in the winter of 1581-82, Sidney was a member of his
escort back to Flushing. In June 1584 Anjou died, and the question of the Queen's marriage ceased to occupy the first place in
the minds of her advisers.

The time had come when a decision must be taken about
English intervention in the Netherlands. By this time, Sidney
seems to have come to the conclusion that this was not, after all,
the best place for action, but that Spain should be crippled by
attacking the source of her wealth in the Indies, and establishing
English bases there. This view may have been partly a natural outcome of his increasing interest in exploration and colonisation.

During the ten years of his frustration, Sidney had held trifling
offices at Court such as that of Cupbearer to the Queen, he had
become a Member of Parliament in 1581, and in 1583 he was
made General of the Horse and given some junior appointment
in the Ordnance. That year, too, he was knighted, but it was a
hollow honour. Elizabeth was bestowing the garter on Count
Casimir of the Palatinate, and Sidney was to receive it for him as
proxy. Only someone of rank could act in this capacity, and so
Sidney acquired his knighthood—a somewhat doubtful expression
of the Queen's favour. Only in the summer of 1585 was he at last
given a post of real responsibility as Joint Master of the Ordnance
with his uncle, the Earl of Warwick.

There had been plenty of time for other interests, and he had
followed with great keenness the activities of English seamen. He
had invested modestly in each of the voyages of Frobisher in 1576
and 1577 in search of the North-west passage to Cathay, and
again in 1578 in the expedition that was an unsuccessful attempt
to found a colony in the land round Frobisher Bay. He wrote
excitedly to Languet after the second voyage about the alleged

discovery of gold and asked his advice about the working of ores. Languet was cautious in his reply, and the tests carried out soon proved his pessimism to be justified.

Sidney's interest in American projects was not based on a desire for wealth. He thought in strategic terms and also of the possibility of founding places of refuge for persecuted Protestants. At the same time he was willing to support Sir Humphrey Gilbert's policy of selling his rights in American lands (not yet discovered) to Roman Catholics so that they could found a colony, thus providing a solution to a religious problem. Nothing came of this scheme; but a bigger disappointment for Sidney was the failure of Humphrey Gilbert's half-brother, Sir Walter Raleigh, to establish his Virginian settlement of 1584, for this had held the possibility of being the desired naval and military base against Spain.

There was, however, still more hope in the West than in Europe. Just before Frobisher's third expedition he had written to Languet 'For my own part, unless God powerfully counteract it, I seem to myself to see our cause withering away, and am now meditating with myself some Indian project'. It is, indeed, likely that he had often considered sailing with one of these expeditions, as he may have thought earlier of joining William the Silent or Casimir as a private volunteer. In 1585 he attempted decisive action.

Drake, who had returned from his triumphal circumnavigation of the globe in 1580, was preparing at Plymouth a new expedition ostensibly as a reprisal for a Spanish attack on a British ship, but which it was hoped would lead to the conquest of Spanish settlements in the West Indies. In September 1585, when even Elizabeth's belated promise of help to the Netherlands did not seem to have brought an appointment for Sidney any nearer, he resolved to join Drake on the expedition he had helped to plan. There ensued a picturesque and undignified episode, not entirely to Sidney's credit, which does much to reveal his weariness with his lot and the despair to which he was being reduced.

That Elizabeth would give her permission for Sidney to go was unlikely. He did not ask it. With the excuse of setting out to meet one of the claimants to the Portuguese throne[13] who was

13 Philip of Spain had acquired the Portuguese throne in 1581; hence England's interest in the pretender.

about to arrive in England, he slipped away and joined Drake at
Plymouth. How far Drake had committed himself in the matter
is not clear. It is probable he never intended Sidney to sail with
him in this surreptitious manner. It is certain that he notified the
Queen as soon as he arrived. Elizabeth sent a messenger with
letters to Drake, the Mayor of Plymouth, and to Sidney himself,
forbidding him to leave England. On receiving news that the
messenger had started out Sidney contrived a fantastic, and
scarcely hopeful, plot. Disguising himself and a number of his men
as sailors, he led the party out to lie in wait for the Queen's
envoy whom they held up and robbed of the letters. Naturally, it
was not long before the true nature of the incident was discovered.
The Queen's anger at the whole affair seems to have been
tempered by a belated recognition of Sidney's ardent desire for
active patriotic service. She dispatched a second messenger—this
time a peer of the realm—and he brought with him also the
appointment to the Governorship of Flushing.

In the summer of 1585 Elizabeth had at last decided to send
help to the Netherlands in their struggle against Philip of Spain.
William the Silent had been assassinated in 1584, but his son
Maurice still strove valiantly. He was offered English men and
money in return for the cession of Flushing and Brill as temporary
cautionary towns. In November, Sir Philip Sidney entered upon
his office; in December, Leicester arrived with an army.[14]

The remaining eleven months of Sidney's life were by no means
easy. Widespread sickness in a garrison already inadequate, the
discontent of the Dutch inhabitants and other local troubles,
were only part of a burden increased by difficulties with the Queen
over supplies, and the ineptness of Leicester. His conscientious-
ness together with his dashing military exploits soon won him the
respect of the city authorities; his gallant death gave him a place
in the annals of their country. In England the story of his death
has been too frequently narrated to need elaboration. The camp
near besieged Zutphen; the inadequate ambush set to intercept
Spanish supplies; Sir Philip Sidney's quixotic—and chivalrous
—throwing away of his thigh piece because the Lord Marshal
lacked his; the horse shot under him; the musket ball shattering
the bone above the knee, and the noble gesture of giving up his

14 See William the Silent, p. 188.

drink of water to the dying soldier who was being carried past him, are all well-etched scenes in an oft-told tale.

Sidney died a little more than three weeks after he was wounded, on 17 October 1586, at the age of thirty-two. The States of Zealand applied for the honour of his burial, but his body was brought back to England on his own boat, the Black Pinnace, and landed at Tower Hill to lie in St Paul's. No monument was ever erected, and since the great fire of 1666, the exact place of his burial has remained unknown. The funeral, which had to be postponed because of the financial difficulties which were perpetual in Sidney's family, at last took place on 16 February 1587. It was the most magnificent that had ever been accorded to any Englishman not a sovereign and it was followed by a prolonged chorus of public praise from his many friends and from some few who were his enemies.

Why should this be? Sidney's was a short life and, one might say, without spectacular achievement. He was distinguished in his day not by any particular attainment, but by his manner, his conversation, his quality of character and mind, and his gift for friendship—in short by his personality. When a man's reputation is of this kind rather than resting on work that can outlive him and which posterity can evaluate afresh in each generation, it is difficult to supply convincing reasons for it. True, Sidney's contribution to literature remains, but valuable as some of it may seem to us now, it was not the basis of his enduring fame.

The emphatic grandeur of his funeral, the flood of elegiac poetry, popular ballads and prose memorials, the months of mourning observed by those of gentlemanly rank, all testify to the deep impression he had made on the national consciousness. He was honoured by Oxford and Cambridge in Latin, Greek and Hebrew, as well as in English; foreign universities paid their tributes; poets hastened to acknowledge their debt to him, King James VI of Scotland contributed some Latin verses. The less articulate sections of the nation, assisted by Thomas Lant's roll of thirty-four engravings, began to make of his name a legend that has persisted.

It would be easy to dismiss Sidney as an overrated personality whose name has been kept bright simply by being constantly repeated, but this would be to deny all contemporary evidence.

There must be some reason for the esteem he commanded in his own day. It would have been some quite exceptional quality in a young man that called forth tributes from statesmen, scholars, princes and poets, and won the friendship of mature and experienced men of the world. Languet, the most intimate and dedicated of his friends from the older generation, was by no means alone in his estimate of Sidney's abilities. Famous scholars such as Petrus Ramus, the critic of Aristotle, and the two printers Henri Estienne and Andrea Wechel (in whose house at Frankfurt Sidney first met Languet) had felt they could converse profitably with the youth of seventeen, and had remarked his high promise. Eleven years later the irascible but intellectually influential Italian philosopher, Giordano Bruno, visiting England, found in Sidney one of the few men of learning with whom he was not impelled to quarrel, and dedicated an important work to him.

He won the respect of men as opposite as Don John of Austria and William the Silent who, after his meeting with Sidney during his embassy of 1577, pronounced him likely to become 'one of the ripest and greatest counsellors of Estate'. Henry of Navarre found him 'fit for friendship with a king', and Philippe du Plessis-Mornay, who represented Navarre in London, was among his intimates. It was Mornay's wife who described Sidney as 'the most accomplished gentleman in England'.

Among his own countrymen, he held the respect of statesmen like the great Lord Burghley and Sir Francis Walsingham whose daughter Frances he married in 1583. And two epitaphs on English tombs have their own brief eloquence: Fulke Greville had himself commemorated as 'Servant to Queen Elizabeth, Counceller to King James, friend of Philip Sidney', and Dr Thomas Thornton, a great Latin scholar of Christ Church, had inscribed on his tomb at Ledbury 'tutor to Sir Philip Sidney'.

Further testimony to the respect of scholars is to be found in the number of books dedicated to him—a greater number than to any contemporary of similar rank—and the range of their subject matter shows how wide were his interests. Philosophy, theology, linguistics, medicine, poetry and horsemanship are all represented.

His discriminating patronage of men of letters is one of Sidney's services to his age, and those who dedicated their work to him were conscious of honouring something more than a dilettante interest in literature; he was felt to be involved in the subject matter of the proffered work. For Alberici Gentile who published a book *On Ambassadors* in 1584, he was 'the perfect ambassador', and for his friend Edmund Spenser whose aim, moral as much as artistic, in writing *The Faerie Queene* was to 'fashion a gentleman or noble person in vertuous or gentle discipline' Sidney had been an ever present model as well as a prime source of encouragement of the work. *The Faerie Queene*, intended as a great national poem, was dedicated to the Queen. *The Shepheardes' Calender* is 'entitled to the noble and vertuous gentleman, worthy of all titles, both of learning and chevalrie, Philip Sidney'. Indeed, references to Sidney are scattered throughout Spenser's work, and *Astrophel* is a pastoral elegy on his death.

Sidney's personality may not always have made as immediate an impact as all this suggests. He had been a serious, thoughtful boy, perhaps unduly staid. His school-fellow, Fulke Greville, said he had never known him 'other than a man'. Languet, in a letter advising him not to study geometry, quaintly adds, 'You are not over-cheerful by nature, and it is a study which will make you still more grave.' A melancholic strain developed and persisted in his character so that throughout his life he was subject to fits of acute depression. Perhaps they arose from the very intensity of his idealism[15] which made him quickly critical of things as they were and sometimes impatient of other people. In some departments of conduct he certainly showed more idealism than judgement. He was extremely sensitive with a shyness that had to be overcome, or at any rate masked, in the interests of his destined career, and he inherited from his mother nerves all too finely set. He had a fiery impulsive side to his nature which more than once betrayed him into injustice. We read of an occasion when he impetuously charged his travelling companion with having cheated him over a bill which the innkeeper had in fact presented twice; and he once wrongfully and violently accused his father's secretary of opening his private correspondence, on very scanty evidence.

We can set against these indiscretions a more common attitude

15 It is noticeable that in all the English arts of the time the hopefulness of the Renaissance spirit is somewhat diluted by a sense of the vanity of worldly things.

of humility, and numerous instances, in his active life, of great self-control. He was a loyal and dutiful son and an affectionate kindly elder brother. His friendships were based on a delicate perception of other people's feelings and were graced by infinite tact.

Sidney was kind and generous, though he was usually short of money. His family, though distinguished, were not wealthy and his father had spent freely in the Queen's service without reward, or even compensation. For some years Sidney occupied a brilliant position as the heir of his childless uncle, the Earl of Leicester. It was a position of hope rather than substance, and when Leicester married the widow of the Earl of Essex, and in 1581 had an heir, the hopes faded and Sidney had to reconcile himself to a lifetime of straitened circumstances.[16] But his generosity persisted and not only to those around him and to those who served him. He concerned himself with unknown scholars and artists who seemed to him men of promise, and he sent one young student up to Cambridge at his own expense.

Perhaps Sidney took himself somewhat too seriously: we are not made aware of much sense of humour in all we read about him.[17] It was inevitable after all that had been impressed upon the boy about the nobility of his inheritance that there should be something of haughtiness and aloofness in the man, in spite of the warmth of his chosen friendships; but he was modest in expression and had the restraint and gentleness of manner recommended to Castiglione's courtier. It is possible that his gravity and reserve in an age much inclined to flaunting, are qualities that have recommended him to a nation that is alleged to take its pleasures seriously. Certainly the weaknesses he had were redeemed by sincerity; there can be no doubt about his genuineness.

Sidney was distinguished among the men of his time both by his talents and the breadth of his interests. In one respect he ful-filled an old Greek ideal revived to adorn the English Renaissance. He responded notably to Aristotle's injunction: 'Learn to play

16 The boy, in fact, died in 1584, and Leicester died (in 1588) without leaving any legitimate children. Sidney's brother, Robert, was created Earl of Leicester in 1618.

17 There are, however, pleasant glimpses of ironic humour in *The Apology for Poetry*.

the flute—but not too well.' He pursued many activities creditably without being the outstanding practitioner of any: it was this that made him touch the age at so many points. His quixotically heroic death—for in all knighthood there is an element of the quixotic—has stamped itself on the imagination of succeeding generations of Englishmen so firmly that he remains one of the best remembered of historical figures.

If it is a quality of greatness that it can contain opposite virtues without their cancelling each other, Sidney was in many respects a great man. He had the courtier's grace without his licentiousness; he strove for virtue without priggishness. Possessed of a strong practical mind that hated pettifogging theory, he was equally capable of deep thought and prompt action.

He lived at a time when the Renaissance in England was quickening to its full flowering. Through his interests and activities we get glimpses of all the great movements that were agitating Europe; in his personality we can recognise the new ideal of manhood that was being fashioned out of a dying medieval tradition and a revived Italian sense of civility; in his writing we can feel the new impulse that was informing English literature. His many-sidedness made him a typical child of the Renaissance spirit and his life had incarnated that spirit in an English form.

## FURTHER READING

H. R. FOX BOURNE. *Sir Philip Sidney: Type of English Chivalry in the Elizabethan Age*. Putnam 1891.

MONA WILSON. *Sir Philip Sidney*. Duckworth 1931.

E. J. M. BUXTON. *Sir Philip Sidney and the English Renaissance*. Macmillan 1954.

BALDASSARE CASTIGLIONE. *The Courtier*. Dent (Everyman).

PHILIP SIDNEY. *Astrophel and Stella*.

—— *An Apology for Poetry*. (Ginn and Co. 1931, together with Shelley's *A Defence of Poetry*.)

# Cervantes

(1547-1616)

*As the light shines more brightly when it is dark, so hope must be firmer under trial; to despair then is the act of a coward, and there is nothing so pusillanimous as the surrender of a hard-tried man . . . to desperation*

*For I would have you know, Sancho that there are two kinds of lineages in the world; those which trace their descent from princes and monarchs, and which little by little time has diminished and reduced to a point, like a pyramid upside down, and others which derive their origin from common folk, and climb step by step till they achieve the dignity of great lords. So that the difference is between those that were and are no longer, and those who are but once were not.*

IN 1588, TWO years after the death of Philip Sidney at Arnhem, the conflict between England and Spain reached its climax with the launching of the Spanish Armada. Its defeat marked the beginning of Spain's rapid decline from a position of European supremacy to the national abasement which characterised the reigns of the successors of Philip II.[1] In contrast, it marked for England the beginning of a period of fulfilment when, relieved of the shadow that had so long hovered over the triumphs of its seamen and the brilliance of its Court, the nation experienced a new security and a great upsurge of spirit. The Renaissance movement, now extending beyond the confines of scholars and courtiers, received its most complete expression in the literary achievement which was to give to Europe its greatest man of letters.

There are some half-dozen figures in European literature who stand out like great peaks above the normal heights of attainment, not only because of their indubitable genius, but because, so obviously transcending national boundaries and belonging to all time, they have remained among the permanent influences of Western man. Of these, Shakespeare's is the first name that springs to mind; few would deny the claims of his great Spanish contemporary, Miguel de Cervantes.

It is interesting to recall that at the period of the Armada Cervantes played a humble part in its preparation, for in 1587 he held some sort of post in Seville as a Commissary of the Government involving work connected with the provisioning of the fleet. It was by no means a satisfactory post. At this time—eighteen years before *Don Quixote* was to be published—Cervantes's fortunes were very low, but already he had lived through experiences and adventures far beyond the imaginings of most ordinary men, and if he had never written at all, his career (had we, in that case, known of it) would arouse our interest, and his personality com-

1 Philip III 1598-1621
  Philip IV 1621-1665
  Charles II 1665-1700 (the last Habsburg)

mand our esteem. Apart from authorship, glamorous adventures and the nobility of his character, he is also interesting because, in following his life, we are brought into touch with so many different aspects of the Renaissance world, aspects which are reflected in *Don Quixote* and his other works, and which are a significant part of social history.

Miguel de Cervantes (he later added the surname Saavedra) was born in the Spanish university town of Alcalá de Henares in 1547. It was the year in which died both Henry VIII and Francis I, and with the death of two of the three monarchs who had been the 'new men' of the early sixteenth century, one could say that the first phase of the Renaissance outside Italy was over. During their reigns the pattern of Europe had been much changed. The permanent division into two religious groups had become a certainty, even though Pope Paul III had summoned the Council of Trent partly in the hope of ending the schism. The other great European struggle was passed on to the next generation, and Francis I's son, Henry II, continued his war against the Habsburgs; but it had ceased to be a war for Italian possessions, being concerned instead with securing the eastern boundaries of France.

French pre-eminence was, in any case, doomed. Soon the country was to be engulfed by the terrible wars of religion, and for the next forty years, pride of place would go to Spain. The Spanish grandee became the exemplar of Europe's ruling class.

Spain had been unshaken by the Reformation. It had remained firmly Catholic, and its apprehension of the Renaissance had been less secular than that of Italy. Even the greatest Spanish contribution up to this time, that of overseas discovery, had been envisaged partly as missionary enterprise. The results, however, were largely temporal. Columbus's opening up of the New World had been followed by Cortes's conquest of Mexico and Pizarro's acquisition of Peru. Spanish power and Spanish wealth were immense, and when, in 1556, Charles V[2] abdicated from his vast responsibilities and his lands were divided between his brother and his son, the reign of the young Philip II began on a note of high hope.

Miguel de Cervantes was the fourth child and second son of an ill-qualified apothecary surgeon. His life, like his great novel, was

2 See William the Silent, p. 171.

episodic. Phases of it are still obscure to us, and the well-authenticated episodes do not link neatly together. It is a life that seems to proceed in jerks.

The exact date of his birth is unknown, but he was certainly baptised on 9 October 1547. The father was feckless and the family poor, and as a result they made numerous moves during Cervantes's boyhood—to Valladolid, Córdoba, Seville—presumably in search of better opportunities. By the time he was nineteen Cervantes was living in Madrid, where he seems to have attended classes at local schools and colleges. The atmosphere of the city must have been stimulating. It had been the capital of Spain only since 1561, but it was already established as the centre for the court; thirty miles out in its countryside, the great building of the Escorial, which combined the functions of palace, church, convent and mausoleum, was proceeding rapidly. Begun, at the Command of Philip II, in 1563 to celebrate a victory over the French, it was to be by its completion in 1593, one of the most remarkable buildings in Europe.

There was in Madrid a lively interest in the theatre to which Cervantes was much drawn. He had opportunities for meeting travelling players, and from his love of drama an interest in other forms of literature developed.

He had always been given to reading anything he could lay hands on 'even', as he said himself, 'torn scraps of paper lying in the street'. October 1568 is the date of his first recorded piece of writing. Philip's third Queen had just died, and a Madrid professor published a commemorative work. He described it as having been written by his 'pupils' and Cervantes was responsible for six of the contributions, but unfortunately we have no precise information about his attendance at any educational institutions.

If Cervantes as a youth entertained any hopes of supporting himself by his pen he must have been forced to abandon them, for later this same year he left Spain for Italy, in the retinue of the papal legate, Acquavita, who was returning home. His original intention in making this journey is not clear, but the lure of Italy was still strong for the adventurous spirit and the inquiring mind. Practical considerations directed him into a kind of auxiliary military service with the Spanish garrisons then in Naples and Sicily. For the next twelve years, Cervantes's life was entirely dominated by the prevailing political considerations, so that it is necessary at this point to understand something of the general situation.

Ever since Louis XII of France had been compelled to evacuate Naples in 1504[3] and leave it to the Spaniards, the south of Italy had remained firmly in the grip of Spain.[4] Milan too, which had fallen to the Emperor Charles V, was in 1545 bestowed upon his son Philip. A succession of popes and the rulers of the smaller duchies were overawed by Spanish garrisons dotted about the peninsula. The one Italian state that retained its independence and preserved something of the old spirit was Venice. Elsewhere Italy was an exhausted and almost ruined land. Even Venice, exulting in the splendid sunset of Italian Renaissance art, had acute problems. Everywhere to the west was the alien Spaniard; to the east, the graver menace of the Turk. Since a quirk of fate had decided that Cervantes's life should be involved in this threat, it is time to glance at the affairs of the Muslim world.

Throughout the seventh century the Arabs had carried their Muhammadan faith from their own country ever further westwards, seeking to gather the converted and the conquered (for them one implied the other) into the Empire of Islam. The peoples of the Levant, of all the north African coast, and of most of Spain, were by the early eighth century dominated by the Muslims.[5] They failed, however, to penetrate into Asia Minor which persisted as the centre of the Byzantine Empire.

The Moors, who had been the Muslim conquerors of Spain, were forced to renounce their religion or leave the country at the beginning of the sixteenth century, and the infidel was thus removed from Europe.[6] But since the eleventh century another danger for both Arab and Christian alike, had been present in the east. From Central Asia, tribes of Turks, known as Seljuks, had

3 See Francis I., p. 107-108.
4 In spite of one attempt at reconquest by the French in 1528 and one by the Neapolitan Pope Paul IV in 1557.
5 The name of the Prophet is also rendered in English as Mohammed and Mahomet, and that of his followers as Moslems.
6 When Ferdinand and Isabella reconquered the last Moorish kingdom of Granada in 1492, they guaranteed their new subjects religious toleration, but in 1502 they were compelled to accept Christian baptism or go into exile. By an ordinance of Philip III in 1609 all were forcibly expelled.

been penetrating the territories of Islam, accepting its faith as they furthered their conquests. By 1071 they had also succeeded in conquering most of Asia Minor from the Byzantines. Soon the Turks were masters of the Muslim world. During the period of the Crusades their Empire passed through many vicissitudes, but by the mid-thirteenth century the Turks were strong again with their power firmly based on Egypt, and during the fifteenth century another branch rose to supremacy as the Ottoman Empire of which the centre was Asia Minor. By the early sixteenth century it had not only taken over the African and Asian lands of previous Muslim powers but had extended into Europe almost to the borders of Austria. The fall of Constantinople in 1453 is the most dramatised incident in the advance.

Of all the Italian states, it was Venice with her eastward overseas possessions that was most concerned with the advance of the Turk. As she was increasingly left to deal with the problem single-handed, she pursued a mixed policy of trading, bribing and fighting as circumstances seemed to demand. She always maintained a representative in Constantinople.

When Cervantes was serving in Italy in 1568, the Spanish authorities were concerned not only with the maintenance of their power in their Italian possessions, but also with the appeals from Venice for help against the threatened aggression of the new Sultan Selim II.

Whatever Cervantes's intentions had been when he left Spain, he made one attempt at civil employment. He was, for about eighteen months, a steward (or some similar officer) in the household of Acquaviva; but in 1570 he resigned his post and enlisted as a private in a famous Spanish regiment. It was a critical moment. The Sultan was threatening to seize Cyprus from the Venetians, and in the late summer Philip II responded to the plea of the Pope, and sent his fleet to join that of Venice. There seems to have been little harmony between the Christian forces and the campaign was a disaster. Cyprus fell to the Turk.

The allied fleets retired to their winter quarters in Naples and Messina, but Christendom was now thoroughly alarmed. In May 1571, the Pope (Pius V), Spain and Venice formed the Holy League for the recovery of Cyprus, and the united fleets were put under the command of the renowned Don John of Austria, illegitimate half-brother of King Philip II. In September, Cervantes sailed with the fleet from Messina on the galley *Marquesa*, and was in the thickest of the fighting at the famous Battle of Lepanto on 7 October. At the time the engagement began he was ill with fever, but he insisted on taking part, finding it better, he said, 'to die fighting for God and the King than to go below deck and save my life'. He was in one of the hottest spots, and received three gunshot wounds—two in the chest, and one which maimed his left hand for life.

Lepanto was hailed throughout Christendom as a great victory, but no liberation of Cyprus followed, and further reflection made it clear that at best the Turkish aggression had been checked. By April 1572 it was realised that a new expedition would be necessary.

Cervantes had spent some of the intervening time in hospital in Messina, and on recovering his health he was transferred to Corfu in a new regiment with which he probably took part in the indecisive battle of Navarino in October. This second expedition was a failure from the outset; it started too late in the year and it was not well supported from Madrid; its outcome decided Don John to withdraw his forces to Messina. In March 1573 Venice signed a separate treaty resigning Cyprus, and the Holy League was dissolved. Spain, however, decided to continue the struggle against the infidel. Cervantes returned to the humdrum life of a garrison soldier at Messina.

More adventures awaited him in the autumn when he took part in a Spanish expedition, again under the command of Don John, to wrest Tunis from the Turks. This they at first succeeded in doing, but the triumph was short lived, and in less than a year the Turks had recaptured the city. By then Cervantes was back with the garrison at Naples. Don John, the hero with whom he was always so proud to have fought, was soon to be removed to another sphere of activity with his appointment as Governor-General of the Netherlands.[7] Meanwhile the changed situation gave Cervantes an opportunity for taking stock of his position.

The man who was to write *Don Quixote* must have been reflective: poverty and destiny had determined he should be a man

7 1576. See William the Silent, p. 182.

of action. We have seen that the question of whether the profession of arms was compatible with or opposed to learning was an urgent one for the men of the Renaissance.[8] Cervantes always held there were two roads to honour. 'The lance has never blunted the pen, nor the pen the lance', said Don Quixote early in his adventures, and in the second part of the book there is more than one discussion which suggests that he held the lance in greater honour, 'for though Letters may have been the foundation of more estates than Arms, still soldiers have an indefinable superiority over men of letters, and a certain splendour about them which puts them above everybody'.

Cervantes had the temperament for both, and his few years of military service abroad had already given him much material for his writing, as well as considerable insight into human nature. His immediate need was work to maintain himself which would give him better opportunities to pursue his literary aims: the obvious post to seek would be in the public service.

In September 1575 he obtained permission to return to Spain, and, presumably because of his distinguished conduct as a soldier, he carried with him commendatory letters to King Philip, from Don John, the Viceroy of Sicily, and other distinguished persons. These letters were to be his undoing.

Early on 26 September, when his boat and two others were off the Rhône delta, they were attacked by a Squadron of Algerian pirates. They fought their assailants gallantly from daybreak to dusk, but in the end they were worn down and Cervantes, with his younger brother Rodrigo, who was also a soldier, was captured and taken bound on a pirate ship to Algiers. There he became the slave of one Dali Mami.

The Muslim immediately had him placed under specially strict surveillance because the letters of recommendation found on him suggested that he was an important and probably wealthy person who could be expected to provide a large ransom. Cervantes was confined in a dark dungeon and chained to the wall with gyves on his ankles and manacles on his wrists. After some months the strict confinement was relaxed because he was becoming ill and his master feared he might lose a valuable hostage. He was then permitted to move about the town and at the first opportunity he

8 Cf. Sidney, p. 194.

began to organise ways of escape for himself and his fellows.

Cervantes was twenty-eight years old when he was captured, and he was destined to spend five years fighting for his freedom. Fight he certainly did, and the story of his captivity is an inspiring one because it is a story of undimmed hope, courage, loyalty and self-sacrifice in circumstances that would have defeated all but the finest natures. Also this series of adventures provided an experience on which he was to draw for his later literary work.

The inset story of 'The Captive's Tale' in *Don Quixote* tells us a good deal about the lives of the thousands of Christian slaves held as prisoners in Algiers at this time. The mere contemplation of an escape required rare courage, for as Cervantes went about in his comparative freedom, he became increasingly aware of the horrors to which the prisoners were subjected, and he actually saw sentences of death carried out by the hideous means of impaling and burning alive. He remained undaunted. The captive in the story might be Cervantes himself speaking: 'I never gave up hope of gaining my liberty, and when the result did not shape with my design in such plans as I contrived, worked out and put in practice, I never gave up, but immediately devised some new hope, never mind how slender and weak, to keep me going.'

His first escape attempt was made in the spring of 1576. Cervantes and seven companions, including his brother Rodrigo, set out on a march of well over 200 miles across wild mountainous country to reach Oran which was at this time in the possession of Spain. They had a Moorish guide who deserted, so that they were eventually forced to turn back to Algiers and surrender themselves to their masters. Surprisingly, the group as a whole do not seem to have been very seriously punished, though Cervantes himself was for a time more rigorously confined.

The second attempt, some eighteen months later, was more spectacular. In the intervening time, Cervantes had succeeded in getting a letter delivered to his parents by a ransomed captive who was returning home, and they sent money through a priest which proved sufficient to ransom his brother, but not the highly valued Miguel. So Rodrigo returned home and was able to assist in the organisation of the next plan for escape. This involved some fifteen to twenty men slipping away and hiding themselves in a cave in a garden near the sea. They were aided by a Spanish gardener in the service of the Viceroy. Rodrigo was arranging for a frigate to be sent from Majorca, and directly it appeared the fugitives, having been joined by Cervantes, were to go to the beach to be taken on board. Everything went as planned until the arrival of the boat, and then, when the sailors were attempting to land, they sighted some Moors and had to put to sea again.

When they returned to make a second attempt, they were immediately taken prisoners. A Spanish renegade who had been carrying food to the cave, having become fearful that the whole plot, and his own part in it, would be discovered, had betrayed them.

A new Governor named Hassan Pasha had just arrived from Constantinople, and Cervantes was taken before him. He had insisted that he alone was the instigator of the plot; that the other men in the cave were ignorant of his intentions, and had been induced by him to flee so far. Under threat of death he still firmly refused to implicate his comrades.

His bearing must have impressed Hassan Pasha for not only did he spare his prisoner's life, but he bought him from his previous master. So important a person of such high courage must surely be worth a magnificent ransom.

In the bagnio[9] of Hassan Pasha, Cervantes was at first chained to the wall of his dungeon, but after a few months he was allowed greater freedom again, and immediately he began to organise a third attempt at escape, which this time did not proceed very far. The plan necessitated getting letters through to the Spanish Governor of Oran, and the Moor to whom they were entrusted was captured, so that the whole scheme was quickly rendered abortive. Cervantes was sentenced by Hassan Pasha to a punishment of two thousand strokes, but for some reason it was never carried out.

Cervantes was irrepressible. It looked as though all thought of escape was hopeless, but his pride and self-respect which were unfailing throughout his captivity, would not let him desist from his struggle with fate. As Don Quixote was to remark later, 'The sorcerers may destroy the outcome, but not the effort'.

His fourth and last attempt was complicated, requiring a more psychological approach. He gained the help of a Spanish renegade by working on his doubts about his new faith, and of a Valencian

9 A bagnio was a prison house for Christian prisoners.

merchant who traded in Algiers by appealing to his desire for profit, and through them made plans for the purchase of an armed frigate which should be brought to Algiers to rescue some sixty Christian prisoners. The whole plot was mysteriously betrayed to the authorities by a Dominican monk whose motives remain unexplained. The Valencian was so terrified of what threats might wring from Cervantes that he offered to pay his whole ransom if he would immediately sail alone with him to Spain. This Cervantes scornfully refused to do. He merely assured the merchant that nothing would make him involve anyone else, and went into hiding.

From this precarious safety he emerged to give himself up to Hassan because he was afraid that some of his companions might be put to the torture in an effort to make them reveal what they knew about their leader. Cervantes was brought before Hassan bound and with a rope around his neck, but again it seems that the superb courage of his bearing induced the Dey (or Governor) to spare his life. The almost uncanny moral effect of his personality is suggested in the story of 'The Captive's Tale' when the narrator says: 'The only one who held his own was a Spanish soldier, called something de Saavedra, for his master never so much as struck him, nor bade anyone else strike him, nor even spoke a rough word to him, though he did things which those people will remember for many years, all in efforts to recover his liberty; and the rest of us were afraid that his least actions would be punished by impaling, as he himself feared they would be more than once.' On this occasion he was merely more closely confined for the next few months.

Cervantes's conduct throughout his captivity was beyond praise —our knowledge of it rests, not only on the hints in his own writings and statements, but on the authority of reliable independent witnesses—although in terms of reality the prospects were almost uniformly dark, and it was only after the failure of the fourth escape plan that some light appeared in the sombre skies.[10]

10 If it seems improbable that so many opportunities of escape would have presented themselves, one has to remember that Algiers had a very mixed and mobile population including renegades, affluent merchants and other Christians; and that there were some 20,000 slaves to guard.

Back in Spain, his ageing parents had been trying to assist their son both by appealing to those in high places, and by trying to scrape together enough money for the ransom. The family accumulated some 300 ducats and in May 1580 two monks of the Trinitarian Order, whose members devoted themselves to the freeing of Christian slaves, arrived in Algiers with the ransom money. Hassan, however, demanded 500 ducats for Cervantes. By begging from Christian traders, and using some of the general fund of their Order, the monks managed to raise the required sum by September. That month Hassan's term of office ended, and he was about to return to Constantinople. His slaves, including Cervantes, were already on the boat when the ransom was finally paid.

At last Cervantes was free, and five weeks later he sailed for Spain. He spent two months in Valencia and by Christmas was back in Madrid.

Paradoxically his days of enslavement were days of hope; he returned to Spain and freedom to encounter days of despair. His old and ailing parents were living with his youngest sister Magdalena in circumstances of great poverty. His elder sister Andrea was a widow living with her daughter in a separate apartment of the house. Rodrigo, his only surviving brother, was with the Spanish army going to Portugal.[11] It fell to Miguel to support the household.

He would have preferred now to renounce the military life, and to pursue the adventure of literature which had always beckoned him. But money had to be earned. He attempted to secure various minor official posts—and does seem to have been sent on one mission to Oran—and then returned briefly to the army to fight in the campaigns in Portugal and the Azores. He remained in Portugal about a year, and was there when Philip made his formal entry in July 1581. Then he returned to Madrid.

Now the lure of literature was stronger than all else, and he gave himself up to a bohemian life on the fringes of the literary society of the capital, at the same time beginning to write for the stage. Between 1582 and 1587 he wrote a number of cloak-and-

11 This was at the time when Philip II was claiming the throne of Portugal. It was in fact united to Spain for sixty years (1581-1640). It was necessary to establish the union by force of arms.

dagger plays which were quite unsuccessful, and of which few survive. He also wrote the first part of a long pastoral work, part in verse, part in prose, called *La Galatea*. Later in *Don Quixote* and in his story *The Colloquy of the Dogs* he came to ridicule the pastoral fashion, but at this stage he was content to use a conventional form.

To this period belongs the birth of his natural daughter Isabel. Little is known of her mother, who was Portuguese, but Isabel appears at intervals in her father's life story and, since he never had legitimate children, the relationship was important, if not always gratifying, to him.

At the end of 1584, the year in which *La Galatea* was published, he married Catalina de Palacios Salazar y Vozmediano, a girl still in her teens who owned a small estate at Esquivias about twenty miles from Madrid. If his wife's social station was somewhat higher than his, it was not particularly exalted, and the estate does not seem to have been a very valuable one. In any case, the restless bohemian Cervantes was not able to settle down on it for any length of time, and much of his life was always to be spent apart from his wife.

He was making little progress in his new profession, and in 1587, forced to seek something more regular, he went to Seville to take up the work connected with provisioning the great Armada. This was a time of declining fortune, and sheer mischance seemed ever to dog his footsteps. He was involved in an absurd scrape when, in the course of his provisioning duties, he tried to collect wheat from an ecclesiastical institution, and was consequently ex-communicated. With the restoration of the grain the ban was removed, but Cervantes, who was always a loyal Catholic, would have felt the sting of the punishment.

After the defeat of the Armada, he was retained in some minor post with the royal galleys, but he was poor and aimless. He applied unsuccessfully to the King for four different posts that were vacant in the Indies. He made an agreement with an old stage friend to write a number of plays, but it was never fulfilled. He spent a brief period in prison either for debt or for some irregularity connected with his work.

Cervantes was not dishonest, but he was not the man to keep accurate accounts, especially in circumstances of peculiar difficulty.

Problems arose over deficits and he was dismissed the service.

He now passed into a period of dire poverty when he had to support himself by any odd jobs he could get, and in pursuit of them became familiar with the underworld of Seville. This experience was later to provide him with valuable material for his short stories, especially for one of the most brilliant, *Rinconete and Cortadillo,* which gives an illuminating picture of the social conditions of Seville at the time, and provides an interesting comparison with the contemporary England of the ' rogues and vagabonds '.

By 1597 both Cervantes's parents were dead and he had no personal reason for returning to Madrid, though he was ordered to find sureties that he would present himself there with his accounts. Apparently no sureties were forthcoming, and he again saw the inside of Seville jail. For the next six years little is known of his movements, although there is some evidence that he led a wandering life in Don Quixote's countryside of La Mancha.

Spain itself was passing into dark days. The defeat of the Armada had put a period to her greatness and under Philip III who came to the throne in 1598, the social and economic decline set in. Yet, in spite of external gloom, these years must have been for Cervantes a period of the most intense and vivid life of the imagination. When he reappears in Madrid in 1603 most of *Don Quixote* (Part I) has been written and he is seeking a publisher. The Accounts Department were still wanting him, and he may have come to the capital primarily to have his accounts audited, but whatever the reason for his coming, the importance of the visit is that during it *Don Quixote* was accepted for publication.

He had evidently found a patron in the Duke of Bejar to whom the book is dedicated in conventional style. It was published at the beginning of 1605 and was immediately a huge success, running through four editions in seven months. In spite of this, and of having had an advance from his publisher, Cervantes's financial position did not much improve; he continued to mismanage his finances, and *Don Quixote* did not bring in all it should because of the numerous pirated editions put into circulation.

Cervantes was never to escape adventures or be long without misfortune. At this time, he moved with his sisters and daughter to Valladolid, possibly because the Court was temporarily established there, and at his home in a tenement in the Calle del Rastro, a bizarre calamity befell him. One night, a dissolute young nobleman who had been wounded in a street duel was found dying on Cervantes's doorstep. He was carried inside and tended by the family, but he died before he could name his slayer. As a result of magisterial investigations, Cervantes and members of his family were lodged in jail on suspicion for two days. It is certain the affair was no concern of theirs; they seem to have been the victims of the spite and gossip of various female neighbours who were hostile to Cervantes's daughter.

Isabel de Saavedra does not emerge as a very attractive person, and her later life is entangled in lawsuits of a somewhat shady character. Altogether there is little suggestion of domestic comfort for Cervantes during these years in Valladolid. His wife, who at first had joined him there, was already back on her Esquivias estate by the time of the assassination incident.

If Cervantes's household was a difficult one to live with, it was also a strain on his finances. He found himself obliged to sign away the rights of *Don Quixote,* and by the end of 1607 he moved back to Madrid. There he was to spend his remaining years in close touch with the intellectual and literary life which had been rekindled by the return of the Court in 1606. He joined various societies in the city—a Literary Academy and a newly formed Confraternity of the Unworthy Slaves of the Most Holy Sacrament, a brotherhood of a type that was being formed at this time to resist Protestantism. Cervantes, always devout, turned increasingly as he grew older to the comfort of his faith. His Confraternity was attached to the monastery of the Trinitarians, and he went often to its sanctuary. He was now in his sixties; life was becoming lonelier. Both his sisters died, and his relations with his daughter weakened because of disagreements with her husband. Literature remained a consolation and his prime endeavour.

In 1613 he published the work that was to rank second to his world famous book—the *Twelve Exemplary Novels.* These short stories[12] are of considerable interest for the picture they give of

12 Three of the most attractive, ' Rinconete and Cortadillo ', ' Man of Glass ' and ' The Colloquy of the Dogs ' are available in an English translation by Samuel Putnam.

seventeenth-century Spain, for their autobiographical element and for their combination of realism with humanity.

It is probable that most of this book was written after the publication of the first part of *Don Quixote*. The prologue, which certainly was, has the ring of confidence: it is also interesting for two other reasons. Here we have a self-portrait which gives us some impression of Cervantes's appearance[13] 'This man you see here with the aquiline countenance, the chestnut hair, the smooth untroubled brow, the bright eyes, the hooked yet well proportioned nose, the silvery beard that less than a score of years ago was golden, the big moustache, the small mouth, the teeth that are scarcely worth mentioning (there are but half a dozen of them altogether, in bad condition and very badly placed, no two of them corresponding to another pair), the body of medium height, neither tall nor short, the high complexion that is fair rather than dark, the slightly stooping shoulders, and the somewhat heavy build—this, I may tell you, is the author of *La Galatea* and *Don Quixote de la Mancha*.'

The other point of interest in this prologue is the announcement of a second part of *Don Quixote*. 'You shall see, and shortly the continuation of Don Quixote's exploits, and Sancho Panza's drolleries.' Before he could make good this promise, one last misfortune was to befall him. In 1614 a spurious sequel to Part I was published under the pseudonym of Alonzo Fernandez de Avellaneda. The real identity of the author remains one of the puzzles of Spanish literature, but that it was conceived in malice by an enemy of Cervantes is obvious from the extraordinarily offensive nature of the preface. He was hurt by the personal attack and worried about his own second part which was only three-quarters finished. At least he was goaded into completion. At the end of 1615 the genuine sequel was published, and the spurious version receded into the shadows.

The complete work was acclaimed enthusiastically. During the last ten years there had been repeated reprints of Part I, and it had been translated into English and French. In the course of time the whole novel was to be translated into the majority of the languages of the world.

13 There is no authentic painting of Cervantes.

It is difficult to suggest briefly what constitutes the greatness of *Don Quixote*. The certainty is that it is one of the books that grows with the centuries, and thus takes its place with the handful of classics at the core of the European literary tradition.

Cervantes's original aim as stated by himself was simple: 'the whole of it is an invective against books of chivalry' and 'my sole object has been to arouse men's contempt for all fabulous and absurd stories of knight errantry'. The orders of knighthood with origins far back in the ninth and tenth centuries had by the eleventh century established a firm ethical code which had certainly done something to mitigate the brutality of medieval warfare, but which was increasingly encumbered by a fantastic ritual. By the later Middle Ages, the institution was decadent, and the ideal it had sought to enshrine impoverished by its very extravagance. We have seen that as it faded from the Renaissance world, something of its idealism was adapted to the new conditions, informing the dreams of the warrior knights of Francis I, and, further modified, serving as an example for the sixteenth-century Spanish grandee and the English courtier.

The literature inspired by the self-conscious days of chivalry persisted. An enormous output of extravagant romantic tales in pretentious style fed the melodramatic taste that is present in every age. Cervantes deplored it, though he must have read a great deal, and it is made clear in the sixth chapter of *Don Quixote* where the knight's friends, the priest and the barber, decide which of his books to burn, and again in the conversation with the landlord during the adventures at the inn (Chapter 32) that he did not regard it all as equally regrettable. His intention remained, however, to extinguish by ridicule the relics of the old chivalry and the books of knight errantry.

Paradoxically the book that was to do this is itself a novel of knight errantry, but taken as a whole *Don Quixote* is a paradoxical book treating as it does of the paradox that is human nature.

The reasons for its first popularity are not far to seek. It contains a wealth of interesting material drawn from Cervantes's rich experience of life. Its episodes, haphazard in order, linked by an itinerary that seems to be mainly chosen by Don Quixote's horse Rosinante, open up a marvellous panorama of sixteenth-century life. All the people of Spain seem to pour through Cervantes's pages and it is an authentic countryside that provides a background for their activity.

Also Cervantes possessed great gifts as a narrator. He is a compelling story teller, and even if he is lured by the fecundity of his imagination into too many inset tales which can become tedious to modern taste, we are, after all, grateful for those whose details add so much to our knowledge of his own life and circumstances.

The deeper significance of the book was gradually revealed. It is concerned with the incongruity between the ideal and the actual, and puts in unique manner man's persistent inquiry: which is reality, which is illusion? A perpetually urgent question is symbolised by Cervantes in the eternally valid characters, the knight, Don Quixote, and his Squire Sancho Panza; the one endowed with the idealism that can be ensnared by illusion, the other embodying an earthly common sense which may, however, fail to catch the falling star. The knight, 'of the Sorrowful Countenance' as he was to be styled by his squire,[14] is sometimes a sad figure, often he is amusing, frequently inspiring. For the essential thing about Don Quixote is that although he is sometimes visited by the fear that his illusions may be illusions, and is increasingly aware of the gap that exists between the world of his dreams and the world of reality, the outcome of his intimations is not bitterness; his essential hopefulness remains, and in the sunny climate of his story we are led to accept his conclusions that mankind errs much more frequently through foolishness than through wickedness, and that most trials are after all, supportable. As Sancho echoes him, 'There's a remedy for everything except death'.

Sancho Panza shares his master's tolerant humanity, and combines it with a salty humour all his own. In action, he is often less than heroic, but he has a resilience which is as impressive as it is amusing, and a cheerfulness which breaks through all his grumbling. His entry into the book is a crucial factor in elevating it from a mere satire on knight errantry.

The book, episodic though it is, has a broad pattern, and an overall coherence. In the course of its two parts the hero sallies

14 Though he himself characteristically changed it later to the resounding ' Knight of the Lions '.

forth three times on his adventures. The first excursion, which
occupies only the first five chapters of the book, he undertakes
alone. For the second set of expeditions, lasting for the rest of
Part I, he is joined by Sancho Panza, and the great complementary
partnership has begun: they set forth representing mankind.

Throughout these adventures Don Quixote is plainly mad. He
was so at the beginning and his madness is increased from the time
his housekeeper, at the end of the first journey, invents an
enchanter to explain the disappearance of his library. Enchanters
play an important part in his hallucinations henceforward. But in
a late chapter of Part I we are prepared by his intelligent discourse to the company at the inn, for the Don Quixote of Part II
who, in the words of one of his hosts, is 'mad in patches, full of
lucid streaks'.

Part II is in no way inferior to the earlier book; indeed it
might be said that it gains in subtlety, and is better constructed.[15]
It is enriched by the greater emphasis placed on minor characters,
and by the superb conversation of Sancho Panza. Don Quixote's
own character develops, and is nobler and more dignified; he
passes out of his phase of acute madness. We notice that whereas
in Part I all the absurd mistakes arose from his own delusions, in
Part II the deception is almost always contrived by other people.
Indeed the adventures of the second book are more fantastic than
hallucinatory.

Sancho Panza too has developed and thus the relationship of
master and man has changed into one of closer companionship. If
Don Quixote more often doubts, his squire has acquired more
confidence, or perhaps simply more conceit. His experiences have
improved his understanding, as his creator himself remarks, even
though his untrained mind can frequently only express its new
findings in a string of proverbs. By the end of the book, Don
Quixote is not only prepared to overlook his squire's mockery, but
even on occasion defers to his judgement. 'Every day Sancho, you
grow less simple and wiser'.

The knight is compelled to make the concession, for the enemy
Doubt is gradually defeating him, and the last chapters are a
tale of failing conviction. We have long been aware that he is, by

15 The later chapters are enlivened by some incongruous—if understandable
—attacks on the author of the spurious version.

the world's standards, less insane. He shows increasing sense in his conversations with other wayfarers; inns are now inns and no longer castles with moats and drawbridges; he is prepared to revise his views of some of his own adventures, and is not completely deceived by the last trick played upon him.

But the approach to Reality is painful. It represents defeat, and the acknowledgment of a non-ideal world in which men condemn other men to the galleys, and warn those who would succour them, that they had better not inquire why. Unusual fits of despondency descend on Don Quixote after his defeat by the sham Knight of the White Moon at Barcelona. He had agreed, if he were defeated, to forsake arms, and to withdraw to his village, and, accepting every humiliation that follows as a just chastisement, he turns towards home, riding slowly and unarmed while Sancho leads his ass Dapple, piled with his master's armour. He is going home to die, for as he 'had no privilege from Heaven exempting him from the common fate, his dissolution and end came when he least expected it', but not before a moment of blinding clarity had revealed to him the foolishness of all knight errantry.

*Don Quixote* is a very long book, but it is simple to read; it was written for everyone. Because of its broad humanity it takes a place as a European legend, and its hero has become a household word. It expresses perfectly something that man repeatedly needs to say, and it stands as a testimony to his noblest characteristic: the enduring capacity to rise above misfortune.

With the publication of Part II of *Don Quixote* Cervantes achieved fame. He never acquired wealth, and his remaining days were few. In the spring of 1616, he was attacked by dropsy, and it was on his deathbed that he wrote for his last work.[16] a dedication that was also a farewell. He had already received extreme unction, and with 'foot already in the stirrup' he could only lament the many works still unfinished. He died on 23 April at the house of a priest in the Calle de Leon, Madrid. By a coincidence the date of his death is the same as that of Shakespeare but this is because England had not yet accepted the reformed calendar, inaugurated by Pope Gregory XIII in 1582; Shakespeare did in fact survive his great contemporary by ten days.

16 An extravagant romance called *Persiles and Sigismunda* published posthumously.

Cervantes was buried in the Trinitarian Church attached to the Convent of the Carmelite Nuns, clad in the habit of St Francis. When, later, the Order changed its premises, the body was removed, and his final resting place is unknown.

The fame of Cervantes persists because of a book that has survived all changes in literary fashion, but the man himself is worthy of his immortality. He was one in whom adversity brought out the best; no one can have whined less about the malignity of fate. We have the testimony of his fellow captives for his good temper, patience, resourcefulness and humour, his serene courage in the face of death. His weaknesses were venial; his heart could err, but it could never despair. He had, indeed, all the qualities of his own hero.

In many ways Cervantes recalls the other great figure of Spain's Renaissance period. Columbus was a major participant in the opening up of a new era which had wrought a changed world by the time Cervantes died. The one opened the door to Spain's grandeur, the other had to witness its decline. As they are placed at either end of their country's period of greatness, one is struck by certain similarities. Both were responsible for great achievements which brought them little wealth, and only temporary fame in their time. Both had to live out an old age neglected by a new generation which had ceased to be interested in the adventures and experiences of which they were justifiably proud. Both tempered disillusionment with mysticism. They had each, in their diverse ways, opened up vistas greater than they realised, and were to have the revived and sustained homage of posterity.

If, in the sphere of action, Columbus's discoveries may be said to have emphasised the passing of the Middle Ages, Cervantes has done much to laugh away their superstitions and their shibboleths. As always in history, there was much to shed—and much to preserve. Preservation is one of the tasks of literature. Out of a timeless book one knight and his squire have ridden on into the modern world.

# FURTHER READING

W. J. ENTWISTLE. *Cervantes*. Oxford University Press 1940.

S. J. ARBO. *Cervantes; Adventurer, Idealist, Destiny's Fool*. Translated by I. Barea. Thames & Hudson 1955.

CERVANTES. *Don Quixote*. There is a good translation by J. M. Cohen, published by Penguin Books.

—— *Three Exemplary Tales*. Translated by Samuel Putnam. Cassell 1952.

# Bibliography

This bibliography, which includes general as well as further bio-graphical works, is necessarily very selective. A number of works of which the titles may at first sight seem somewhat irrelevant are, in fact, illuminating in the context of this book. Some of these (which are reasonably accessible) are mentioned here both as an acknowledgement of my own indebtedness, and as a guide for those readers who wish to pursue ramifications. Titles of books recommended for further reading at the ends of chapters are not repeated.

## General

ASCHAM, ROGER. *The Scholemaster*. 1570.

AYDELOTTE, F. *Elizabethan Rogues and Vagabonds*. O.U.P. 1913.

BARKER, ERNEST. *Greek Political Theory*. Methuen 1918.

BELL, MARY I. M. *A Short History of the Papacy*. Methuen 1921.

BERENSON, BERNARD. *Italian Painters of the Renaissance*. 1894-1907. Phaidon Press 1952.

BERTRAND, L. and PETRIE, C. *The History of Spain*. Eyre & Spottiswoode 1945.

BINDOFF, S. T. *Tudor England*. Penguin Books 1950.

BLACK, J. B. *The Reign of Elizabeth*, rev. edn. O.U.P. 1959 (Oxford History of England).

BLOC, MARC. *Feudal Society* (1940), tr. L. A. Manyon. Routledge & Kegan Paul 1961.

BOWRA, C. M. *The Greek Experiment*. Weidenfeld & Nicolson 1957.

BRINTON, SELWYN. *The Golden Age of the Medici*. Methuen 1925.

BRYCE, J. *The Holy Roman Empire*, rev. edn. Macmillan 1956.

CAMBRIDGE MODERN HISTORY, vol 1 *The Renaissance*; vol. 2 *The Reformation*. C.U.P.

NEW CAMBRIDGE MODERN HISTORY, vol. 1. *The Renaissance*; vol. 2 *The Reformation*. C.U.P.

CLARKE, M. V. *The Medieval City State*. Methuen 1926.

DAVIES, R. T. *The Golden Century of Spain.* Macmillan, re-issue 1954.

ELTON, G. R. *Reformation Europe 1517-1559.* Collins. 1963.

ELYOT, THOMAS. *The Governour.* 1531.

ERASMUS. *Epistles of Erasmus,* tr. F. M. Nicols. 3 vols. Longmans 1901-18.

—— Translated works, various editions.

FINLEY, M. I. *The Ancient Greeks.* Chatto & Windus 1963.

FRUIN, R. *The Siege of Leyden,* tr. Elizabeth Trevelyan. Humphrey Milford 1927.

HALE, J. R. *England and the Italian Renaissance.* Faber 1954.

HAY, DENYS. *The Italian Renaissance and its Historical Background.* C.U.P. 1961.

JACOB, E. F. *Italian Renaissance Studies.* Faber 1960.

KITTO, H. D. F. *The Greeks.* Penguin Books 1951.

LAVISSE. *Histoire de France,* vol. V. H. Lemmonier.

LEFRANC, ABEL. *La Vie Quotidienne au Temps de la Renaissance.* Librairie Hachette 1950.

LEWIS, BERNARD. *The Arabs in History,* rev. edn. Hutchinson 1959.

MACHIAVELLI. *History of Florence.* 1532.

MADARIAGA, SALVADOR DE. *Don Quixote.* O.U.P. 1935.

MATTINGLEY, GARRETT. *Renaissance Diplomacy.* Cape 1955.

MORE, SIR THOMAS. *The Correspondence of Sir Thomas More,* ed. E. Rogers. Princeton U.P. 1947.

—— Translated works, various editions.

MOTLEY, J. L. *The Rise of the Dutch Republic.* 1856. Murray 1904.

—— *The United Netherlands* Murray 1904.

NEWTON, A. P. ed. *The Great Age of Discovery.* Univ. of London Press 1932.

PEARS, STEUART. *The Correspondence of Sidney and Languet.* 1845.

PIRENNE, HENRI. *Medieval Cities.* Princeton U.P. 1925.

POLLEN, J. H. ed. *St Ignatius Loyola.* Burns & Oates 1913.

PRESTAGE, EDGAR. *The Portuguese Pioneers.* A. & C. Black 1933.

—— ed. *Chivalry.* Kegan Paul 1928.

ROBINSON, CYRIL. *A History of Greece.* Methuen 1929.

SEIGNOBOS, CHARLES. *A History of the French People*, tr. W. Alison Phillips. Cape 1933.

ROWSE, A. L. *The England of Elizabeth*. Macmillan 1951.

SIDNEY, SIR PHILIP. *The Poems of Sir Philip Sidney*, ed. W. A. Ringler. O.U.P. 1962.

STOBART, J. C. *The Glory that was Greece*. Sidgwick & Jackson 1911.

—— *The Grandeur that was Rome*. Sidgwick & Jackson 1912.

SYMONDS, J. A. *Renaissance in Italy*. Smith Elder 1880-1909.

WIND, EDGAR. *Pagan Mysteries of the Renaissance*. Faber 1958.

## *Biographical*

ALLEN, P. S. *The Age of Erasmus*. O.U.P. 1914.

ARMSTRONG, E. *Lorenzo de' Medici*, rev. edn. Putnam 1908.

BAILLY, AUGUSTE. *François Ier, restaurateur des lettres et des arts*. Librairie Arthème Fayard 1954.

BELLONCI, MARIA. *The Life and Times of Lucrezia Borgia*. Weidenfeld & Nicolson 1953.

BRANDI, KARL. *Charles V*, tr. C. V. Wedgwood. Cape 1939.

BRENTANO, FR. FUNCK. *Luther*, tr. E. F. Buckley. Cape 1939.

CAMPBELL, W. E. *Erasmus, Tyndale and More*. Eyre & Spottiswoode 1949.

CELLINI, BENVENUTO. *Autobiography*, various editions.

CHABOD, FREDERICO. *Machiavelli and the Renaissance*, tr. D. Moore. Bowes & Bowes 1958.

DYKE, PAUL VAN. *Catherine de Médicis*. Murray 1923.

—— *Ignatius Loyola: Founder of the Jesuits*. Scribner 1926.

FARROW, JOHN. *The Story of Thomas More*. Collins 1956.

GUTKIND, C. S. *Cosimo de' Medici*. O.U.P. 1938.

HACKETT, FRANCIS. *Francis I*. Heinemann 1934.

HALE, J. R. *Machiavelli and Renaissance Italy*. Eng. Univ. Press 1961.

HOLLIS, CHRISTOPHER. *Sir Thomas More*. Sheed & Ward 1934.

HOUBEN, H. H. *Christopher Columbus*, tr. J. Linton. Routledge 1935.

HUME, MARTIN. *Philip II of Spain*, rev. edn. Macmillan 1916.

HUNTER, G. K. *John Lyly. The Humanist as Courtier*. Routledge 1962.

KELLY, J. F. *The Life of Cervantes*. Chapman & Hall 1892.

LOTH, DAVID. *Lorenzo the Magnificent*. Routledge 1930.

MADARIAGA SALVADOR DE. *Christopher Columbus*, rev. edn. Hollis & Carter 1949.

MANGAN, J. J. *Life, Character and Influence of Desiderius Erasmus*. Burns & Oates 1927.

MATTINGLEY, GARRETT. *Catherine of Aragon*. Cape 1942.

MERRIEN, JEAN. *Christopher Columbus: The Mariner and the Man*. Odhams 1958.

MORISON, S. E. *Admiral of the Ocean*. O.U.P. 1942.

MORRIS, CHRISTOPHER. *The Tudors*. Batsford 1955.

NEALE, J. E. *Queen Elizabeth*. Cape 1934.

PAUL LESLIE. *Sir Thomas More*. Faber 1953.

PIUS II. *Memoirs of a Renaissance Pope*, tr. F. Gragg, ed. L. Gabel. Smith Coll. Mass. 1937.

PREVOST, JEAN. *La Vie de Montaigne*. Librairie Gallimard 1927.

SCHEVILL, RUDOLPH. *Cervantes*. Univ. California P. 1919.

SEEBOHM, FREDERIC. *The Oxford Reformers*, rev. edn. Dent 1938.

SHELLABARGER, SAMUEL. *The Chevalier Bayard*. Skeffington, n.d.

TERRASSE, CHARLES. *François Ier: Le Roi et le Règne*. Grasset 1943, 1948.

VILLARI, P. *The Life and Times of Savonarola*. Fisher Unwin 1898.

WALDMAN, MILTON. *Elizabeth and Leicester*. Collins 1946.

WALLACE, M. W. *The Life of Sir Philip Sidney*. C.U.P. 1915.

WALSH, W. T. *Isabella of Spain*. Sheed & Ward 1931.

—— *Philip II*. Sheed & Ward 1938.

YOUNG, G. F. *The Medici*. Murray 1924.

# Index

*(References are given for the subjects of the chapters only when their names occur in other parts of the book.)*

Don John of Austria, 182, 204, 211, 220, 221, 222

*Don Quixote*, 216, 221, 223, 228, 230, 231-34

Drake, Francis, 208-9

Dudley, Ambrose (Earl of Warwick), 198n, 207

Dudley, Robert (Earl of Leicester), 167, 188, 198n, 200, 201, 206, 209, 213

Egmont, 172, 175, 177

Eleanor, (Queen of France), 121, 123, 126, 127

Elizabeth I, 134, 167, 177, 178, 182, 196-209 passim

Erasmus, 5, 29, 30, 31, 34, 125

Escorial, 218

Essex, Earl of, 202, 213

Etampes, Duchess of (Anne de Heilly), 119, 120, 127, 128

Ferdinand of Aragon, 78, 85, 86, 88, 92, 95, 96

Ferrante, (King of Naples), 18

Ficino, Marsilio, 12

Field of the Cloth of Gold, 32, 100-3, 118

Fisher, John, (Bishop), 38, 44, 56, 71

Florence, 1, 5, 9-24, 117, 153

Foix, Gaston de, 111

Fontainebleau, 123, 124

Francis I, 32, 135, 217, 231

Francis II, 117, 121, 123, 125, 136, 199

Frederick Henry of Nassau, 187

Froben, Johannes, 58, 71

Frobisher, 207, 208

Gérard, Balthasar, 187

Gilbert, Sir Humphrey, 208

Gozzoli, Benozzo, 13

Granvelle, (Bishop of Arras), 169, 172, 173

Greeks, (Ancient), 1-5, 29, 71, 77, 141, 147, 151, 157, 159, 213

Greville, Fulke, 198, 201, 202, 211, 212

Grocyn, 29, 30, 48

Guise family, 136, 150, 155

Haarlem, Siege of, 179, 181

Henry VIII, 28-45 passim, 58, 100-104, 126, 128, 217

Henry II (Fr.), 121, 123, 125, 128, 135, 136, 149, 172, 199n, 217

Henry III (Fr.), 135, 137, 139, 152, 154, 155, 186, 199n, 206

Henry (IV) of Navarre, 137, 155, 188, 199, 211

Henry the Navigator, 76

Holbein, 34, 61,

Holy League, 220, 221

Holy Roman Empire, 104-6, 132, 167-9, 189

Hôpital, Michel de l', 137, 151

Horn, 172, 175, 177

Huguenots, 135, 137, 157, 178, 182

Humanism, 4, 33, 147, 163, 197

Innocent VIII, (Pope), 20

Inquisition, 168, 173

Isabel, (daughter of Cervantes), 227, 229

Isabella of Castile, 78, 85, 88, 89, 91, 94

John II, (Port.), 78, 85

Julius II, (Pope), 57, 63

*Julius Exclusus*, 57n

*La Galatea*, 227

*Lady of the May, The*, 201

Languet, Hubert, 200, 201, 204, 205, 207-8, 211, 212

Latimer, William, 29

League of Arras, 182

Leicester, Earl of, (Robert Dudley), 167, 188, 198, 200, 201, 206, 209, 213

Leo X, Pope, (Giovanni de' Medici), 20, 21, 59, 64, 65, 114

Leonardo da Vinci, 19, 114, 115